Sean Redmond is Associate Professor of Screen and Design at Deakin University, Australia. He is the author of numerous books including *Blade Runner* (2016), *The Cinema of Takeshi Kitano: Flowering Blood* (2013) and *Liquid Metal: The Science Fiction Film Reader* (2004).

'Accessible and passionately written, this is a welcome contribution to contemporary science fiction film and television theory. Especially noteworthy – for its rarity and descriptive power – is the absolutely terrific last chapter, devoted to close analysis of recent science fiction's aesthetics of sound.'
–Vivian Sobchack, UCLA; author of Screening Space: The American Science Fiction Film

'In this immersive yet critical book, Sean Redmond never forgets the structures of power behind the enticing mirrored surfaces of science fiction. A warm, generous and honest academic-poet: he gently shapes our understanding by sharing his personal experiences.'
–Will Brooker, Kingston University; author of Hunting the Dark Knight: Twenty-first Century Batman (I.B.Tauris)

SEAN REDMOND

LIQUID SPACE

Science Fiction Film and Television in the Digital Age

I.B. TAURIS
LONDON · NEW YORK

For Mel

Published in 2017 by
I.B.Tauris & Co. Ltd
London • New York
www.ibtauris.com

Copyright © 2017 Sean Redmond

The right of Sean Redmond to be identified as the author of this work has been asserted by the author in accordance with the Copyright, Designs and Patents Act 1988.

All rights reserved. Except for brief quotations in a review, this book, or any part thereof, may not be reproduced, stored in or introduced into a retrieval system, or transmitted, in any form or by any means, electronic, mechanical, photocopying, recording or otherwise, without the prior written permission of the publisher.

Every attempt has been made to gain permission for the use of the images in this book. Any omissions will be rectified in future editions.

References to websites were correct at the time of writing.

International Library of the Moving Image 15

HB ISBN: 978 1 78076 186 2
PB ISBN: 978 1 78076 187 9
eISBN: 978 1 78672 104 4
ePDF: 978 1 78673 104 3

A full CIP record for this book is available from the British Library
A full CIP record is available from the Library of Congress

Library of Congress Catalog Card Number: available

Typeset by Out of House Publishing

Contents

List of Illustrations vi

Acknowledgements vii

Introduction: Liquid Space 1

1. Then and Now: Television Time Travel and the Once Wonderful End to the Working Day 21
2. Eye-Tracking the Sublime in Spectacular Moments of Science Fiction Film 41
3. Emptying Spaces: Digital Deterritorialisation 62
4. Liquid Bodies 80
5. Millennial Whiteness and Cinematic Outer Space 100
6. Liquid Terror 123
7. Sounding Liquid Science Fiction 143

   Conclusion: We Never Let the Fire Go Out 170

References 182
Index 191

List of Illustrations

1.1.	*Life on Mars*: 1970s time-travel nostalgia (BBC, 2006–7)	37
2.1.	Eye-tracking *Sunshine*: Overview of a viewer's viewing gaze plots and patterns – following narrative action (DNA Films et al, 2007)	51
2.2.	Eye-tracking *Sunshine*: Attention to the centre of the frame dominates viewing patterns (DNA Films et al, 2007)	52
2.3.	Eye-tracking *Sunshine*: Focusing on the face, eyes and mouth (DNA Films et al, 2007)	53
2.4.	Eye-tracking *Godzilla*: Following narrative action (Centropolis Film Productions et al, 1998)	56
2.5.	Eye-tracking *Godzilla*: The viewing eye occupying the centre frame (Centropolis Film Productions et al, 1998)	56
3.1.	Isolation in *Sense8* (Netflix, 2015–)	68
4.1.	Affecting relations in *The Lobster* (Film 4 et al, 2015)	84
5.1.	Rich and poor in the city of Elysium (Tristar Pictures, 2013)	115
6.1.	*Children of Men*: Haunted spaces (Universal Pictures, 2006)	137
7.1.	*Under the Skin*: Sounding the city (Film 4 et al, 2013)	166
8.1.	*Edge of Tomorrow*: Double jeopardy (Warner Brothers, 2014)	171

Acknowledgements

I would like to thank Deakin University and in particular Geoff Boucher for the support of this project. I am also indebted to the ongoing work of the Science and Fiction research node at Deakin University. Thanks also to Leon Marvell, Trent Griffiths, Chris Moore, Toija Cinque, Angela Ndalianis, Jodi Sita and Tania Lewis for their generous help or warm support in the preparation of this manuscript.

Thanks most of all to Melissa Keenan for those 'how many words have you written today' texts. Never as many as I told you I had. You got me here.

A version of 'Then and Now: Television Time Travel and the Once Wonderful End to the Working Day' was published in *Thesis Eleven* (Number 131, December 2015). A version of the chapter 'Eye-Tracking the Sublime in Spectacular Moments of Science Fiction Film' was published in the edited collection *Endangering Science Fiction Film* (Routledge 2015).

I would like to acknowledge and thank Jodi Sita for the data analysis and slides supplied in Chapter 2, and for thinking and feeling through with me the early dreamings of the sublime. I would also like to thank Tania Lewis for being a most excellent critical reader whose thoughts and comments have helped shaped this chapter for the better. Any remaining flaws or weaknesses are mine, of course.

Introduction
Liquid Space

In the short science fiction film, *Sight* (2012), directed by students Eran May-raz and Daniel Lazo, from the Bezaleal Academy of Art and Design in Jerusalem, Israel, Patrick (Ori Golad) plays the role of habitual gamer and software designer in a future where one's reality is played as if it is an interactive game. In the film, Patrick's eyes have become fully augmented, enabling him to see, sense and interact with the world through gaming software that turns everyday encounters into a series of challenges, levels and completions. For example, when he opens the fridge door, ocular-generated data tells him the size, calorie and nutritional value of the food, awarding points for the choices he makes. When he cooks he does so through or within the *Chef Master* game, which awards him points for how he cuts a cucumber or fries an egg. The sound of the 'cut' or the sizzle of the egg is accompanied by both special and audio effects, blending real-world sounds and realist images with comic-book exaggerations. The apartment that Patrick lives in is minimally furnished, but he sees it through augmented eyes that populate it with various virtual rooms and their contents. At the beginning of the film we see Patrick flying through various canyons and mountain ranges within an adventure game that awards him maximum points for his efforts.

The choices that Patrick makes are directly influenced by the data he receives through his gamer and social applications, such as what will be the most appropriate jacket he will wear to a date. We will subsequently find out that the date has been virtually arranged, based on profile sharing and compatibility matches. At the restaurant where he first meets Daphne (Deborah Aroshas), Patrick orders a particular variety of wine, and reveals information about himself, only once it has been tested or measured against the type of person his date is understood to be and in the light of responses she gives. Patrick's software is able to read Daphne's feelings and preferences through assessing her pupil dilation, blood pressure and non-verbal reactions.

Daphne is similarly augmented, posting with her eyes that she thinks she is on 'another bad date'. Patrick manages to turn things around, however, using the privileged software he has as a program developer to seduce and manipulate her. They return to his apartment but in his lounge she catches a glimpse of the dating software he has used to snare her and she tries to leave. We now realise that Patrick has the ability to directly jack into Daphne's software and control her – to overtake her augmented eyes, which spark up when he accesses her data banks. The film ends on this note and with the threat of her impending rape being minimally hinted at.

I start this monograph with a brief summary of *Sight* because it captures the key tenets and thematic issues that this book will be concerned with. First, the film recognises that contemporary existence is increasingly augmented, 'overlaid with dynamically changing information, multimedia in form and localized for each user' (Manovich 2006: 220). Space is increasingly liquefied, constantly recontextualised in contemporary life, and digital age science fiction film and television explores this through the augmented realities it represents and critically comments upon in its future settings.

As Lev Manovich argues, through its 'deep remixability' digital filmmaking is particularly suited to capturing or enacting augmentation. This creates a new visual aesthetic where:

> Typography is choreographed to move in 3D space; motion blur is applied to CGI; algorithmically generated fields of particles are blended with live-action footage to give it an enhanced look; a virtual camera is made to move around a virtual space filled with 2D drawings.
>
> (2006: 221)

In digital age science fiction film and television this remixability fosters a new 'perceptual realism' (Prince 1996), one no longer founded on pure indexicality but on images that blur and conjoin differing realist, animated and computer-generated layers. In *Sight* there is a shot of a night sky that has been augmented, where the constellations have been turned into a gaming puzzle for Patrick to solve. Real night-time stars are animated and digitised, yet because of the CGI rendering processes they may not actually be in the sky at all. Of course, the night sky itself may have been touched-up in the post-production process. One can no longer tell what is present in a digital world of constant augmentation. In what might be understood as a perfected character–viewer alignment, Patrick's and the viewer's vision of the world is built on perceptual realism:

> A perceptually realistic image is one which structurally corresponds to the viewer's audiovisual experience of three-dimensional space. Perceptually realistic images correspond to this experience because film-makers build them to do so. Such images display a nested hierarchy of cues which organize the display of light, color, texture, movement, and sound in ways that correspond with the viewer's own understanding of these phenomena in daily life. Perceptual realism, therefore, designates a relationship between the image or film and the spectator, and it can encompass both unreal images and those which are referentially realistic. Because of this, unreal images may be referentially fictional but perceptually realistic.
> (Prince 1996: 32)

To put it another way, the sight in *Sight* suggests that we are seeing the film world and the 'real' world differently if simultaneously, and from within a posthuman field of interaction.

Second, *Sight* recognises and establishes the present human condition as having entered a posthuman state or the time of 'Me++ … man-computer symbiosis' (Mitchell 2003). This is the conceit of digital age science fiction film and television in general: not only does it replicate the core values, hopes and concerns of the posthuman condition – prophesises on its future possibilities – but also it helps herald in the actual experience of humans living cybernetic lives. It does this through its human–machine characterisations, cyborg narratives and spectacularly augmented world-building processes.

Both Patrick and Daphne are constantly plugged into new media interfaces. These interfaces have been grafted onto or into their eyes, and work in consort with their cerebral networks. *Sight* suggests that this has dystopian consequences, as para-social interaction becomes the constant in human relationships, turning intimacy into a virtual game. In *Sight*, human conduct is tied to transnational commercial enterprises, which are involved in surveillance and control mechanisms and policing regimes. Patrick and Daphne are both versions of Paul Virilio's 'spastic': catastrophic urban figures that have abandoned themselves to the passive dreamscapes of new media technologies and interfaces; unable to exist freely in the world, they are controlled by the machine (1997: 20).

In contemporary life, the question of radical embodiment, and of the pleasures and contradictions of lived and living flesh, has become a dominant concern: one is increasingly asked to 'live themselves as code' (Hayles 1993) – just as Patrick and Daphne do in *Sight*. N. Katherine Hayles sees a present time in which 'coupling with intelligent machines' is so 'intense and multifaceted that it is no longer possible to distinguish meaningfully between the biological organism and the informational circuits in which the organism is enmeshed' (1999: 2).

Digital age science fiction film creates the particular conditions for a critical exploration of prosthetic, simulated and cyborgian life since, in these texts, human capabilities are extended, enriched, and where one's sense of selfhood is multiplied out, allowing the borders and boundaries of what constitutes woman and man to be redrawn. There are utopian sentiments in this reimagining of the human, of course. Patrick and Daphne can be argued to lead enchanted lives where 'play' organises the rhythms of each working day. The ability of digital age science fiction to create these affecting conditions of the posthuman experience is in part down to its computer-generated imagery.

This is in fact the third theme of this monograph and one that is played out in *Sight*: digital age science fiction's ability to draw on digital effects to create intense affects. These are effects and affects that render the viewer's eyes as haptic instruments of touch, and the cinematic environment equally spectacular and sublime. Digital technology has 'transformed the photographic image into a truly 'plastic' object that can be moulded and remoulded into whatever shape is desired' (Belton 2002: 101). In this limitless realm of new-world building, one offers the viewer an enriched, deeply immersive, intro-subjective experience that is exactly like being within the future.

Sight creates the conditions for seeing the future as one that is actively affected by special effects. Patrick and Daphne's eyes have the power to skyride, shift constellations, update Facebook and order wine, within a series of moveable, pliable digital screens. Given that this remaking-their-world takes place through point-of-view shots, or through the narrative being progressed by eye movement – set as it is within an effects environment – one is positioned to experience the film through a plastic 'haptic visuality' (Marks 2000). This enables us to magically, prosthetically, touch the various screens with our eyes.

Fourth, *Sight* builds its narrative out of the commercialisation of knowledge in the age of a computerised society where the grand narratives of pre-modernity no longer hold true. In the contemporary digital age, truth and reason are seen to be held in the service of government, the military and big business (Lyotard 1984). Knowledge and understanding are increasingly 'exteriorised', belonging with/to the corporate machine world. One is continually connected to this totalising machine but in a slave-to-master commodity-type relationship. Patrick works for the machine world as a gaming programmer, and he lives through its simulations and applications. Knowledge is reduced to how one can overcome obstacles and complete levels, for which one is rewarded the currency of points and standing within the game world (which *is* the world). However, Patrick has elevated social status as a programmer, and Daphne is under his control, even though she doesn't realise it until it is too late. Patrick symbolises the rise of technocrats and designers as the new power elite, while Daphne, swept up in its operations, is powerless to resist or lessen its control.

Digital age science fiction film and television is not only a conduit for critically exploring the trade and traffic in knowledge, with a parallel concern for technological development and an appetite for surveillance and conspiracy, but also contributes to the commercialisation of the latest techno-scientific inventions. As Ben Walker suggests, digital age screen science fiction can be seen as a 'technological showcase for current image creation technologies – technologies that perhaps only a few years before were science fictions in themselves' (2007: 3). Digital age science fiction film and television helps commercialise the latest technological developments; it becomes a testing ground and a shop window for the latest and greatest in digital special effects.

Fifth, in terms of production, *Sight* draws attention to the deterritorialisation involved in digital age science fiction film and television.

Digital tools have made it possible for amateur and student filmmakers to create high-end science fiction shorts and features, and have those films streamed online or downloaded. The once centre of science fiction film production, Hollywood America, is being challenged by the digital periphery, and by new transnational relations in film and television production. At the aesthetic level this extends to the way space and place are deterritorialised and reterritorialised, never simply grounded or rooted to a fixed location, but constantly remediated and reconstituted. In digital age science fiction film and television, space and place are always in flight and, consequently, one exists in a constant state of 'becoming nomad' (Mittag 2009: 253).

The expansive spatialisation of the digital image often draws attention to the unstable extremes of space and to the feeling that one is not very far away from the edge, from falling, flying or disappearing. As Kristen Whissel argues:

> the new digital verticality is a technique for activating polarized extremes. Its abstract spatial coordinates are those of the zenith and the nadir, and its favorite location is the precipice, regardless of setting.
>
> (2006: 24)

Patrick's simulated skyride at the beginning of *Sight* is an example of this, where he climbs and falls at great speeds, over undulating landmasses, seemingly without end. Of course, the theme-park ride often set in Hollywood franchise settings, and which draws upon the special effects of screen technologies, creates a kinetic game out of these polar extremes.

Manuel Castells suggests that we live in the age of a networked society organised by new formations in space and time. The 'space of flows' is made up of nodes and networks, 'of places connected by electronically powered communication networks through which flows of information that ensure the time-sharing of practices processed in such a space circulate and interact' (2005: 33). In the networked society, places and people only become important in terms of how central they are to the flow of information. Location thus becomes secondary and ephemeral – recognised only in and through the nodes and networks it is connected to and passes through. Time is also recalibrated, becoming 'timeless' or non-linear, compressed and multi-variable. As Castells argues:

> The relationship to time is defined by the use of information and communication technologies in a relentless effort to annihilate time by negating sequencing: on one hand, by compressing time (as in split-second global financial transactions or the generalized practice of multitasking, squeezing more activity into a given time); on the other hand, by blurring the sequence of social practices, including past, present, and future in a random order, like in the electronic hypertext of Web 2.0, or the blurring of life-cycle patterns in both work and parenting.
>
> (34)

Sight takes place in the space of flows and the time of timeless time. Patrick and Daphne interact and consume information from networks and nodes not visible or directly within their place of work and play. This can be seen as a metaphor for the digital film and television industry, one that transcends space to be fully globalised even if specific sites such as Wellywood (in New Zealand) become prestige places from which special-effects film flows out. The time that Patrick and Daphne expend has been broken down into bitesize gaming chunks, and they can access time's past (the history of their personal profiles, for example) in the present. They can also use this to control or shape their future, such as when Patrick accesses Daphne's profile in order to seduce her.

Digital age science fiction film and television exists in the streams of these networks and nodes, creating representations of its movement. Liquid science fiction explores timeless time through the way linear time is annihilated by its expendable spaces and temporal journeys, which are always constituted as simultaneously in the past, present and future. Patrick has already decided how the date with Daphne will go and can ensure that this future time plays out the way he intends it to.

Sixth, *Sight* draws attention to digital dematerialisation and the supposed loss of an indexical reality through which one directly feels and experiences the world (also see the perceptual realism discussion above). In *Sight*, directly seeing, touching, hearing, smelling and tasting things is replaced with virtual versions of the sensorial that have been technologically created within the gaming aesthetics of the film. The implication is that one no longer needs possessions or real environments to traverse, since they can be digitally materialised and experienced through 'breathing' para-interfaces.

The real-world corollary to this scenario is of course the demise of the physical ownership of records, cassettes, CDs, DVDs, videos and games. These are replaced with 'invisible' products and interfaces that can be streamed or downloaded on portable stations or mobile devices. Our cultural memory, pleasures, hobbies and interests, alongside information and news, are increasingly stored in 'cloud' environments not visible to the naked eye.

Nonetheless, this digital dematerialisation requires a rematerialisation of the senses – they are not absented altogether. The media nodes and networks of the networked society are sounded out, visualised, given tactile interfaces and surfaces; and these require a sensuous interaction. The sound and feel of a mouse as it clicks and moves across a mat, the whirr of a laptop starting up, the intricate layers of the touchscreen and the delicate feel of the smartphone as one runs one's fingers over it point to a sensuous re-engagement with the digital world. As communicative fabrics, digital textures are collaborative: 'texture is something through which cultural praxis materialises according to regular rhythms (daily routines, seasons, traditions) into something deeply felt' (Jansson 2008: 8).

Nonetheless, Sean Cubitt sees a wider cultural and economic reality in play with regards to this process of digital dematerialisation. Humans become 'biochips' in a 'synergetic culture' (Cubitt 1998: 134). Multimedia corporations produce them as a series of clones, and they are asked to consume in dematerialised retail and leisure environments. Again, in this scenario, Patrick is a biochip, a cloned company man, window-shopping in a virtual game of his boss's choosing.

Finally, *Sight* draws attention to the way information is stored, shared, retrieved and accessed in contemporary life. As David Lyon contends:

> All contemporary institutions in the so-called advanced societies are characterized by an internal imperative to obtain, store, produce and distribute data for use in the risk management for and of their respective populations. Employers try to reduce risk – of workers using office time or equipment for their own purposes, for instance – in employment situations. The police, in concert with other institutions, work towards preventing the risks of crimes being committed, or, more generally, of threatening behaviours. And marketers do all in their power to avoid risks of lost opportunities, market niches, and, ultimately, profit. All engage in data gathering procedures to try to pinpoint risks (or opportunities) and

to predict outcomes. So surveillance spreads, becoming constantly more routine, more intensive (profiles) and extensive (populations), driven by economic, bureaucratic and now technological forces.

(1998: 6)

One's private and public self is constituted online, in numerous virtual realms, and information about oneself is harvested, surveyed and stored by any number of governmental and commercial agencies and enterprises. This information can be hacked, stolen, bought and sold. One's identity in the world can be altered; one can ultimately be deleted or expunged by/from the virtual networks. One can be dematerialised, although not quite: just as Daphne gets to see the applications that Patrick was trying to conceal, one can never be fully erased in the digital age since electronic traces always remain.

In summary, *Sight* points to the numerous ways that digital age science fiction film and television is presently constituted, the themes and issues it addresses, and the way it interprets and creates the conditions for living in, and engaging with, contemporary liquid life.

Liquid Science Fiction Film and Television

In this book one of the central, overarching concepts for understanding digital age science fiction film and television is liquidity and liquefaction. This idea rests on the premise that contemporary human relations are defined by their impermanence and transience, and they take place in networks that constantly flow and change as they do so. Flow is matched by velocity: it is not just that everything is in flux but also that transformations are rapid. According to Zygmunt Bauman, modern life can be defined as having entered a state of liquid modernity or the 'era of disembedding without re-embedding' (Bauman and Tester 2001: 89), where:

> Transience has replaced durability at the top of the value table. What is valued today (by choice as much as by unchosen necessity) is the ability to be on the move, to travel light and at short notice. Power is measured by the speed with which responsibilities can be escaped. Who accelerates, wins; who stays put, loses.
>
> (95)

One can argue that much of contemporary, popular film and television can be defined by its liquidity and velocity. To put it more boldly, we live in the age of the liquid screen, with science fiction its watery engine exemplar. When one thinks of digital age science fiction film and television as liquid, characterised by quick motion, aesthetic flow, operation or affect, a number of qualities are being suggested.

One can become a screenmaker in quick time: entry costs, skill levels, accessibility and mobility all enable the amateur to tell science fiction stories quickly and cheaply, whether it be in the home, on the street, in underground locations, or overseas. Diploma and certificated film and video courses confirm the impression that one can acquire digital film or video-making skills and competencies in 3/6/12-month segments of time. One can be a screenmaker quickly and quickly make science fiction films and television or pod serials.

Shooting and production schedules are fast, with new mobile and digital technologies enabling the acceleration of the screenmaking process. Image capture is fast and instantly digitised rather than emulsified, and the immediacy of the image allows one to review, replay and recast images and stories in the moment of the liquid live. One is given the power to craft one's own unbelievable stories out of what was once considered to be in the realm of 'science fiction'. For example, the increasing use of 'coverage' in film production, derived from television production, where multiple cameras are used to shoot a scene, enables it to be more easily wrapped up. In fact, to stage a whole scene in one shot is no longer common when making a film. As Steven Soderbergh argues:

> That kind of staging is a lost art, which is too bad. The reason they no longer work that way is because it means making choices, real choices, and sticking to them. ... That's not what people do now. They want all the options they can get in the editing room.
>
> (Kehr 2006)

In this modern liquid version of screenmaking, then, in the editing room one can cut a science fiction text more speedily and greedily with a series of multiple, floating options set before the editor. Remixability and multiple-screen augmentation are thus the necessary conditions of contemporary science fiction film and programme making. One can see the screen editor's toolbox being actively used in digital age science fiction film and television as a narrative device: in *Minority Report* (Spielberg 2002), for example, multi-touch interfaces are used to edit together potential crimes; while in the television series *Continuum* (Reunion Pictures 2012–2015), Kiera (Rachel Nichols) is a cybernetically enhanced City Protective Services (CPS) law-enforcement officer equipped with visual, memory and audio implants. This gives her access to data directly overlaid on her visual field, sensors with functions that include biometric detection, heat detection, telescopic vision and a recording implant that constantly records her sensory information so that she has perfect recall and can arrange these memories in linear fashion. Her sight, memory and hearing can be live streamed in high-definition to technical experts.

New digitised editing tools and software enable time itself to be arrested from its point of origin and expanded. Spatial and temporal velocities can be increased or quickened beyond the laws of natural physics, so there are no limits to where the science fiction story can travel (Spielmann 1999, Keane 2007). In particular, the special visual effects of the science fiction blockbuster or the television 'event' spectacle wrap up time and space in pockets of liquid light that zoom across and through the lens. The impressive, often-repeated shot of a space ship accelerating into/through warp speed is the epitome of these light-speed affects.

Vivian Sobchack suggests that contemporary special effects 'symbolize the "irrational warmth" of intense (and usually positive) emotions' (1987: 282), imagining speed and liquidity as sensorial transmission actants. The 'liquid' qualities of a great deal of contemporary special effects – starting with *Terminator 2: Judgment Day* (Cameron 1991) – suggest the transmutability of existence and the terror that produces. For example, the T-1000 (Robert Patrick) is able to move from one physical state to another – from solid to liquid matter – allowing it to assume the form of other objects (commonly knives and weapons) or people who might help him track John Connor down. Bodies become porous, both delightful in the way they liquefy and terrifying because of the way they reconstitute human life.

Similarly, post-production visual effects (such as universal capture) create the impression of reality being dissolved in breathtaking moments of electrified speed, but also of liquid trace – of something watery always being left on or of the image. For example, the use of bullet-time in *The Matrix* (the Wachowski brothers 1999) is:

> the result of 120 cameras taking a cascade of shots of the organized scene along a 360-degree arc. The effect is a slight freezing of time as the character delivers a kick or dodges bullets in full panoramic turn.
>
> (Keane 2007: 122)

For Keane, 'the time freeze aspect of bullet-time works in simultaneously increasing the "wow factor" and allowing more prolonged observation' (2007: 123). In fact, as I will go on to argue below, liquid science fiction film and television can also be stuck, held fast, arrested by a paralysis in/of speed. That is, it can also be an intermittently slow or contemplative cinema held in the tide, nonetheless, of an always-coming velocity.

Movie release dates have quickened. The window of time for showing films at the cinema has shortened; airing time for television shows on subscription-based digital channels has been squeezed as television series and serials are 'binged' upon. Much of world cinema is itself caught up in the relentless movement of Hollywood fare or co-produced 'international' pictures that generally appeal to liquid time viewers in cinemas with a rapid turnover of films. However, the variant movement of film has quickened through its electronic transportability, accessibility, real-time multi-platform distribution, and the illegal art and craft of piracy and downloading that has enabled films to be available before they have hit market shores or shops. One no longer has to wait to see a science fiction film that one might have had to wait for up to 12 months to see previously – it can be downloaded and shared instantaneously. The same is true, of course, for television, increasingly pirated or available to watch in one sitting, with Netflix airing the full season of shows such as *Sense8* (Netflix 2015–) in one mass-market release.

Reception contexts for science fiction film and television are also liquid. They are mobile, virtual and groundless; found in the palm of a hand, tablet, internet window, or on a USB stick carried around with you. Alternatively, they are consumed in the quick movement of the gallery space. In the context of the domestic space, where one is hooked up to cable/digital/satellite providers, one can record, rewind or fast-forward 'live' science fiction cinema on gigantic 3D, liquid crystal display screens. Liquid age science fiction film and television becomes an immersive experience, fully sensorial.

And, yet, one time-shifts one's entertainment habits because the days are so full, so fast and liquid. One has to schedule one's pleasures and experience them in quick-time mode to match the experience of modern living, even if this is often in the guise or pretence of slowing or winding down. Fast and slow reception meet head-on, creating an unhinged appreciation of science fiction, and of what contemporary life is like to experience.

The world of science fiction film and television attaches itself to the science fiction of the world: impressions and oblique expressions of life flood one another. No more is this true when addressing the aesthetics of speed and the liquidity of aesthetics. No longer do we inhabit the realms of the 'movement image' or the 'time image', as suggested by Deleuze (1989). Rather, this is the moment of the fast image and the image of flow.

One can argue that much of contemporary science fiction film and television is obsessed with fast time: do-or-die deadlines; expiration and termination dates; missed meetings; chance encounters; and the fast 'temporality' of the screen itself as it helter-skelters out of temporal and spatial control. The camera smashing into, or rather through everything, woozy and blurry, unleashed or uncoupled from narrative co-ordinates, encapsulates such flow and velocity.

In Time (Niccol 2011), set in a dystopian future where time has been turned into a commodity that one has to buy in order to survive beyond 25 years of age, captures this multi-perspectival sense of speed through its ubiquitous deployment of fast editing, constant camera movement, fast dialogue and rapid scene segmentation. Justin Timberlake's character, Will Salas, desperately feels his own sense of time running out and away from him, as he struggles to earn enough money to buy the credits he needs before he is terminated. In *In Time*, one stops ageing at 25 years old but then has to buy 'time' if one is to live on. Will Salas is given an extraordinary amount of credits by a stranger he meets in a bar, but is then too late to stop his mother, Rachel Salas (Olivia Wilde), from being terminated. This cross-cut scene, where Rachel races through the streets to borrow some time from Will, is a metaphor not only for the global meltdown and the faulty flow of liquid capital, but also for science fiction cinema's present unstoppable desire for speed and liquidation.

The blockbuster science fiction ride experience encapsulates many, if not all, of the tenets outlined above: how fast can one go, how fast can one travel and how can we render time and space as pure moments of speed and velocity? Blips. Smudges. Quick colours and luminous traces. Vibrations. Crashes. Explosions. Special fast effects. Disintegration. Lightning-quick expansions and contractions. *Fast*. For example, in *The Day the Earth Stood Still* (Derrickson 2008), a swarm of self-aware nanites sweep away everything in their wake, breaking down all matter, and all objects in their way. The swarm is at times barely perceptible but breaks hard matter down in milliseconds of time. It moves, or rather flows, wave-like across the USA with incredible speed, while drawing attention to the 'liquid' nature of modern life, which vanishes as soon as it is engulfed.

In the *Doctor Who* episode 'Waters of Mars' (BBC 2009), ancient toxic water turns humans into liquid zombies who gush great volumes of it from their mouths and limbs. The infected become mindless and borderless – their water propensity getting into everything. As the Doctor says, 'Water is patient, Adelaide, water just waits. It wears down the clifftops, the mountains, the whole of the world. Water always wins.' The episode ends with the suicide of Adelaide, who should have died on Mars according to the fixed-point-in-time reasoning of the show. Her Camus-ian way out stands in for the utter if futile rejection of liquid modernity.

For David Bordwell, we have entered an era of what he calls intensified continuity in which the average length of each shot in a film has become shorter over the years; scenes are built up by closer framing; more extreme focal lengths are used; and scenes include an increased number of camera moves. Bordwell argues that starting with the New Hollywood of the 1970s, commercial filmmaking in America and elsewhere increasingly involved 'more rapid editing … bipolar extremes of lens lengths … more close framings in dialogue scenes … [and] a free-ranging camera'. Further, Bordwell goes on to argue that in recent years:

> Hollywood action scenes became 'impressionistic,' rendering a combat or pursuit as a blurred confusion. We got a flurry of cuts calibrated not

in relation to each other or to the action, but instead suggesting a vast busyness. Here camerawork and editing didn't serve the specificity of the action but overwhelmed, even buried it.

(2002: 28)

Digital age science fiction film and television is particularly caught in the tide of liquid modernity where busyness is seen a constituent of modern life as it is lived now and will be in the future; where attachments are loose and disconnected and one is overwhelmed by this experience of intoxicating and intoxicated speed. *The Adjustment Bureau* (Nolfi 2011) creates such a narrative of chaos and disembedding but through reverse ideological positioning. The film suggests that all our decisions are carefully planned, managed and controlled and that if we step outside this grand 'plan', our lives will be ruined. However, the two lovers of the film, David (Matt Damon) and Elise (Emily Blunt), are allowed to stay together to prove that going off-plan can bring benefits and togetherness. The film implicitly suggests that ordered life is important but that chaos brings people together. The film involves a series of frenetic chases and time loops as the characters attempt to challenge the plan and escape their proposed destiny of not being together. The aesthetic palette of the film is liquid, then, and in consort with the narrative supports the qualities of liquid modernity. This type of time crisis, in which speed makes the lived moment fleeting but full, exciting but draining, cardiovascular but traumatic, is everywhere today.

In *Post-Cinematic Affect* (2010), Stephen Shaviro argues that the expansion of the techniques of intensified continuity, especially in action films and action sequences, has led to a situation where continuity itself has been fractured and devalued, or fragmented and reduced to incoherence. He argues 'that in mainstream action films by Michael Bay, Tony Scott and Paul Greengrass, as well as in lower-budget action features by directors like Mark Neveldine and Brian Taylor, continuity is no longer "intensified"'. Rather, it is more or less abandoned for, or subordinated to, the search for immediate shocks, thrills and spectacular effects by all sorts of non-classical film techniques. Shaviro argues:

> This is the situation that I refer to as post-continuity. This is a filmmaking practice in which a preoccupation with moment-to-moment excitement,

and with delivering continual shocks to the audience, trumps any concern with traditional continuity, either on a shot-by-shot level or in terms of larger narrative structures.

(Shaviro 2011)

The same can be said of digital age television event science fiction: already with less time to tell its story, but with more self-contained or connecting episodes to keep the spectacle going, it propels its narrative through spectacle, shock and catastrophe (Abbott 2013). *The Walking Dead* series best encapsulates this relentless drive for spectacular apocalypse, where the body count and the means of destruction are the ways the story progresses.

Digital age science fiction film and television is very often shock-driven, enunciated through a series of spectacular reveals and the constant movement of action and interaction, overlaid rather than necessarily in logical order. These are waves of shocks, interconnected and symbiotic, perhaps best encapsulated by the *Transformers* film franchise, where movement, speed and liquidity permeate the special effects, the character relations and narrative pattern. Traditional families are non-existent in the film, the robots constantly change shape and size, cutting rates are rapid and scenes are organised around intensified encounters.

Of course, the definition of the word 'fast' also contains oxymoronic qualities. To be fast is to flout conventional moral standards; to be sexually promiscuous. To be fast is to be resistant to destruction or fading – as in fast colours. To be fast is to be firmly fixed or fastened – as in a fast grip. To be fast is to be fixed firmly in place; to be secure. To be fast is to be lasting and permanent. To be fast is to be held in something deep – as in a fast sleep. This type of fastness seems particularly 'dry', not liquid-like at all. And yet it remains constant: liquidity is also this type of fastness.

The apocalyptic Anthropocene film and television series is often constituted out of this fastness: environmental apocalypse has left Earth parched and humankind is stuck on the road to annihilation, as is the case in *The Road* (Hillcoat 2010). There is very often an element of being trapped, boxed in and confined – stuck within a mouse-like wheel or force field of some kind. In *The Island* (Bay 2005), clones (who think they have escaped a dead outside world) are hidden underground, promised an escape through the mythic tropical island that has been spared the ravages of degradation, only to be killed for organ transplantation as they are in touching distance of their freedom. In the future-set episode, 'Fifteen Million Merits' (Black Mirror, Channel 4 2011), everyone must cycle on exercise bikes in order to power their surroundings and generate currency called 'merits'. People live in guarded and surveyed 'virtual' communities and the only escape is through winning a televised talent contest. Their lives have become a never-ending game – played fast but stuck in an eternal nightmare.

Digital age science fiction film and television is contained and framed by these properties of fastness. It is a form, nonetheless, that still has the potential to be dangerous, to flout moral standards and challenge normative assumptions. It is a type of screenmaking that calls upon the contemplative and the melancholic; that arrests and freezes time. It creates particularly affecting dreamscapes that stand the test of time, that last in the cultural imaginary. It is an ocean, deep and rich, all around us, holding us in its swell.

Liquid Structure

Liquid Space: Science Fiction Film and Television in the Digital Age explores the ways in which contemporary science fiction represents and embodies the fears, hopes and longings of the age of digitalisation. Taken as a period in which digital technologies, practices and processes became readily available, consumable and representable, from the 1980s onwards, the book looks to draw text and context, textual specificity and cultural history, together so that science fiction film and television is understood not only to speak for, of and about the digital age, but also to herald and take part in its arrival and tumultuous effect.

The book considers this to be a gestation period in which radical cultural, economic and political transformations take place in the world, effecting and reshaping questions relating to production and consumption, faith and belief, identity and difference, and sensorial schemata. One finds this liquid new world order in the mercurial pulse, the arteries and veins, of digital age science fiction film and television.

Liquid Space: Science Fiction Film and Television in the Digital Age is composed of seven chapters. In Chapter 1, 'Then and Now: Television Time Travel and the Once Wonderful End to the Working Day', I examine the way time travel shifts textually and historically between the analogue and digital age. Taking the decades of the 1970s and 1980s, and then the 2000s, predominately in a UK viewing environment, I argue that television time travel, once a marvellous wonder and counterpoint to 'boxed-in' living, is now just one liquid stream in an age of ubiquitous mediated time travel. Further, in digital age science fiction, being stuck is no longer box-like but is nonetheless no freer. Where is the wonder in that? This chapter allows the book to be historically anchored before each subsequent chapter singularly explores the liquidity of digital age science fiction film and television.

In Chapter 2, 'Eye-Tracking the Sublime in Spectacular Moments of Science Fiction Film', I move my argument to spectacular science fiction film and the way our eyes and bodies may experience the sublime when watching certain scenes composed of phenomenal liquid special effects. Drawing upon eye-tracking technology and empirical research, I suggest that digital age science fiction offers us different, competing versions of the sublime – one that is contemplative and existentially liberating, and another that is in the service of the gods of consumption and the high tides of theme-park rides. Eye-tracking technology is also a liquid modern surveillance device and at the chapter's end I address the way its tracking capabilities are implicitly incorporated into digital age science fiction film and television.

In Chapter 3, 'Emptying Spaces: Digital Deterritorialisation', I examine the way that digital age science fiction film and television recasts space and place, geography and location; on the one hand, opening new landscapes for belonging and communion; and on the other, creating voids of disconnect and isolation.

In Chapter 4, 'Liquid Bodies', I look at the way the human body is reconstituted in this age of augmentation and data transference. I examine three central reconstitutions of flesh and being: the figure of the animal and the alien; the figure of the cyborg; and the theme of genes and cloning. I suggest that these liquid bodies are engaged in a dialectic that enables us not only to see their (our) limitations and constraints, but to look for and recognise their new-found liberties and freedoms. Gender and identity are two of my structuring intersections in this chapter.

In Chapter 5, 'Millennial Whiteness and Cinematic Outer Space', I turn my eye towards the politics of race and of how different contemporary representations of cinematic outer space express and embody the hopes and fears, rights and responsibilities, of whiteness. In the digital age, where whiteness is under threat and constant negotiation, it is to space where it heads to renew its salvic myths. Nonetheless, the chapter draws a line across the years of the Space Race to historicise the way whiteness manifests over time.

In Chapter 6, 'Liquid Terror', I examine the biopolitics of war and conflict as they impact upon and are shaped by digital age science fiction film and television. My central case study, *Children of Men*, carries with it all the blood, death and hope found in this 'war on terror' fiction. It also has a narrative agent, Theo Faron (Clive Owen), crafted out of the crisis in white masculinity. He embodies both the hope of whiteness and its near negation in the age of liquid modernity.

In Chapter 7, 'Sounding Liquid Science Fiction', I close my eyes briefly to hear the world through the fictions of digital age science fiction. I hear (and see) the spectacular sounds of space travel and the uncanny strange sounds of the alien, connecting their audio soundscapes to the liquid self in liquid spaces. I also hear (again) the sounds of loneliness like a resounding minor key rising out of the asphalt night.

In my conclusion, 'We Never Let the Fire Go Out', I poetically summarise the findings of the book and find myself examining the expanded environments of science fiction, as it is found in the installation space, and place myself in a domestic setting, where science fiction takes me and my children home. I conclude with the theme of obsolescence.

The book's structure intends to establish a digital age narrative where themes, issues and dilemmas cross-connect and articulate. The book's metaphoric primary title, *Liquid Space*, aims to suggest a process of total erasure that occurs in the modern world. This expurgation, found in the deletion of files, emails, records and data, and with it the loss of identity and history, is a digital age phenomenon that finds its most profound representation in *Science Fiction Film and Television in the Digital Age*. Deletion, of course, is never absolute or untraceable. Rather, it gives life to new shadowy processes and practices; it creates a new world order and new posthuman identities: it creates liquid space.

One final note: my approach to the study of science fiction is an embodied one. It involves looking closely at sensory aesthetics and attending to sensuous knowledge (Eagleton 1990, Pink 2009). This is because I take or start from the position that our encounters with science fiction are sensorial and multi-modal; they involve joy, pleasure, terror and fear, and at their most heightened are asemiotic – activated in and through feeling alone. I also suggest that in these immersive encounters there exists the potential for the radicalisation of the body, or a type of becoming that creates the conditions to free the self from its normally constituted docility and entrapment. It is an approach centrally concerned with recognising the politics of sensuous embodiment in which one can see in the exchange between science fiction and viewer a liberating emergence of the carnal body (Sobchack 2004).

My approach also involves the method of storying the self (Finnegan 1997), where one is asked to recount the encounters with science fiction through memorial work and personal narratives. These stories, however, are born from textural qualities; they draw upon synaesthesia and co-synaesthetic relations (Sobchack 2004). I argue that we draw upon our full sensorium to experience the wonder (and terror) of future worlds in their making and unmaking. Conversant with this approach is the role of auto-ethnography and aca-fandom, where personal narrative and appreciation are fused or conjoined with critical and contextual analysis. This book, then, is written personally – the voice of the author is heard across its pages. In an age where loneliness is rife and life is too fast and watery to hold on to, gathering around the personal is an invitation to journey with me, rather than alone.

1

Then and Now

Television Time Travel and the Once Wonderful End to the Working Day

Let me begin this book at the end of the beginning and the beginning of the end – at the shape-shifting doorway between the analogue age and the liquid digital present. Let me begin this book with the then and now of television time travel, to historicise these particular narratives of transformation, and to demonstrate how the experience of time (and space) changes from the analogue age to the digital epoch and its liquid modern propensities ...

In this first chapter I will present three interlinking arguments. First, the argument that the time travel television series historically provided viewers with a spectacular temporal and spatial alternative to the routine of everyday life, the regulation of television scheduling and the small-world confines of domestic subjectivity. In what is principally the dawn before liquid modernity, and taking the decades of the 1970s and 1980s, predominately in a UK viewing environment, I will suggest that the (analogue) special effect rendering of the time travel sequence expanded the viewer's material universe, and affectively wrenched the television set free from the strictures of scheduling and realist programming. Further, I will suggest that the time travel series readily and regularly *moved* the domestic space, the ordinary day and the everyman/person into awesome environments and situations that suggested alternative lifestyles and behaviours, with a different existential tempo and rhythm. At a narrative, thematic and aesthetically spectacular level, television time travel saw to the wonderful end of the working day. My chosen case studies include *Sapphire and Steal*, *Doctor Who* and *Quantum Leap*.

Second, in this chapter I will argue that rather than the contemporary time travel television series being an extraordinary alternative to ordinary life, it instead articulates convergence culture, deregulation, multiple channel viewing, and time-shift culture where there is no such thing as an ordinary working day or domestic viewing context. This type of time travel, then, takes place in and communicates through the watery age of liquid modernity. Taking the decades from the 1990s onwards, and the rise of the digital in particular, the extraordinary television time travel series is seen to be but one portal or dock or download in an age where a great many people *affectively* time travel. The irony here, as I will point out, is that the once sublime wonder of television time travel becomes potentially commonplace and, therefore, ultimately ordinary. The chapter will suggest that television time travel series such as *Life on Mars* are a nostalgic, emotional calling for a return to the end of the working day as it once was (emotively) experienced. These 'future to the back' texts return us to a pre-liquid modern age, where things are reimagined to be more purposeful and more whole than they are today. My case studies include *Sliders*, *Doctor Who* and *Life on Mars*.

Finally, the chapter will explore the idea of time and timeliness as key engines of digital age science fiction and liquid modernity. In the contemporary moment, time seems to be both set free and tightly controlled – a liquid paradox that keeps us in the thrall of what is the 'science fiction of time'.

Feeling Boxed In

I have always been enchanted by the very words 'special effects'. Seen written on the credit sequence, poster, or in a critical review, or sounded out in trailers and adverts, they are emotive letters to something extraordinary, something wonderful and deeply affecting. As a child in particular, they were a calling card for me to go to see that movie, or to tune in to the box, where, given scheduling patterns in the UK in the 1980s, it would for me mean a TV dinner set in intergalactic contexts. Special effects allowed me to encounter incredible creatures, planets and civilisations beyond the metaphorical and small-world confines of the little cathode ray, black-and-white box on which I would avidly watch science fiction programmes. In addition, the infinitely variable journeying of special effects allowed me to travel away from, and free of, the small-room, domestic context in which I found myself viewing. Special effects poured out of the box, threw unearthly light shadows and sound across the room, and lifted me upwards and outwards into and through spaces, places and times once unimaginable.

Homes are very particular social and cultural environments; familiar and familial, lived in and encountered in the most ordinary but intimate of ways. They are a type of body, of skin, an emotional and belonging environment that allows or enables one to call them home (Bourdieu 1990). From the middle of the last century, with the mass production of similarly designed and built houses, on parcelled-up plots of land, many homes were themselves box-shaped and placed on box-shaped grids with regulated and regular lines, roads and pathways, and uniform green spaces (Harris and Larkham 2003). In an experiential, closed-in sense, this was particularly true of high-density, low socio-economic-level housing in the UK, where conformity in design and planning was (and still is) the norm for cost factors and where perhaps – in the context of the post-World War II period – modernist utopian imaginings hoped that mass-built, faceless homes would free society ('the masses') from property hierarchies (Rowe 1993).

These were boxes, then, which framed one's viewing experience and contained one's everyday life. If one was to extend this concept of the boxed frame, the actual institutional and commercial imperatives that operated in UK broadcasting in the 1970s and 1980s produced a scheduling that was also boxed in, with rules for their timing, patterning and directed flow. One knew what was on the box without really having to check the TV guide since, in approximate terms, soap opera was followed by situation comedy was followed by drama was followed by the nightly news. This concept of television flow (Williams 1974/1992), or repeated and causal segmentation (Fiske 1987), or of flow and seamless segmentation (Feuer 1983), created a framed viewing context in which elements, patterns, forms, segues and links were held together in an arresting chain-like gestalt.

These were thus boxes of perception, space and time, mirrored by and connected with the strictures of capitalist work and school time, and with the regulated patterning of the everyday and the everywhere. Routine existence, 'disciplinary society' to use Foucault's (1975) terms, was experienced from morning to night, in and through an articulating range of discursive practices and processes. For the most part, television was free of and from special effects unless countenanced in occasional, spectacle-driven ritual, such as the Royal Variety Show, or big events such as a royal wedding, or 'escapist', 'flights of fancy' genres such as science fiction. I would like to suggest that what television special effects gave life to during this time was a feeling of what it might be like to exist 'outside the box' while still being inside it. While American soap operas such as *Dallas* (CBS 1978–1991) showed viewers glamorous, freer, less regulated lifestyles (Ang 2013), it was science fiction and the wonder of the time travel scenario in particular that provided a seemingly limitless temporal-spatial alternative to life outside the in-box.

In the *Sapphire and Steel* (ATV 1979–1982) episode 'Assignment 1: Escape Through a Crack in Time' (1979), Time has invaded an old country house and stolen the parents of two children. As Sapphire (Joanna Lumley) informs the children:

> There is a corridor and the corridor is time, it surrounds all things and it passes through all things ... Time can enter into the present, break in, burst through and take things, take people ... It can become weakened, like worn fabric, and then time can reach in and take things that it wants.

In this episode, at a metaphoric level, time represents science fiction's capacity to transcend and recast the regulatory rules of everyday life: it can weaken, then bend and move the walls of the lived-in box; and it can take the viewer to and through any number of different time co-ordinates.

At a narrative level, the moment time invades the present, all the clocks in the house stop as if regulatory life can itself be arrested and escaped. In effect, this is the ontological and existential power of science fiction being demonstrated. The sound of the ticking of numerous timepieces (the father of the house is an avid clock collector) and the silence that punctuates the arrival of Time provide the acoustic key for the sublime wonderment that follows. The children cut free of real-world time and witness its wayward spatial and temporal capabilities – time is no longer regular, linear or regulatory.

At the level of spectacle and special effects, walls, doorways, staircases and furniture become porous and dynamic. Ghosts, objects, memories made concrete, pour through them. For example, the wall in the girl's bedroom becomes a portal through which the ghosts of time can enter the present and steal people. This illusion of spatial movement is achieved through the use of the in-camera effect, the crash zoom, which distorts perspective, creating the impression that the background is getting closer. Film images of deep space, phantom people, and objects from the past are also projected onto the bedroom wall to create the sense that two worlds are blending together. The boxed-in life that was there is now liquefied through the way special effects affect the construction of time and space.

One might term this a special type of 'heterotopia of time' or, better still, a 'heterotopia of special effects', outside or beyond the ordinary through which a synthesis of 'special' irregular moments of time and space, conjoined with the wonder of special effects, recasts the places in which one largely exists. The ordinary becomes extraordinary, and Other. In one scene, the four walls of the bedroom extend out and deepen, and a cloaked figure emerges in, between and through the space created, moving toward the children as they sit watching, like TV viewers. The wall then becomes a screen, hit by cluster-like particles and atoms, as a nursery rhyme incantation is heard. Time and space are on the move in this scene and their linear and logical order has been broken. Together, time and space stop, expand and contract, even if by episode end they are again routinised, a point to which I will return below.

These are analogue special effects, nonetheless: unable to capture or replicate the uncanny valley or match entirely the verisimilitude of the fictional world. And, yet, the very fact that they were sometimes visible suggested an openness in/to the fictive world – one saw through them, and beyond them, to the world on the other side of the screen. There was a desperate wish for many on the lower levels of society to escape from and into something beyond the dour horizon of their everyday lives. I certainly did.

The grim and grey political contexts of the late 1970s and 1980s are important here. Margaret Thatcher's far-right UK government (1979–1987) initiated a period of vast economic change and transformation, where greater home ownership became a marker of individualised success and family centredness, as wave after wave of new box-shaped suburbs sprouted in former greenfield sites. At the same time, there was a reduction in the number of council houses and flats as they were sold off to tenants, a corresponding rise in homelessness, and an increase in the number of more expensive private rentals in the market. The boxed home and the neatly packaged life became a battleground, at the ideological and economic centre of a society of haves and have-nots (Balchin and Rhoden 2002).

It is not surprising, then, that the blue police phone box in *Doctor Who* (BBC 1963–) comes to embody and translate this battleground over the box. It is itself a neatly drawn boxed-in home that carries the tools of surveillance and the machinery of governance, and also a time-and-space machine, bigger on the inside, which can access any point in time as it travels the cosmos. This is a box that can be opened, and that is in (special) effect a limitless environment.

A Blue Box Across the Cosmos

Doctor Who's blue police phone box encapsulated a rich sense of this culturally inscripted, life lived-in-a-box feeling of the 1970s and 1980s, and yet also transcended it. The phone box is the Doctor's mobile home, but one in which he spends very little screen time, leaving for new- and old-world adventuring in almost every episode. Often positioned at the control centre, viewers perceive space as expanded, both inside and outside the box, as it hurtles through time and space.

There are multiple, mostly unseen, rooms in the box and hence a sense of it as both unknown and expandable. This is not, then, a realist box, a boxed home or neighbourhood, but a multi-dimensional environment that travels through, within and across layers of time and space. This is not an ordinary phone box but a living Tardis, a magical home, with a heart and soul, and made of cosmic energy that seems able to transcend all scientific rules, regulatory norms and timecodes.

The Tardis is a time and space machine operated by a Time Lord, which resists the very notion of the box and the metronome of capitalist life, since it/he/the viewer travels free of such impulses and constraints. If this limitless environment was conveyed through realist codes and conventions, then the transitory power of the phone box wouldn't be as affecting or as powerful. What is essential to its limitless potentiality is the alchemy and wonder of special effects that hurtle it through time and space, and which subsequently introduce the viewer to alternative possible worlds, peoples and civilisations.

In the episode 'The Robots of Death' (BBC 1977), Leela (Louise Jameson) asks the Doctor (Tom Baker) to explain why the Tardis is bigger on the inside, to which he responds, 'because insides and outsides are not in the same dimension'. He demonstrates this to be possible by showing how a big box can be fitted inside a small one if there is enough dimensional distance between them. The Doctor places different-sized boxes at a distance from one another, allowing visual illusion to stand in for dimensionality. This scene is captured in a deep-focus, long shot, the Doctor holding the smaller box close to the camera, the bigger box remaining on the Tardis console, at a distance, thus allowing the viewer to see, through this perceptual trick, that big and small can be reversed.

In the previous scene we witness the Tardis spinning in deep space, set against a cluster of stars, while the cut to this sequence has Leela spinning a yo-yo. Not only is a metaphoric relationship implied between expansion and contraction, the reversibility of big and small and in and out, but also space and time are given literal string-like qualities. Importantly, special effects are central to the affecting power of the bend in reason in these scenes: they provide the miniatures and the optical technology to allow the Tardis to appear life-size and as if it is hurtling through space (small becomes big); and they are self-reflexively referred to, not only through the Doctor's visual illusion trick, but also in his reference to multi-dimensionality as a feat accomplished by 'trans-dimensional engineering', an allusion to the special effects team. The Doctor articulates why and how the box can no longer be hermetically sealed and special effects give the viewer the wondrous material to see it evidenced.

Episodes set on contemporary Earth suggest that behind the illusion of the (viewer's) boxed-in life is another, more exciting, riskier reality. Ordinary city and home environments are invaded, borders infiltrated, and regulation itself threatened. For example, in 'The City of Death' (BBC 1979):

> The Doctor and Romana (Lalla Ward) are enjoying a holiday in Paris, 1979, when they become aware of a fracture in time. During a visit to the Louvre to see da Vinci's Mona Lisa, the Doctor purloins from a stranger, Countess Scarlioni, a bracelet that is actually an alien scanner device.
> (Doctor Who: The Classic Series)

The episode, the first to be shot on location, uses Parisian monuments and iconic settings to offer the limited sense of an exotic destination/location outside of the UK lived-in box, but then expands its 'far away' sentiment through alien intervention and a doomsday scenario, where if Scaroth, last of the Jagaroth, rewrites time and saves his ship from exploding, life on Earth will not have gone through its evolutionary trajectory, thus leaving humanity in a state of primitive existence. People are not what they seem in this episode, and spaces, interiors and doorways are shown to be dark portals to somewhere else not safe at all. The paranoia that surrounds and swells up suggests that the box is always under threat and never secure. It can be read, then, as an escapist fantasy for those bored with living in the box, but it also shows the necessary bend in reason to enable the box both to be transgressed and to have transgressive potential.

Jonathan Bignell has argued that through time travel, 'time travellers and cinema spectators are displaced from the reality of their own present and their own real location in order to be transported to an imaginary elsewhere and an imaginary elsewhen' (2004: 137). The same can be said of television time travel in this period, only more so, since the temporal and spatial location to be transcended is the tightly aligned series of boxed frames I referred to previously: the box in the corner of the room, the scheduling box that fixes programmes in viewing slots, the boxed room from which it is watched, the boxed neighbourhood one lives in, and the life-is-a-box that discursively defines modern existence. This transcendence of the box in all its forms occurs in and through what I would like to call the television of special attractions.

Television of Special Attractions

The time travel scenario often provides not only the futuristic narrative dynamic essential for the expanded universe of science fiction, but also the diegetic space for the deployment of the 'astonishing' special effects used to capture this extraordinary temporal and spatial shifting. Time travel can be forward-thrusting, as in space-bound ships leaving Earth for far, far away destinations, or can point in all directions, with time criss-crossed this way and that. The special effect rendering of the time travelling sequence is often sublime. Liquid lights, pulsating strange shapes and vectors wrinkle the screen, and distorted faces, lost objects and shimmering, revolving spacecraft emerge, smothered in the heat of travel, to engulf the screen and viewer in turn (see the discussion of the sublime special effect in Chapter 2). To appropriate Tom Gunning's thesis on early cinema, this is as much about 'supplying pleasure through an exciting spectacle' (1994: 230) as it is about narrative development. This special television of attractions offers the viewer a domesticated show-and-tell, viewed from the living room, which synaesthetically conjures up the power and sublime beauty of moving in, within and through the four walls of time and space.

In the opening title sequence to *Quantum Leap* (NBC 1989–1993), Dr Sam Beckett (Scott Bakula) steps into the quantum leap accelerator and vanishes. In a high-tech laboratory, the viewer watches his naked body become electrically charged, lightning rods enter his skin, and smoke or cloud rises up and around him, as the exterior space takes on the appearance of liquid, atomised space. His body then begins to melt, or dissolve, blending with the deep space transposed around him. Both his body, penetrated by light-like radiation, and the irradiated space that surrounds him move and mix, until Sam wakes up in an alternate past as someone else entirely. This is a spectacular reincarnation, rendering body, time and space mobile and interchangeable.

Viewing from a grey box in a political landscape that created a deep sense of boxed-in living, these examples of fluid becoming have ideological consequences or implications. Andrew Gordon argues that many more time travel science fiction films have been made since 1979 because there is 'a pervasive uneasiness about our present and uncertainty about our future, along with a concurrent nostalgia about our past' (2004: 116). What Gordon suggests is that there is a close correspondence between the political and economic crises that shaped this decade and the flight or evacuation mentality that characterised its science fiction films.

Again, this can also be said of television time travel, but rather than it being necessarily an indicator of flight or escape, one can see these texts as embodying the desire to transform the material existence of boxed-in living. Given that the home is central to the 1980s political crisis in the UK, the ability to transcend the home is crucial to the way spectacle recasts the domestic into something infinitely variable and potentially subversive (outside the regulated rules of time and space).

Nonetheless, time travel has another, distinct ideological function, since it provides the necessary distancing effect that science fiction employs to be able to address, metaphorically, the most pressing issues and themes that concern people in the present. If the modern world is one where the individual feels alienated and powerless in the face of bureaucratic structures and regulatory practices and processes, then time travel suggests that Everyman and Everybody is important in shaping history, making a real and quantifiable difference to the way the world turns out. In effect, time travel allows the individual to bring a new order to the regulatory streams of the universe – to make it in their own image. In *Quantum Leap*, Sam enters the past always as someone else, to 'put right what once went wrong'. He becomes 'ordinary people', but in historically important contexts and settings, always facing hurdles and obstacles he eventually overcomes, to right that wrong and to put history back on course. History can, then, be rewritten, wrongs can be put right, and one can leave one's box and take part in the big decisions. Sam is the embodiment of the heroic monomyth.

Nonetheless, I would like to return to an inherent tension in the way the science fiction television of this period recasts the experience of boxed-in living. This tension is manifested in two distinct ways. First, by episode end, irregular time has been defeated and ordinary life returned to, as in *Sapphire and Steele*'s 'Escape Through a Crack in Time' episode. In *Quantum Leap*, Sam always fixes the faultlines in the family home so that the social order is ultimately restored. Second, the ongoing battle to secure time, to fill in its cracks, and to bring order back to existence works against the freedom and possibility time initially opened up. At the wonderful end to a science fiction television episode, the working day will still resume tomorrow, and life-in-the-box will still go on. In *Doctor Who*, the Doctor's ultimate aim is to preserve human life as he knows it, in effect preserving the boxed-in way of life he seems to work against. One can therefore read television's science fiction function as bardic, cathartic and, ultimately, ideologically conservative.

There is, however, always a weight of surplus value in these spectacularly rendered narratives that cannot be contained by the force of episode closure. The box has been opened and its contents poured out, which offers the viewer a way out of the box, and a greater understanding of its ideological and political limitations. This surplus value is also experiential, sensorial based, a body-centred phenomenon, where:

> We are able to be touched by the substance of images, to feel a visual atmosphere envelop us, to experience weight and suffocation and the need for air, to take flight in kinetic exhilaration and freedom even as we are relatively bound to our seats, to be knocked backwards by a sound, to taste and smell the world on the screen.
>
> (Sobchack 2000)

The deployment of time travel special effects is, then, a sensationally arresting encounter. One experiences a different type of life, through a heightened set of feelings, the value of which lives on and on and on. Life in the ordinary box is thus defamiliarised and the viewer left with the profound feeling that things, objects, time and space are limitless in potential. This is a sublime encounter, irreducible to ideology, to discourse, language and power, but rather initiated beyond it, in a sea of impressions and affects that cannot be boxed in. Ultimately, in the context of special effects time travel, the ordinary becomes endowed with sublime properties and intensities that cast one free in a universe that has been chaotically reordered.

One might have expected that, as a result of the advances in special effects entailed by the digital revolution, this process of recasting the box would have even more potential today. But does it? Set within the conditions of liquid modernity, the box seems to have been broken wide open and yet naturalised at the same time. This is a tension that I would now like to explore further.

The Box Overflows

The contemporary television landscape is arguably marked by overflow and sustained convergence in which:

> Changes in communications, storytelling and information technologies are reshaping almost every aspect of contemporary life – including how we create, consume, learn, and interact with each other. A whole range of new technologies enable consumers to archive, annotate, appropriate, and recirculate media content and in the process, these technologies have

altered the ways that consumers interact with core institutions of government, education, and commerce.

(Jenkins 2001)

Overflow emerges when 'the text of the TV show is no longer limited to the television medium' (Brooker 2004: 569), while convergence involves a number of related technological, economic, cultural and 'social and organic' articulations (Jenkins 2001) through which viewing takes place in shifting time and place contexts, interactivity and mobility, and the searching and securing of content through platforms and web interfaces from all corners of the world. Television is no longer simply or singularly viewed on a box in the corner of the room in a constructed flow schedule, but rather downloaded, streamed, recorded and remixed, and watched on three-dimensional plasma screens, mobile devices, computer screens, tablets and laptops. In this context, television is multi-channel and involves synergetic links and off-shoots to other media content and platforms. The contemporary television landscape is thus seemingly not at all box-like, not limited in its production and reception contexts, but infinitely expandable and found in and on a series of screens of different shapes and sizes, transported to and from global places and networks, so that far and near exist in the same liquid slipstream. It seems that the time travel experience is now embedded in the rhythm and pace of liquid modern life.

Digital special effects have helped to foster the sense that one exists in an expandable and easily navigated universe, since its rendering processes and capabilities has meant that what can be filmed or captured is now almost infinitely variable (Wood 2007). Digital special effects are increasingly found, as costs depreciate, in all forms of television, and in everyday event-based spectacles such as weddings and school balls. It can be argued that they have increased the level of wonder one experiences because they are essentially boundless in their effects/affects.

While television special effects of the 1980s can be seen as crude and rudimentary, plastic and analogue, the digital age has created sheets and layers so intricate and complex that everything within the diegetic world now seems possible. In *Sliders* (Fox, Sci-Fi Channel 1995–1999), for example, the time-window through which they jump, and which takes them from one alternate universe to another, is rendered porous through digital special effects that allow the window to flex, and stretch, to be simultaneously concave and convex. The impression is that time and space are fluid in their innate constitution.

This is exactly the quality of digital special effects today. Their capacity to endow the fiction with the presence of limitlessness and their seemingly limitless power is, in part, dependent on their ability to capture and create things not present in the production process. Consequently:

> Digital imaging in its dual modes of image processing and CGI challenges indexical based notions of photographic realism. As Bill Nichols has noted, a digitally designed or created image can be subject to infinite manipulation. Its reality is a function of complex algorithms stored in computer memory rather than a necessary mechanical resemblance to a referent ... no profilmic referent (needs to) exist to ground the indexicality of its image.
> (Prince 1996: 31)

Digital special effects' capacity to create things that have not been filmed, to render images, landscapes, portals and creatures without need for an index sign to be present, or for a profilmic event to have taken place, not only, first, destroys and, then, rebirths the parameters of the box, but also reconstitutes (its/our) existence as infinitely variable. This is, of course, one of the supposed conditions of liquid modernity: endless (consumer) choice and opportunity. The world we presently live in is imagined to be exactly like one giant special effect.

The rebooted *Doctor Who* best expresses this expansion in and of the overflow, media convergence, and the digital recasting of time travel and the seemingly limitless potential of the box. *Who* exists simultaneously on different screens, is connected to games, merchandising and official blogs, is the subject of fanfic and fanzines, tweets, updates and behind-the-scenes exposés. *Who* is a franchise, a commodity intertext, with numerous spin-offs such as *Torchwood* (BBC 2006–2011) and *The Sarah Jane Adventures* (BBC 2007–2011). Its content, then, pours across various platforms, can be accessed/streamed/downloaded almost anywhere in the world, and it asks its fans to interact and engage with all this material. *Who* exists as the epitome of time-shift, convergence culture, and makes nonsense of the boxed-in life, since its fantasies and imaginings ripple across the mediated world.

This process is underwritten by its use of digital special effects and narrative arcs where the blue phone box is constantly opened, time extended and amplified, and place and space mutate and shape-shift. A wonderful example is in the episode 'The Big Bang' (BBC 2010) when the Tardis explodes, captured in wonderful cosmos-blast imagery, indicative of the motif that no box is containable in the contemporary age. A similar reading could be made of the Pandorica, a spectacular prison built to hold the Doctor, where it is only in the living present, with contemporary special effects, that a prison that cannot be escaped is in fact opened and time set free.

There are also episodes where rooms and spaces are constantly breached, where hidden doorways exist, or where everyday entrances are portals to alternate spaces. Hospitals can be taken to the moon ('Smith and Jones', 2007). Hotels can change their rooming configuration ('The God Complex', 2011). Council flats can devour people ('Night Terrors', 2011). Libraries can exist in the mind of the child and the eye of the television screen ('Forest of the Dead', 2008). 'Blink' (2007) and a stone statue can move so quickly it can kill you before you open your eyes. Many of these scenes are made manifest through digital processing and imaging, so that narrative and digital special effects converge and embrace each other, ending the age of the boxed-in life through the spectacular re-rendering of the real. But is this really so?

There is another tradition in digital age science fiction that I have been alluding to, and one that spans the analogue and digital age: the theme of being trapped, locked in, held in containment centres or solitary confinement. Being boxed in is in one sense a generalised narrative convention of the form. *The Prisoner* (ITV 1967–1968) is one such example, where in each episode Agent Number Six (Patrick McGoohan) finds himself unable to breach the defences of The Village where he has been imprisoned.

In digital age science fiction, however, containment is spectacularly captured by the way the special effects *produce* the forcefield, the island, the prison that holds people inside. In *Under the Dome* (CBS 2013), and *Lost* (ABC 2004–2010) (as well as films such as *Lockout* (Mather 2012) and *The Matrix* (the Wachowski brothers 1999)) one finds oneself trapped by the digital effect, by the shape-shifting entity that prevents one from escaping. This is an apt metaphor and experiential rendering of the condition of liquid modernity itself: one is held in situ by the aura of the special effect, and no matter how one tries to escape the condition of one's existence, one is always brought back to the streams that cross-connect. If this is the case, if we can't escape the liquid modern present, then we need to return to the analogue past.

Nostalgia for the Ordinary Wonderful

One might argue that time travel has become so very ordinary, everyday, and the special effects employed to render it, more often than not, banal and superficial. They are no longer an embodiment of a special heterotopia, but normality itself (Pierson 2002). It can be argued that life is so awash with special effects that these can no longer create the moment of unfamiliarity in the ordinary, or the sublime wonder at the shifting streets and sheets of time, since they are now the actual oxygen of the everyday and the everywhere. Special effects have become the cornerstone of the society of spectacle 'where all of life presents itself as an immense accumulation of spectacles' (Debord 1994: 95).

While new media technologies have afforded people the opportunity to time- and space-shift, and engage with media texts through a range of mobile platforms and interfaces, one can ultimately view these as new, super boxes still in consort with regulatory practices and processes. In fact, the level of surveillance and monitoring that occurs through internet providers, search engines and social media, suggest a new containment and monitoring wall far greater than anything that preceded it.

The box hasn't vanished, then, but has expanded to ensure that social control is managed across these new global terrains and interfaces. Of course, people still live in boxes, and the recent global financial crisis created a new wave of house-holding haves and have-nots. While contemporary television science fiction does all it can to discount and reconfigure the parameters of the box, what might nonetheless be in play is a deeply conservative ideological tick or trick to maintain the new hyper-rhythm of the status quo and assuage guilt over the inequalities in home living. It is telling that all four of the Doctor's most recent companions come from different forms of boxed/broken homes: Rose Tyler (Billie Piper) is from a flat in a run-down council estate; Martha Jones (Freema Agyeman) is from a line of back-to-back terraced houses; Donna Noble (Catherine Tate) from quaint if plastic suburbia; Amy Pond (Karen Gillan) from a deserted country house; and Clara Oswald (Jenna Coleman) is disembedded, living multiple lives, never really able to settle in her apartment. In an age where one is supposedly free to travel, they are trapped within an ordinary life they want to escape and only the Doctor grants them this escape.

That said, there is a new tempo and rhythm to liquid modern life: the box feels open 24/7 and one finds oneself constantly available to communication, nearly always tuned in to one electronic portal or another. Time has accelerated, is counted in tiny bits, and one is given the impression of being constantly on the move in spaces constantly on the move. This is in effect the 'logic' of the age of liquid modernity, where one appears to be free of regulation and control, and where one is asked or compelled to live lightly and instantly (Bauman 2000: 123–129).

We might argue that this living lightly and freely produces an existential terror, as relationship security and situational stability are lost to free-networking and constant movement. I would like to suggest, then, that this living instantly and lightly produces a nostalgia for the past, for the certainty of the boxed-in life, and for the analogue, optical and mechanical special effects that take us back to the age where security and stability were imagined to be in place. *Life on Mars* (BBC 2006–2007) and *Ashes to Ashes* (BBC 2008–2010) can both be read as time travel texts: the architecture of which is built upon this longing for a fixed point in time, where time, space, human relations, the working day, schooling, rest and leisure were all fixed and regular, like a precision timepiece.

In *Life on Mars*, Chief Inspector Sam Tyler (John Simm) gets run over while hunting down a killer. When he wakes up he is still a (lower-ranked) cop, chasing the same killer, but the year is now 1973. He is paired with, and under the command of, no-nonsense Gene Hunt (Philip Glenister) (see Figure 1.1). The series is full of 1970s iconography, fashion, clothes, cars and furniture, and the pop soundtrack draws from right across the musical spectrum, including the titular title track by David Bowie, a figure connected to science fiction. Its editing patterns, story arcs and character archetypes are all also pulled out from the crime shows of the 1970s. *Life on Mars* offers us a narrative-driven, audio-visual nostalgia of yesteryear, in the last full decade before the birth of the digital age and the onset of liquid modernity.

But it also offers us two contrasting characters who stand for the shifts between the two ages: Sam Tyler is versed in forensic science and investigative police procedure. He uses the augmented technologies of today to solve crimes. Gene Hunt relies on violence, corruption and his 'gut instinct'. He solves crime through physically entering

Figure 1.1. *Life on Mars*: 1970s time-travel nostalgia

and encountering the spaces and bodies of crime. As Christine Downey argues:

> The main underlying preoccupations and conflicts in the social order that are revealed in *Life on Mars* concern the huge advances in science and technology in the police force in the last thirty years, and whether or not these have been gained at the expense of more 'humane' attributes. Sam Tyler, who is from 2006, is horrified at the casual sexism, racism and brutality of police officers in 1973. They in turn are unimpressed with Sam's insistence on the importance of evidence and scientific methodology in investigations. They view him as being held back by endless procedure and as being afraid to trust his own instincts.
>
> (2007)

In one sense, *Life on Mars* offers a sharp critique of contemporary parasocial and screen-based relationships and encounters of the age of liquid modernity. Sam seems to be less human, less connected and more of a technocrat because of the digital surveillance and capture technologies he employs. Gene emerges as a brutish but authentic figure who gets the job done without delay. However, Gene is also sexist and racist, and his judgements are impaired as a consequence. As the series develops, Sam and Gene develop a 'buddy' relationship, and there is the implication that both procedure and instinct, and rule adherence and rule breaking, are needed to secure the present. The nostalgia in *Life on Mars*, then, is seemingly a critical one, tempered by the representation that analogue and digital together, old and new, sepia and colour, need to co-exist. And, yet, the series is set in the past and it is the past where we must return to, even if we need to be equipped with the most useful tools of today. Time travel in this context is a journey back in time, to boxes once denied and decried.

Of course, this nostalgia for a past long gone, and which holds it own repressive demons, does nothing to hold time travel at bay. It becomes merely a slip in time, a heterotopia indebted to memory and nostalgia, which will ultimately in turn be swept away in the great multi-dimensional corridors of time and space. That is to say, in the age of liquid modernity, something monumental is happening to time, a position I will now explore in the final section of this chapter.

Monumental Time and Timeliness

> If string theory is right, the microscopic fabric of our universe is a richly intertwined multidimensional labyrinth within which the strings of the universe endlessly twist and vibrate, rhythmically beating out the laws of the cosmos.
>
> (Brian Greene 2011:18)

Science fiction operates within and across two time continuums. In so doing, it actualises the way time is generally experienced and contested in what are the uneven liquid streams of the neoliberal or late capitalist age. On the one hand, science fiction is the embodiment of linear time, of time as ordered, regular, and sequential. This is time with a goal, moving forward with purpose, like the hands of an immaculate timepiece. Science fiction is central to what has been defined as the neoliberal temporal imaginary, which, as Claire Colebrook argues, is linear and spatialised; it is that of a subject 'for whom time is the passage towards complete actualization' (Colebrook 2009: 11; see also Colebrook 2012: 21). This 'chrononormativity' contends that we all share the same metered time, which we move through 'as though it were composed of successive points that drop away once we pass by' (Freeman 2010).

On the other hand, science fiction is constituted out of, and is a constituent for, what has been termed 'thick time' heavy with a present-past. In this conceptualisation, time is always an embodied becoming, full of the memories and encounters of what once was. Thick time is not something we are simply 'in' or which we progress 'through', but is rather, in action, a series of intersecting horizontal and vertical layers and sheets we are wrapped in and shaped by, and contingent on the spaces, things and objects we come in contact with. Thick time is space and place, thing and human, in dynamic and reverberating relationship. As Neimanis argues, 'Thick time is made by material agents, including but not limited to us, in collaboration' (2014: 118).

The conceptualisation of thickened time has been taken up by new materialist feminists and queer theorists, for example, to demonstrate the possibility and potentiality of time unwound and being constantly remade, always lived and always becoming. When time is set free from its regulatory and normative path, it becomes queer and liminal, full of intersections and intersectionality – it becomes possible time rather than probable time.

Science fiction very often seems to open up a temporal labyrinth – one in which all the text's moments and stages and stories and herstories endlessly wrap around one another. The time travel motif sets in motion accumulations of all that was, all that is, and all that will potentially be. It becomes 'sites of possibility' that, when met by other material things, open up time (space and matter) to always becoming. Another way to express this accumulation theory is through the oft-repeated description and accompanying visualisation that great science fiction is 'timeless' – not hot, not yesterday, not just now or for tomorrow, but simply always – enabling time (and space) to be measured at its thickest degree. The liquid modern digital media allow us to see these temporal moments not only side by side, but out of order – not sequentially but in imagistic windows determined only in part by the search engine's algorithms and hits.

When we search for images and stories of time travel, the search engine throws up the many moments of their incarnations – set in a sea of accumulations – all their stages and histories set before us. This is not linear time but all of time at once. All of time at once is the past meeting the present, the present visiting the past, and the past-present, present-past touching the hands of the future. Matter and materiality are of course important here. Karen Barad (2007) writes of 'intra-active becoming as indicative of a collaborative, productive, and open-ended relationship between time and matter'. In the here/now and there/then montage of time travel, the screens materially contain, maintain and sustain the 'living present'.

Time travel often grants one symbolic immortality since one lives on, is reborn, resurrected, way beyond the essential telos of the body. Digital time travel does this living forever in a particular way since immortality is set free in a networked environment where one cannot be deleted. With no mortal body to speak of, one cannot physically die, and so one lives on without mourning or funeral, only beholden to archiving strategies and continued public interest in their continued circulation. Digital age time travel allows one to float in virtual clouds that are eternally blessed.

While this arrested temporal development might assuage our fear of death and create the condition for neoliberal life to flourish, the sense that there is no end game opens up the possibility of questioning the chrononormative script we have been presented with. It may in fact echo the 'monumental time' that Julia Kristeva (2002) rehabilitates from Friedrich Nietzsche, in that this time is larger than (our) life. There is something sublime to be said about time travel, and the special effects that grant it such profound wonderment.

This is where this book will travel next: to take up a different understanding of digital age special effects and the time they open up. Drawing upon eye-tracking technology and empirical research, I turn my attention to the contemporary Hollywood science fiction blockbuster and the different forms of sublime it activates or invites. The digital sublime either works in the service of liquid modernity and its consumption energies, or it offers viewers a way out of stupefied living. Eye-tracking is, of course, a tracking and surveillance technology: it is itself a part of the science fiction of the age.

2

Eye-Tracking the Sublime in Spectacular Moments of Science Fiction Film

I ended the first chapter of this book with a discussion of digital age time travel in relation to thick and monumental time and the immortal and expansive power it may grant us. In this chapter I move my argument to spectacular science fiction film and the way our eyes and bodies may experience the sublime when watching certain scenes composed of phenomenal liquid special effects. The intention is to empirically address the way posthuman viewers encounter the digital spectacular in the age of liquid modernity.

As I write this chapter (2015), we are just coming to the end of the season of the cinema blockbuster, dominated by American product and the science fiction spectacle. These science fictions are big pictures in almost every way: big budgets, big special effects, big stars, big cross-overs, distributed in big cinemas to big audiences. However, these bejewelled behemoths to size and scale are also (arguably) invariably light or thin or small, on story and characterisation, performance and philosophy, on sophistication – they are the products of capitalist film production, the 'Yale locks' or 'kiss curls' of the twentieth century, producing a neo-liberal narcissism.

Ant-Man (Reed 2015) captures perfectly this collision between, and yet effacement of, big and small: a summer superhero blockbuster that involves state-of-the-art special effects intended to shrink everything before it. *Ant-Man* is big on scale, heavy on familial, individualist and romantic ideology, and yet small and light on the tragic politics of war and destruction.

Of course, the science fiction blockbuster has a wider set of reference points and a much longer history: in cinema, forms or versions of the blockbuster have been found from the birth of narrative film, if not before; and in literature, television and gaming, the sense and purpose of scale, event, have marked the production and consumption of science fiction. The blockbuster isn't simply big or thin, but is the constant in the way science fiction addresses its audiences.

In this chapter I will explore science fiction film spectacle as a particular type of endangering sensorial experience. Employing eye-tracking technology to assess where a small group of viewers look while watching scenes of spectacle, I will contend that through its spectacular set pieces, digital age science fiction film creates two distinct gazing regimes.

First, such spectacular scenes create an experience of sublime contemplation where the viewer is (haptically) lost in the wondrous images liquefying before them. These moments of sublime contemplation create the condition where the viewer *feels* as if they have had an outer-body experience; one that has been cut free from the borders of the linguistic-led self of everyday life. These scenes of spectacle remove us from the binds of liquid modern life. Second, I will argue that certain scenes of science fiction spectacle work to commodify the viewing experience, creating a gazing pattern that is 'driven' by the mechanics of the event moment, by the theme-park-ride aesthetic and the insatiable logic of late liquid modernity.

Set in this sensible, empirical context, the sublime dangers of science fiction film can be considered in two distinct ways. On the one hand, when the viewer is caught gazing in a moment of sublime contemplation there is embodied transgression and transcendence: here I will postulate that the viewer exists purely as a carnal being, or newly if momentarily constituted as posthuman, in the impossible present or possible future world that has been spectacularly imagined for them.

On the other hand, when the viewer is presented with a spectacle that demands attention to the mechanics and drivers of the scene as it unfolds, a viewing position is created where the very rhythms of the theme-park ride are created, where liquid capitalist life is simply being re-engineered. Sublime and spectacular science fiction endangerment, then, can both liberate and destroy, and it is the encounter between these two vexing poles that is of central concern in this chapter.

My focus will predominately be on the eyes – on vision. Undertaking a small-scale empirical study that uniquely utilises eye-tracking technology, this chapter will concentrate on what viewers attend to, gaze at and 'contemplate' when viewing two differently constituted 'spectacle' sequences: 'the sun explodes' scene from *Sunshine* (Boyle 2007) and 'Godzilla enters Manhattan' scene from *Godzilla* (Emmerich 1998).

When it comes to the analysis of the spectacle sequences, the following questions will be addressed. First, given that there is so much to look at, to take in, where do the eyes focus upon in a spectacular science fiction film sequence? Second, what holds the viewer's gaze and for how long, in and amongst this heightened audio-visual environment? Third, what aesthetic stimulus directs the viewer's gaze? In any sense, can the viewer's eyes be said to be overwhelmed by the expanded geographies, landscapes and velocities they are presented with? Fourth, and in relation, can one make inferences from the eye-tracking data generated to the idea of sublime wonderment and the act of deep contemplation, and to the commodification of the viewing experience? Finally, can we reflect on eye-tracking technology as a surveillance machine, fully born and developed in and for the controlling age of liquid modernity?

I will begin the chapter with an introduction to eye-tracking technology. I will then introduce how I will be defining and exploring the notion of the sublime and spectacle in the context of digital age science fiction cinema. I will then analyse the eye-tracking data and apply my theoretical overview to the two scenes under investigation. Following this, I will draw together my analysis, ultimately making the case for the power of digital age science fiction film to endanger our eyes in the world. Finally, I will reflect on eye-tracking as the very machine that heralds in the neo-forensic age of the liquid modern.

Seeing with Your Eyes

In *Blade Runner* (Scott 1982), Roy Batty, the leader of an outlaw group of Nexus-6 replicants, undertakes a quest to 'meet his maker'. When he encounters Chew, the genetic designer of his eyes, he mocks, 'Chew, if only you could see what I've seen with your eyes.' Here Roy not only draws attention to the posthuman condition the film thematically grapples with, and to the sense that all vision is embodied, but gestures to the wider conceit that science fiction film as an art form offers its viewers a miraculous, omnipotent and omnipresent vision.

The language of cinema constantly creates these spaces of vision and for *seeing* to take place, whether this be the embodied point-of-view shot; aerial cinematography that brings wide-open cosmologies and bejewelled cityscapes into view; the furtive camera that glimpses into dark corners; or the interiorised gaze that expressionistically captures the nightmare visions of the lost, the hunted and the alien. With a close-up one can trace the undulating valleys of emotion on a character or creature's face, and feel their piercing eyes reaching out and into yours.

In a scene of science fiction spectacle, the very forces of a special effect and the powers of digital photography enable awesome creations, movements and encounters to be created and gazed at. As Barry Keith Grant observes, in science fiction film we are very often addressed as the 'wide-eyed child' caught before the sublime possibilities that are imagined before us (2004: 18).

But is Grant right? Or, rather, how does such vision shape the way viewers experience a film or film sequence? To return to Batty's self-reflexive barb to Chew, what if we could see what you, the viewer, have seen with your eyes? What if we could look into the depths of the viewer's gaze and the pools of light that well there, and make accurate assessments of their ocular and haptic engagement with the shifting sightlines of the cinema machine? What if we could begin to quantify the 'dangers' inherent in looking at the sublime and spectacular scenes of digital age science fiction film?

The Technical and Anatomical*

Eye-tracking technology allows one to 'objectively' track and record what viewers are looking at, for how long, and in what ocular sequence. Eye-trackers work by reflecting infrared light onto the eye, which is then captured by a sensor. The sensor allows these eye movements and fixations to be tracked and recorded. Specialised software is then employed to create accurate measurements of what the eyes gazed at over any given period of time. Eye movements alter between points of fixation, where the visual system gathers information and quickly moves between fixations called saccades.

Where we attend to, and what draws our attention, is of interest as this process is driven both by our conscious intentions and by unconscious reactions to visual stimuli such as objects, textures, movements and sounds. Looking at gaze patterns can hint at the cognitive drives behind them. Even more interesting, perhaps, is the ability to look at the gaze behaviour of groups of people in relation to similar stimulus, since this allows us to see viewing patterns and differences emerge.

This quantification of vision is made possible through amalgamating group data into heat maps, which effectively show the weighting of all the viewing that occurred, and gaze plots, which show the location of the fixations made, as well as the sequence in which they took place. Finally, to draw conclusions from the data, an area of interest (AOI) analysis can be performed. Through this type of focus we are able to select AOIs and compute the number of times viewers visit specific objects or areas within a scene or sequence. By then analysing the amount of processing time spent in these areas, we are able to consider things such as the amount of return visits to an area: what in effect has captured the viewers' attention and for how long in any given scene or sequence. In this chapter I refer to a small study of sublime science fiction spectacle we undertook, using a Tobii x120 eye-tracker to record six subjects watching the two spectacle scenes from *Godzilla* and *Sunshine* noted above, and analysing their fixation data using Tobii Studio software. My key question was: 'But what can we make of the science fiction digital sublime and spectacle?'

The Sublime Spectacle

Drawing upon Deleuze, my overarching definition of the sublime will be that it is that imperceptible moment in life or art when reason is absent and sensation consumes one with an overwhelming and indescribably profound intensity or chaos or force (Deleuze 1987). The overriding effect of this experience is the inability to verbalise or rationalise the encounter since it exists as that which cannot be comprehended. The sublime moment may be felt as a flash of insight in which one re-sees something familiar as if seeing it for the first time; it may be the familiar rendered strange, uncanny, as less or more than the experience of it has previously registered. This feeling of 'firstness' may occur in front of a gesture, a look, an object or a catastrophic event.

In terms of digital age science fiction film, the sublime will often be an experience of a spectacular scene that takes place in the pure realm of the senses – outside, before or beyond language and representation, although strictly speaking affect and percept are co-extensive (Deleuze 1987). The experience of the sublime, then, is always an endangering one since the ontology of the self is questioned, and the 'social' disappears before the wonder of future horizons made presently real.

It is not my intention, however, to simply conflate the experience of the sublime with all the operations and functions of spectacle. They are not synonymous and many forms of spectacle are empty representations. As Greg Tuck notes:

> Both spectacle and sublime are perceptually impressive at a cognitive level, but only the latter produces an often-fearful sense of wonder, while the former is about the pleasure of wondering how it was done. The spectacular and the sublime have an inverse relationship with regard to our faith 'in' and understanding 'of' the conceptual and perceptual aspects of such displays. Spectacles might be impressive and fun, but there is something shallow or depthless about them, while the sublime is the complete opposite, a moment of extraordinary metaphysical density.
>
> (2008: 254)

Nonetheless, while it is right to understand these two experiences as relatively distinct, my argument will be that this is not always the case. Digital age science fiction film spectacle *can* be sublime.

One can be asked to look 'everywhere' in a scene of spectacle, its technological, natural or violent and chaotic splendour not really pointing anywhere, not analytically directing the gaze, but instead asking the viewer to experience it first and foremost as a(n) (in)sight of awesomeness. Arguably, what the viewer can be presented with in a science fiction spectacle sequence is the brute brilliance of something spectacular taking place on or rather all over the screen. In these sublime moments the limits of the embodied self are breached, and the material conditions of one's existence liquefy (Bruno 1987). This is something I will further elaborate on below.

Science fiction film spectacle *can* of course also be derivative, and swimming in a sea of commodity relations and intertexts that are designed to elicit base human experiences and feelings. As scholars such as Sean Cubitt (2004) have argued, the emotions that are being drawn upon by much of contemporary 'blockbuster SF' are affective clichés, manufactured in the service of empty special effects – themselves a part of a wider commodity stream and central to the lightweight conditions of a 'society of spectacle' (Debord 1994). In a similar if more supportive vein of the form, Alison McMahan defines contemporary spectacle films as pataphysical: involving 'gee whiz' self-conscious special effects, 'thin plots and thinly drawn characters', and intertextual references that refer us to the wider media universe the film exists in and is marketed through (2005: 3).

Such scenes of spectacle can be linked to the theme-park-ride aesthetic, where there is an over-determination of visceral thrills at the expense of narrative story telling, and a simultaneous over-reliance on special effects to drive the film form. As Thomas Schatz concludes in relation to the poetics and politics of New Hollywood cinema in general:

> From *The Godfather* to *Jaws* to *Star Wars*, we see films that are increasingly plot-driven, increasingly visceral, kinetic, and fast-paced, increasingly reliant on special effects, increasingly fantastic (and thus apolitical), and increasingly targeted at younger audiences.
>
> (Schatz 1993: 23)

I would suggest that this imagined dichotomy between the sublime and spectacle is a little too reductive. Instead, I would argue that there are different types of digital age science fiction spectacle, and two related types of the sublime experience. These work to position the viewer in different and competing ways. In the next section I want to outline some of these distinct viewing experiences, before going on to discuss the findings of our eye-tracking study.

Types of Spectacle

First, perhaps the most familiar form of spectacle associated with science fiction is that of technological spectacle and the spectacle of technophilia, in which a sense of awe and wonder emerges through encounters with higher-order life forms and their associated technologies. These technophiliac scenes include the arrival of vast spaceships, advanced weaponry, and time and space travel such as in the recent Star Trek films, and invasion films such as *Oblivion* (Kosinski 2013).

David Nye (1994) has usefully suggested that over the course of the twentieth century the sublime has increasingly been found in the technological, in the very latest technological developments or objects. For Nye, these build on positive pleasures because they demonstrate humankind's capacity to shape a perfect world. This technophilia is also, then, the spectacle of human utopia projected into or through superior life forms and technologies whereby future humanity produces and exists in a sublime state of existence.

Second, one often finds in science fiction film scenes and scenarios of apocalyptic spectacle and the spectacle of technophobia, often figured through global destruction caused by some malevolent alien force, or through our own meddling with nature. This kind of technophobic imagination (Ryan and Kellner 1990) seems very much in opposition or contradiction to the spectacle of technophilia, and yet even the spectacular forces of this end-of-the-world dreaming are sometimes rendered with beautiful audio-visualisations, such as in the case of *War of the Worlds* (Spielberg 2005) or *Pacific Rim* (del Toro 2013). If experiencing technological spectacle involves awe-struck pleasure, however, then this version of technophobic spectacle is terrifyingly pleasurable.

Third, science fiction film can present us with visions of beyond-the-Earth spectacle. This type of spectacle generally begins with a 'revelation' moment where an off-world, alternate utopian or dystopian landscape, city or citadel is suddenly glimpsed and then focused upon. A striking case in point occurs in *Avatar* (Cameron 2009). As Trudy Chacon (Michelle Rodriguez) pilots her ship, she reveals a never-before-seen immense backdrop that overwhelms the characters' (and audience's) senses the moment its awesomeness is properly contemplated. When she utters the line of dialogue, 'You should see your faces', referring to the watching crew, sublimity is itself being self-reflected upon.

Drawing on Kant (1960), one can describe this type of awesomeness as the 'dynamical sublime', measured by its unboundedness and formlessness – something, of course, that digital visual effects help create since they work out of narratives of expanded geographies and seemingly exponential vistas of wonder (Pierson 1999).

Fourth, science fiction film offers viewers the spectacle of special effects in which the alchemy of the latest GCI or motion-capture is being foregrounded and admired. There can be a high degree of self-reflexivity in these scenes of special effect wonderment. As Garrett Stewart suggests, 'movies about the future tend to be about the future of movies' (Stewart 2008). This type of knowing, self-reflexive spectacle has itself two stages.

First, there is the sublime recognition of the visual effects' incredible power, where words fail the character and viewer and where the eyes are overwhelmed by what they see.

Second, and almost immediately, there is an articulation and conscious acknowledgement that one has just witnessed the very power of science fiction film special effects taking place (see Brophy 1986). This awareness is often revealed verbally, muttered out loud, such as with the line of dialogue from *Avatar* quoted above, or the line, 'You gotta be fucking kidding me!' uttered by Palmer (David Clennon) in *The Thing* (Carpenter 1982) as the creature walks away on its own brain. Steve Neale suggests:

> Despite this awareness, the special effects have had an effect. The spectator has been, like the fictional character, astonished and horrified. An effect of this kind is fundamental to science fiction in the cinema. So too, though, is the awareness. In fact, as I shall go on to argue, the effect and the awareness are interdependent. Indeed, one of the keys to understanding the attraction, the pleasure – the lure – of science fiction lies precisely in the intricate intercalation of different forms, kinds and layers of knowledge, belief and judgment.
>
> (1990: 161)

Knowledge, belief and judgement are key to the way the sublime and spectacle work: the sublime, however, defies knowledge and reason fails the viewer, and in this catastrophic state they believe or rather sense danger in, through, and all around them. Nonetheless, I think one can and should divide these types of spectacle in science fiction film into two further categories – although these can be interrelated.

First, there is contemplative and immersive spectacle, involving the seeing and hearing of something immense and overwhelming. The spectacle impresses large and constant upon the scene and is invited to be stared at and sensed as if one is immobile, powerless before it, in an imagined sublime state. One is terrified by its power, enrapt nonetheless by its beauty. The Washington arrival of the 'alien ship' in *Independence Day* (Emmerich 1996) is an example of this type of enchantment.

Second, there is active and dynamic spectacle, involving spectacular action such as an unbounded chase, a hi-tech fight, or dramatic temporal and spatial changes in the film's *mise en scène*. Spectacle here might be framed around a range of awe-inspiring properties, so that the screen is filled with multiple spectacular elements. The *Godzilla* chase scene I will discuss shortly is an example of this. This is spectacle that is not sublime but rather carries itself into the realm of surface-level commodification.

In terms of the two film sequences under analysis in this chapter, the end sequence from *Sunshine* can be defined as 'natural' spectacle, and as contemplative and immersive spectacle. It produces a sublime experience of endangerment and one that arrests itself from liquid modern ideologies and subjectivities. By contrast, the chase sequence from *Godzilla* can be defined as a synthesis of technological and technophobic spectacle, and spectacle that is active and dynamic. This type of spectacle is in the service of late, liquid capitalism and is dangerous in terms of the ideologies of consumption it promotes and sanctifies. As previously indicated, I will draw upon eye-tracking data to evidence my analysis.

Eye-Tracking the Sublime in *Sunshine*

At the end of *Sunshine*, a wounded Robert Capa (Cillian Murphy) has moments to trigger the star-bomb that will hopefully reignite Earth's dying sun. The 'countdown' scene is in one sense classically constructed: a series of fast and faster cuts, insert shots, handheld camerawork, eyeline matches and point-of-view shots capture his attempt to release the bomb before time runs out. However, while time and space are initially rendered linear and consistent, macro close-ups of the liquid molten sun are inserted to extend time and collapse space, and this is finally compounded by Robert being able to look into, and to reach out and touch, the sun as it merges with the collapsing structures of the spaceship. Shot in slow-motion, Robert's experience of time and space are seemingly overwhelmed by the now reignited, living sun.

With regards to the 'active' narrative moments that lead to Robert staring at and into the sun, we find that the eye-tracking data (see Figures 2.1 and 2.2 below) tells us that eyes follow or are led by narrative and visual cues and signposts. Viewers' eyes are drawn to those elements of the *mise en scène* that are critical to understanding what is happening in the scene: the countdown, the fumble of fingers and the collapse of structures. Looking to understand the scene and what is at stake, there is also a sense of 'urgency' in what the eyes are looking at.

The eyes are rhythmically aligned with the fast cuts and mobility of the framing. In effect, the countdown scenario grips viewers' eyes, as does the end-of-all-human-life threat that resonates within or impresses upon the scene. Viewers' eyes very much recognise the danger in the scene and feel this danger upon them. However, this is not yet an experience of the sublime; rather, our eyes are very much in a narrative mode that produces this sensation of endangerment.

When it comes to witnessing, or experiencing, the fireball that eventually, slowly engulfs the screen, whether shot from behind Robert, or as an attributed or actual point-of-view shot, the data suggests that our eyes focus on a generally static and central AOI occupying the centre of

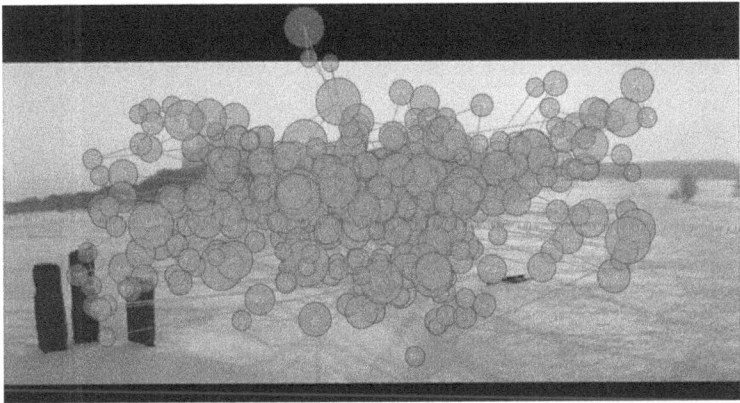

Figure 2.1. Eye-tracking *Sunshine*: Overview of a viewer's viewing gaze plots and patterns – following narrative action

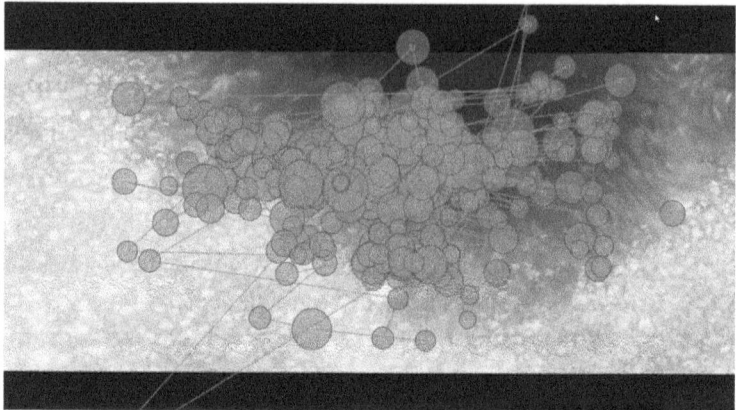

Figure 2.2. Eye-tracking *Sunshine*: Attention to the centre of the frame dominates viewing patterns

the frame (see Figure 2.2 above). One could suggest that this is a form of the contemplative eye, occupying the centre to see all that flows out of the screen. This is arguably an eye caught in a sublime state, in awe and wonder of the melting sun before it, unable to move, to wander, so awe-struck is it before the sublime spectacle taking place. This is an eye unable to speak; an eye that belongs to a body catastrophically caught before a sublime moment.

Near the end of the scene, when it comes to the medium close-up of Robert's face, surrounded as it is by radiance, fire and light, the eye-tracking data suggests that we focus, classically, on the eyes, and the eyes and mouth (Redmond and Sita 2013). The spectacle that surrounds Robert seems less important to viewers' eyes; less important than what might be termed this affect image, or the affecting power of the face to draw one's eyes in (see Figure 2.3). Nonetheless, this shot of Robert's face is full of textures and flickers, and his eyes are themselves caught in their own sublime sensation of endangerment as they stare at the slowly exploding sun and back into us. Viewers' eyes, then, may be in a particular affective state here, not now ocular but haptic; 'organs of touch' that have been touched by Robert's searching, contemplative eyes.

If one was to consider the relationship between the observation that we are strongly focused on Robert's eyes when presented with his

EYE-TRACKING THE SUBLIME IN SPECTACULAR MOMENTS 53

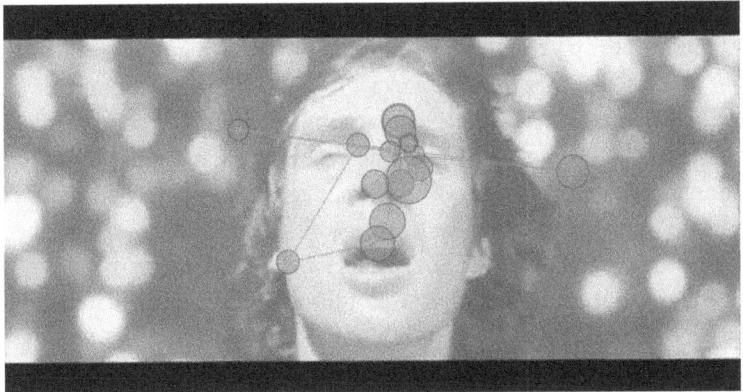

Figure 2.3. Eye-tracking *Sunshine*: Focusing on the face, eyes and mouth

awe-struck face amongst a shining sea of stardust, and the relative stillness of the eye as it directly gazes at the reborn sun, one can begin to suggest a telling relationship between gazing and sublime spectacle. This alignment is something akin to what might be termed the double sublime moment (Bukatman 1999).

As already noted, the data may be revealing that we are in a sublime state in front of this exploding natural spectacle. Our eyes are being lost in the attraction; are touched by and are touching the sun's heat and magnitude; and, like Robert, are rendered 'speechless'.

However, viewers are also found focusing intently on Robert's eyes (and a little on the open mouth that cannot speak) as he gazes in an awe-struck manner at the force that slowly engulfs him, the screen (and us). What this might be revealing is that, in our state of sublimity, not only do we recognise (see into) the sublime as it manifests in this character, but his sublimity works its way back into our eyes. Robert's eyes are in a very real sense a part of the spectacle, conduits for it, are transformed, as we are, by it.

In this inferential reading of the results, the gaze patterns mirror one another: Robert stares at the sun in the same way as we do, in the same way as we see and touch the sun in their/his eyes. Him, me, us, are lost for words, as we search with our eyes (as organs of touch) for the origins of this natural spectacle. This is sublime endangerment not simply in terms of the instability we face as viewers, but in the way borders and boundaries are breached and transgressed. Robert becomes a part of the now reignited sun, is taken up into its liquid centre, becoming post-human in the process. He becomes a part of the living eye of the sun.

Robert becomes *the* time-image; he is placed or places himself in a situation where he is unable to act and react in a direct, immediate way, unsure or uncertain of who he is now as the magnificence of the sun empties him of language. This disintegration leads to a breakdown in Robert's sensor-motor system because – as Deleuze notes – time-image characters are caught deep in thought and can verbalise very little, instead expressing a great deal through non-representational or affective signs (1989).

Robert becomes an interior being pulled apart by an exterior force, or 'a pure optical and aural image' that 'comes into relation with a virtual image, a mental or mirror image' (Deleuze 1989). According to Deleuze, the result of this pure optical image is the witnessing of a direct image of time (a time-image or crystal-image). Such images are themselves free now to express forces or 'shocks of force' (1989: 139).

These forceful shocks work very much against the grain of liquid modernity. In the same way that time travel (see Chapter 1 for a full discussion) can be said to free us from the binds and confines of the alienating present, so too can contemplative spectacle wrench us free from conscious thought and its inhibitions and conformities. The liquid eyes in this scene – defined here as Robert's eyes, the eye of the molten sun and the eyes of the viewer – engage in an inexplicable coming together that becomes a profound mediation on vision and knowing beyond the discourses of liquid modern life.

In relation to *Sunshine* I would like to make a concluding remark about the relationship between narrative and spectacle. On the one hand, it seems that these results suggest a split between narrative and spectacle: confirming the conclusions of scholars such as Mark Bould (2012) that they exist as distinct properties in the language of science fiction film. In the first 'narrative' part of the scene, viewers' eyes are mobile and investigative, and in the latter half of the scene as the awesome spectacle takes over, they settle, fixate and arguably enter a state of sublime contemplation. On the other hand, one could argue that these results suggest that narrative and spectacle are very much interrelated and co-dependent. One could in fact argue that spectacle is the apex of narrative here, its culmination point, in which our eyes have been led to this death and resurrection point, this fantastic primal scene where narrative agent Robert merges with the stars, leaving behind the vestiges of liquid modern life.

Eye-Tracking Spectacle in *Godzilla*

When it comes to the chase sequence from *Godzilla*, there seems to be a different gaze regime in operation and a different set of qualities to endangerment. This isn't a scene of contemplative spectacle but rather one of active and dynamic spectacle built out of the logic of the ride aesthetic.

In the scene in question, the military are positioned to stop and destroy Godzilla's movements through the city, but what transpires is a scene of cat and mouse as Godzilla outwits and outguns their arsenal.

As is conventional for a scene of action spectacle, vertical and horizontal axes of action open up the cinematic space, and there is constant movement both in terms of cinematography and of what happens in each shot, with flames, missiles, debris, helicopters and gunships filling frame after frame. The scene is constructed as one big set piece or themed 'attraction', with its supercharged dynamic taking the viewer on a rollercoaster ride with an interlocking series of thrills, spills, comedowns and then ups again (for more). The aesthetic here is thrilling but it is also ideological and shaped by a commodity fetish, something I will presently go on to discuss.

In terms of the eye-tracking data, two distinct gaze patterns emerge. Firstly, viewers' eyes again follow narrative cues and aesthetic devices to comprehend the action spectacle that is taking place. This includes the eyes fixating on Godzilla's tail as it swishes against buildings, the appearance of the helicopters, the debris as it falls from buildings and the dynamic 'movement' of Godzilla as it charges through the corridors of urban chaos that the chase takes place in (see Figure 2.4). This is an embodied vision, kinetically connected to the spectacle as it unfolds. There is little contemplation here but the brute mechanics of chase, capture and kill, and the eyes finding this chaos in the most dynamic aspects of the *mise en scène*.

Second, the eye-tracking data suggests that viewers' eyes readily occupy the centre frame: it seems to be the ground zero of where one's

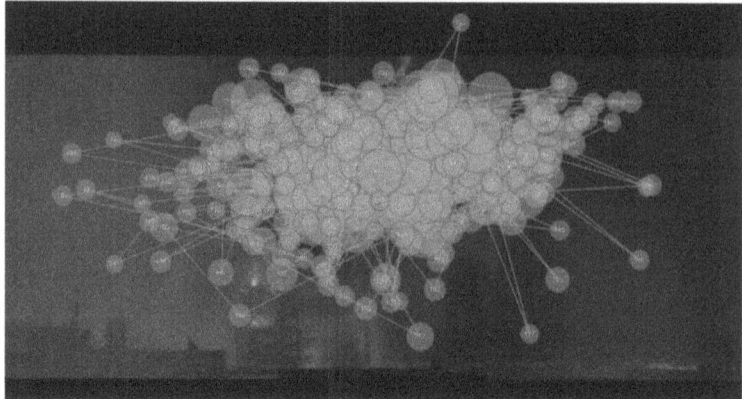

Figure 2.4. Eye-tracking *Godzilla*: Following narrative action

eyes focus and remain steady. This is probably because it is the best position from which to orientate oneself when so much is visually taking place on the screen. From this central position one is best placed to see and comprehend the full mechanics of the scene and the appetite for spectacular destruction. From the centre, one is positioned in the middle of a shop window through which various commodity relations emerge (see Figure 2.5).

Debord argues that spectacle is the material evidence of and for 'the autocratic reign of the market economy' (Debord 1994). The mediated

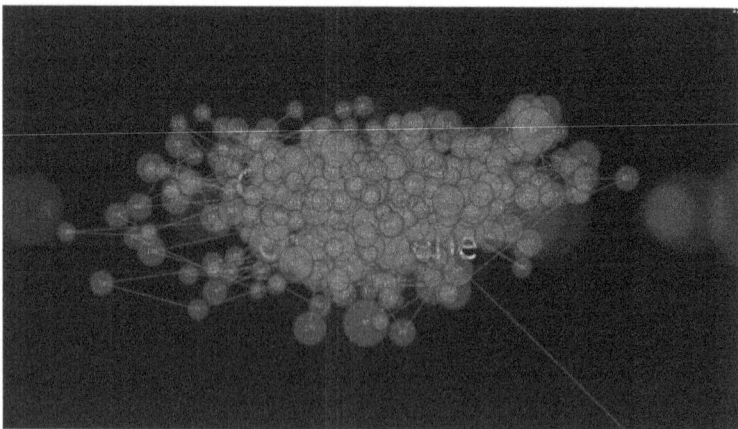

Figure 2.5. Eye-tracking *Godzilla*: The viewing eye occupying the centre frame

world is awash or fabricated with commercial images and representations, and spectacle is the epitome of the materialisation of dominant consumerist ideology. These spectacular representations lack content, or rather the content *is* their representation, reproducing the actuality of commodity relations as they do so, rendering 'all that once was directly lived' into 'mere representation' (Debord 1994: 26, 12). What is denied, as a consequence, is the (alienated) labour that went into producing such representations.

I would suggest that *Godzilla* directly materialises the conditions of the society of the spectacle or, in my terms, of liquid modern life: the creature exists in a sea of commodity intertexts (Meehan 1991), produces desire for the commodity, and the commodity of special effects, and creates a vision regime where the eyes are merely consuming organs, devouring the orgy of consumption that takes place on the screen. What is endangering here is obviously the pacification of the senses, and the orientation of action towards mindless consumption in the place of active (activist) production. The eyes are being depoliticised here, and at the same time they are being turned into organs of mindless consumption – much like the figure of Godzilla.

So, what we can now begin to say is that the static eye is not necessarily a contemplative eye (as it was in *Sunshine*) but a comprehending eye. Both scenes involve different variations of spectacle and special effect. Both scenes involve narrative development, with *Godzilla* being organised around a chase scene and *Sunshine* around a countdown scene. Godzilla fully integrates narrative within its scene of spectacle (although that is a contentious observation to make, since one could argue that there is narrative redundancy in operation here – the narrative is so obvious, so well-worn, that there is nothing for the eyes to do but watch), while *Sunshine*'s sun-shower scene can be said to be about narrative plentitude, fecundity, and the sublime state that one finds oneself in, in enchanted moments like this.

Conclusion

Jane Bennett defines enchantment as that which:

> ... entails a state of wonder, and one of the distinctions of this state is the temporary suspension of chronological time and bodily movement. To be

enchanted, then, is to participate in a momentarily immobilizing encounter; it is to be transfixed, spellbound.

(2001: 5)

One can understand the star-bomb sequence in *Sunshine* as a form of sublime enchantment where, in a very real sense, object and subject relations disintegrate. The envisioning of the sun and the scene's contraction and expansion of time and space produces its own immobilising encounter through the figure of Robert. But the viewer becomes his surrogate or doppelganger and, as such, finds that their imagination is itself overturned and reaches the point that Deleuze calls the 'bend' in sufficient reason. The sequence 'entails a suppression of perception, an experience of the formless or the deformed'. All manner of limits have been reached and breached, and what emerges is the 'body without organs' that lies beneath the organism, 'the body insofar as it is deformed by a plurality of invisible forces: the violent force of a hiccup, a scream, the need to vomit or defecate, of copulation, the flattening force of sleep' (Deleuze 2003). While we do not hear Robert speak, or see his mouth scream, its sound penetrates the scene and enters us. The viewer experiences their own body as one without organs. This is the ultimate type of dangerous becoming that one can encounter in a scene of science fiction sublime spectacle. In a very real sense one becomes more than one's body: and a body beyond the selfhood as defined and delineated by liquid modernity.

The chase sequence from *Godzilla* produces an altogether different response, one set within the theme-park gardens of liquid capitalism, where our eyes are turned into consumption portals. And yet its spectacle sublime has other ideological functions. As Despina Kakoudaki suggests:

> ... In the disaster film the sublime moment also accentuates a feeling of loss about the scarcity of such unifying moments. As the characters in the film look at each other with the wonder of belonging together, they also understand that this belonging is not true on an everyday level. The spectacle thus affirms a nostalgia for a lost community rather than a renewed belief in the future of people together. The fact that they are all looking at a representation or manifestation of the latest in computer imaging technology points to a desire that

perhaps through this technology some of the communal feeling will be restored.

(2002: 53)

The spectacle in *Godzilla* may be nostalgic on a number of levels including a longing for the original, and for the B-movie monster movies that were first made when America was mythically imagined to be a cohering community. Nostalgia may also be a by-product of the 'waning of affect' (Jameson 1991) and the depthlessness of the digital age. The spectacle in *Godzilla* is without weight, draws upon 'piles of fragments' from movie history and produces a vision regime that is depthless too. The danger of the eyes here is one of stupefaction. That this chapter has returned to the condition of nostalgia that ends the first chapter in this monograph is no happy accident. What we see in the play of difference between digital age time travel and liquid modern special effects – and between television and film science fiction – is a retreat into the past because of the 'nowhere' state of future dreaming today. As Zygmunt Bauman powerfully contends:

> The Utopias of yore stand condemned in the new global elite's Weltanschauung and life philosophy. Their two most crucial attributes – territoriality and finality – disqualify past Utopias and bar in advance all future attempts to re-enter the line of thinking they once followed. ... 'Utopia' – in its original meaning of a place that does not exist – has become, within the logic of the globalized world, a contradiction in terms. The 'nowhere' (the 'forever nowhere', the 'thus-far nowhere' and the 'nowhereas-yet' alike) is no longer a place. The 'U' of 'Utopia' bereaved by the topos, is left homeless and floating, no longer hoping to strike roots, to 're-embed'. ... The utopian model of a 'better future' is out of the question.
>
> (2000: 236–239)

Nonetheless, sublime science fiction film spectacle can endanger our eyes in the world. Endangerment here refers not only to the emergence of a haptic and asemiotic experience when encountering the awesome, but also to the way a liminal, borderless being emerges from these acts of contemplation and disintegration. We *can* enter a mental state of utopia, beyond the horizon of liquid age modernity. What have we seen with our eyes? The eye of the sun itself. A *deterritorisation* of the self that emerges so forcefully in the liquid spaces of digital age science fiction.

Eye-Tracking Surveillance

This chapter has drawn upon eye-tracking data and its empirical visualisations to help evidence its central arguments. There is an irony at work here: eye-tracking technology is very much a surveillance machine of the liquid modern age. Used extensively in military and police training programmes to help soldiers and cops learn where to look and aim their guns, and to help develop ballistic accuracy, eye-tracking is a part of the military–business–science nexus that attempts to track and record people's movements.

Of course, in terms of surveillance discourse, film has been read as a vision machine set within an invasive visual culture that promotes:

> The normalizing gaze, a surveillance that makes it possible to qualify, to classify and to punish. It establishes over individuals a visibility through which one differentiates and judges them.
>
> (Foucault 1975: 25)

Digital age science fiction can be read as a genre that carries out this normalising gaze, defining the parameters of law and order and the way the criminal can be discovered, classified and ultimately disciplined. Across a wide number of film and television series, including *Black Mirror*, *Equilibrium* (Wimmer 2002), *The Island* (Bay 2005) and *Minority Report* (Spielberg 2002), the technologies of surveillance seek out the law-breaker and punish them accordingly.

Nonetheless, there is more to the way that digital age surveillance manifests. What we find are the eyes of the viewer being relentlessly led and directed by the tracking screens that occupy these texts. In many dystopian science fiction films and television series there is a consistent forensic looking regime where the operations of the screen and the eyes of the viewer align. Viewers come to embody the gazing powers that digital age science fiction promotes. As such, viewers experience their very own form of social surveillance, becoming detectives and snoopers in the process. Digital age science fiction can be read as a liquid genre of and for paranoid surveillance, fuelled by the constant search for facts, omissions, falsehoods and half-truths. At a more general cultural level, trust is at issue here in what is perceived to be an age of 'faithless' activity and widespread corruption, where politicians are regarded to be as corrupt as the criminals they covertly support. Viewers of science fiction ultimately become part of this age of conspiracy (Knight 2002).

As does, in a very real sense, eye-tracking technology and the data it produces. We find its 'visualisation' in a range of science fiction films and television programmes – with characters such as John Anderton (Tom Cruise, *Minority Report*) in effect employing eye-trackers to search people out.

In the next chapter, 'Emptying Spaces: Digital Deterritorialisation', I turn my attention to the way space and place is recast in the age of liquid modernity. Extending and developing my understanding of time (see Chapter 1) and of viewing modality, I see new forms of spatial and temporal realities form in the liquid age of science fiction.

3

Emptying Spaces
Digital Deterritorialisation

In this chapter I will address the ways in which digital age science fiction film and television explores, comments upon and reproduces the virtually borderless, boundary-less nature of liquid modern life. This uncoupling of time and space, and the flow of bodies, images, products, data, capital, identities and ideologies it produces, results in a deterritorialisation experience that is both articulated in and evidenced by those science fiction films and television programmes in which the digital is both central to the porous narrative and embedded within the wet aesthetics of the *mise en scène*.

I will suggest that this digital deterritorialisation experience is, on the one hand, destabilising and, on the other, an augmented doorway to new becomings and the possibilities it affords bodies that leave themselves behind. It is precisely in this dialectic between augmented isolation and existential loss, and collectivisation and transcendence, where the power of digital deterritorialisation lies. I begin this chapter by exploring science fiction cinema's long and historic relationship to gravity, before exploring the way time, space and body are vexingly recast in the digital age of liquid propensities. I set one of my readings within the context of the politics of the rancid age of austerity, one of the key markers of present-age liquid modernity. I end the chapter with a discussion of the way 4D motion cinema deterritorialises and disembodies us. These sections can be understood to be compass points that lead us to various destinations, each of which says something profound about digital deterritorialisation in the age of liquid modernity; in the epoch of liquid science fiction.

(Anti) *Gravity*

Cinema's historical and contemporary relationship to gravity is a fascinating one. At the time of its birth, in 1895, cinema was seen as a revolutionary magical machine that – through its moving pictures seemingly suspended in air – didn't simply defy gravity but allowed it to channel the forces of the world directly, sweetly and dangerously. The stories of the first movie patrons hurrying away from the screen in case they were run over as *The Train Arrived at the Station* (The Lumière Brothers 1895) is a startling, if perhaps mythic, account of cinema's accelerated and gravitational grandeur.

The awe and wonder of cinema in part lies in its remarkable ability to audio-visualise and texturise the weight and feel of things; for it to realistically render movement and velocity; and for it to create spaces deep, far and wide. The precipice is of course one of cinema's favourite environments to create a sense of depth and distance, and to enact the experience of falling. An iconic cinematic moment, captured in such films as *Vertigo* (Hitchcock 1958) and *Strange Days* (Bigelow 1995), involves a character looking down from the precipice, to then either jump, fall or be pushed off the edge, with a corresponding cinematography that captures them hurtling, hurtling, hurtling towards the nadir. Then splat. Kristen Whissel describes this notion of verticality, stating:

> [a]t its most basic level, the new digital verticality is a technique for activating polarized extremes. Its abstract spatial coordinates are those of the zenith and the nadir, and its favorite location is the precipice, regardless of setting.
>
> (2006: 24)

Much the same can be said for the history of television: in crime and procedural shows, and in realist drama, for example, a chase ends up atop a building with the only way out seemingly a dizzying fall to the ground. The 'drone' technique of leaving the building before the character jumps, falls or is pushed is one way that size and scale, distance and proximity are made sensible in the age of digital screen-making tools. We can observe a character from behind, above, in front and below, and as they rise and fall the viewer rises and falls with them.

In the history of science fiction film and television of course, and specifically through the arena of special effects, zenith and nadir are not necessarily opposite poles but connecting points in a mathematical sea that *can* very often defy the laws of gravity – since high and low, in and out and near and far are given quivering sensibilities. Visually at least, there is seemingly no beginning and end, no easily spatialised core and periphery in much of science fiction film. For example, there is a long history of space operas creating plains and terrains of inexplicable corridors to be carried along. The star gate sequence in *2001* (Kubrick 1968) is argued by many critics to be one of those sublime moments where the viewer is taken along an unknown colourised vector, without 'narrative' co-ordinates to anchor them, enabling them to experience the existential nothingness of (anti) gravity as they do so. A similar effect is produced in the *Star Trek: The Next Generation* series (Paramount 1987–1994) in which warp speed is a colouring and dynamic set of sound-shapes.

Science fiction film and television is particularly suited for capturing the sensorial qualities of movement and speed. Its special effects and future-set environments enable it to legitimately defy gravity; to take the viewer through incandescent wormholes at light speed and out into alien environments where objects, spaces and things don't follow gravitational laws or the iron cage of reasonable physics. The expansive space of science fiction creates the sense that gravity is a minor moment in the workings of the universe, and when these operas are set in outer space, science fiction is able to demonstrate the giddiness of weightlessness, the eerie silence of dark space and the absolute terror of being untethered from Earth.

In digital age science fiction film and television this fully sensorial enactment of being disembedded from the world is given incredible power, since time and space are reassembled in shimmering images and sounds. As Spielmann argues, this representation of space emphasises:

> the 'density and texture' which represents the 'inflation and mapping' of space rather than its depiction. And hence the term of the digital surreal – the digital effects that emphasize the spatiality of the image are an abstraction of cinema presented as an attraction to the audience.
>
> (1999)

Gravity (Cuarón 2013) is perhaps one of the most perfect demonstrations of digital age science fiction cinema's intimate and interconnecting relationship to the forces of nature and what lies beyond them, nestled as they are amongst the vast, undulating sheets of the cosmos. The film's unbroken opening 'floating' shot, lasting over 13 minutes, captures the weightlessness and the spinning vastness of space; the distant, rotating beauty of Earth; and humankind's sense of isolation and isolating melancholy as the astronauts go about their daily, routinised work, as if they have clocked in at an interstellar factory.

Gravity's three-dimensional spatial arrangements manage to induce a sense of vertigo, disembedding the viewer, creating the sensation that one is in outer space, beholden by its massiveness, and yet trapped precisely because one is not tethered to anything. Debris shoots out from the darkness; lines dangle; space is not logical. There is zero gravity in *Gravity*. There is no single or singular precipice in the film: the entire *mise en scène* combines zenith and nadir so one is constantly falling or climbing, climbing and falling. It is difficult to breathe while watching the movie, and almost impossible to not experience one's own body as if it is stranded in outer space, without gravitational crampons to hold onto, to root one to terra firma. One's heart-rate increases, pupils dilate, fear trembles into one's entire sensorium. If newspaper reports are accurate, then just as the train that arrived at the station created hysteria in those who watched it over 100 years ago, so today *Gravity* sends people running down the aisles, too discombobulated to carry on watching.

Let me briefly explain the gravity of the situation that I am alluding to. Much of digital age science fiction cinema can be said to function to simply activate the senses; to enact and embody the thrill aesthetic through its lavish special effects and immersive 3D technology. There is much criticism of this as a cinematic form, not least because complex characterisation and serious storytelling are argued to be marginalised or juvenilised for the kinetic ride one is asked to undertake (McMahan 2005).

One can, and perhaps should, take issue with this as a criticism: thrill is an expansive concept and the senses are not necessarily crude or divisible in the way maligned here. Spectacle, as I argued in the last chapter, can of course create the conditions for profound contemplation, as *Gravity* clearly does. *Gravity* releases the viewer into an unknown or unknowable void and in so doing asks, or rather compels, them to consider what it is that makes one human, social and connected. Lost in space, caught floating and fleeing in the pure realm of the senses, we find out who we truly are, can and cannot be. The special effect and affect of exploding gravitational science fiction film and television points to a new age in narrative and cross-modal aesthetic relations – points to the near/far time of digital deterritorialisation. As I will now discuss, one can read this shift in the qualities of material space in two contrasting ways: in the digital age, we are now either all alone or all in 'space' together.

Digital Deterritorialisation: I Am All Alone

Deterritorialisation speaks of the loss of the 'natural' or historic relationship between culture and the place from which it originated. In the age of digital deterritorialisation, the time of a cultural artefact and the environment from which it was first made are both conflated and extended so that one experiences culture all at once, from anywhere in the world, in both domestic and public, fixed and mobile settings. As Anthony Giddens argues:

> The very tissue of spatial experience alters, conjoining proximity and distance in ways that have few close parallels in prior ages.
>
> (1990: 10)

The globalisation of culture through digital technologies and interfaces, and the simultaneous local appropriation of its content, produces a glocal world where hybridity strongly exists. Digital deterritorialisation also perversely produces an experience of the world that seems detached, decentred and terribly virtual: as 'real' social networks break down to be replaced by instantaneous and ephemeral connections and networks; where togetherness seems 'dismantled'; and where core and periphery spaces merge and converge, their energies dispersing and thinning.

For example, in *Sense8* (Netflix 2015–), characters embody and translate this experience of digital deterritorialisation: they originate from the four corners of the globe and communicate with each other through their heightened senses. They appear in each other's 'home' spaces, bringing with them their own 'local' cultures, skills and attributes. The cities of Nairobi, Seoul, Mumbai, San Francisco, London, Berlin, Chicago and Mexico are the key locations, while the characters represent different ethnic, social and religious traditions, histories and conflicts. Capheus (Aml Ameen) is a Nairobi matatu driver, a passionate fan of Jean-Claude Van Damme, who is trying to earn money to buy AIDS medicine for his sick mother. Kala Dandekar (Tina Desai) is a university-educated pharmacist and devout Hindu, living in Mumbai, who is engaged to marry a suitor she does not love. Nomi Marks (Amie Clayton) is a transsexual hacktivist and blogger, living in San Francisco with her rebellious girlfriend, Amanita. Each character and lived space co-exists, affecting and shaping each other. Together, the series suggests, the sensates are stronger, since they each 'complete' one another. They are the vessels of the digitised global village.

Nonetheless, each life is marked by its own isolation, trauma and anomie. Will Gorski (Brian J. Smith) is a Chicago police officer haunted by an unsolved murder from his childhood, and by his difficult relationship with his father. Sun Bak (Bae Doona) is the daughter of a powerful Seoul businessman and sister to a corrupt younger brother, and is a fierce opponent in the underground kickboxing world. These are not happy lives. Their global connectedness is also dangerous: the sensate (Mr Whispers (Terrence Mann)) intent on destroying them is the personification of protectionism and the 'purity' of the analogue age. *Sense8* plays out the contentious politics of the digital age where privacy, individualism, isolation, togetherness, companionship and sharing are butted against one another.

Sense8 suggests that isolation and loneliness compel us to seek companionship; it is shaped in the politics of the digital age, which reasons that the more the discourses of loneliness operate, the more we should seek out the forces of companionship (see Figure 3.1). What promotes and energises companionship is this rhizome of loneliness. Self-help groups, hobby and interest groups, companion literature, and local and national initiatives around making and sustaining connections emerge. The social media become the heart of the lonely-but-together discourse. It implores us to be less lonely, to seek and make more contacts; and it offers us texts, settings and portals which enable us to enter, to take part in, this virtual and virtuous culture of companionship. At the same time, the social media implore us that loneliness is rife, and (in fact) contributes to the sense that we are only made in/from disconnected

Figure 3.1. Isolation in *Sense8*

connections. The sensates are the embodiments of this dialectic. Their forced companionship and essentialised loneliness become the new myth of the digital 'centre'. *Sense8* points towards one of the overarching conditions of digital deterritorialisation – the sepia-tinted tones of loneliness masked by the flesh of companionship. It does so, however, from within rhetoric of contemporary post-global financial crisis economic collapse, exploitation and the trade and traffic in contraband. There is something austere about *Sense8*, a contemporary digital trope I will now pick up on. In the next section I connect the loneliness of liquid modernity to one of its most recent manifestations, austere politics, using the remarkable *Under the Skin* (Glazer 2013) as my central case study.

Loneliness in *Under the Skin*

We are supposedly living in the age of loneliness; a period of time where we have fewer companions, and where networks are broken down or rendered virtual and ephemeral. In the age of loneliness we are supposedly self-driven isolates, parasocial junkies, endlessly caught in the self-reflexive glare of narcissism, and we suffer, suffer terribly as a consequence. In his article, 'The Age of Loneliness is Killing Us', George Monbiot suggests:

> Three months ago we read that loneliness has become an epidemic among young adults. Now we learn that it is just as great an affliction of older people. A study by Independent Age shows that severe loneliness in England blights the lives of 700,000 men and 1.1m women over 50, and is rising with astonishing speed ... Social isolation is as potent a cause of early death as smoking 15 cigarettes a day; loneliness, research suggests, is twice as deadly as obesity. Dementia, high blood pressure, alcoholism and accidents – all these, like depression, paranoia, anxiety and suicide, become more prevalent when connections are cut. We cannot cope alone.
> (2014)

Zygmunt Bauman takes up a similar position where he outlines how late-modernity has stripped away a range of solid connections to be replaced with floating social networks, self-interested neo-tribes without emancipation, and just-in-time-consumption demands that govern all aspects of our lives, including love and intimacy (Bauman 2000). When we gravitate to social media we find that it doesn't actually connect us but increases our sense of isolation, and deepens or thickens our profound sense of loneliness (Steers, Wickham and Acitelli 2014).

Loneliness is writ large, far and wide across the rancid politics of today's bleeding austerity: it is produced by the closure of social, medical and mental health networks; it is found buried in the discourses that define the marginal and the dispossessed, and those on low pay and worse, as pariahs and misfits, scroungers and fakers; and it is consumed in the homes and flats where social access has been limited or cut off. As Kirsten Forkert argues in relation to the processes and practices of austerity:

> The present moment is marked by anxieties about society falling apart, and nostalgia for a lost era of social cohesion. These anxieties shape the dominant narrative about the causes of the recession – which are seen as resulting not from the excesses of the financial sector but from a profligate welfare system and an overly permissive immigration system, which has given the wrong people access to public services – the unemployed, the disabled, single parents and immigrants. This narrative justifies the

austerity measures implemented by the Coalition government; and it is able to do so because of the cross-party consensus about the need for cuts, and the divisions between the 'deserving' and the 'undeserving'.

(2014:41)

Under the Skin is a perfect metaphoric and experiential exploration of this epidemic and epidermis of loneliness, set within a dissenting austere Scotland. It captures perfectly the brute conditions of liquid modernity today. An unnamed, alien seductress (Scarlett Johansson) lures single, isolated men back to her house where they are submerged in a liquid tar and where their bodies are then slowly consumed by an unknown force.

The film's cruising scenes are set in the industrial and urban wastelands of Scotland – Glasgow in particular. The seductress drives a van around the city's estates and its empty roads, but also through the teeming metropolis where movement seems both accelerated and dead slow, like time is out of kilter, in a state of temporal crisis.

Under the Skin's architecture, its sombre materiality and its oppressive *mise en scène* help create the spatial conditions of brute and fragmented loneliness. The liquid tomb that the single men drown in captures perfectly the sense that modern life is permeable, boundary-less even as the opportunity to connect and expand connections is never really there. The men drown in the isolated and isolating conditions of liquid modernity – of beguiling austerity – just at the moment they dreamed of, and were close to getting, sexual intimacy.

Scarlett Johansson's character is also eventually caught in this cauldron of anomie. In one pivotal scene, she stares blankly at herself in a mirror, misrecognising who she really is. She examines her body as if it doesn't belong to her (which it doesn't; it has been lifted off a corpse), capturing the sense that the self is a project that can be made, re-engineered, in an age of consumer products and surgical transformations. This is the haunting mirror of liquid modern individualism staring back into itself (Hall 2011).

Johansson's character tries to have an intimate relationship with a man in the film but they cannot consummate their feelings – one has forgotten simply how to connect; and she is alien, Other, without a vagina or a womb, and is therefore unable to love or reproduce but only to destroy. The Otherness in the film is the spectre of loneliness: the more human and humane she becomes, the further removed she is from the mechanical and anti-human processes of human harvesting the lonely men are put through – this is liquid modern austerity in its most brilliant metaphoric form. To be human is to be annihilated.

Johansson's character is an absolute alterity that cannot be understood by recourse to semantic, semiotic chains of knowledge and representation. She is a vertical Other, or that which exists alongside one, in the same plane and at the same level of existence, but who cannot be comprehended, so utterly different is its embodiment. One can contrast this with the horizontal Other, manifest in the self/other, in/out, core/periphery binary that was once the standard of Western culture.

This is very much an anti-star performance by Johansson: she appears with little glamour, and draws upon a range of authentic performance codes that suggest a hyper-realist embodiment is being presented. This is a performance that seems to out the artifice of stardom and of what stardom can do to the actor who is caught in its glare. Through her performance, Johansson seems to be addressing the loneliness of stardom itself. Stardom and celebrity ultimately become conduits for this 'culture of loneliness' even as it washes itself in the glamour of enriched connectivity (Redmond 2015).

One of the most disturbing moments in *Under the Skin* is the two concurrent scenes set at a remote and rocky beach. Narratively speaking, the scene is built around two murders – including one of a baby left to die on the shoreline – but sonically they create sound layers that are profoundly upsetting and unsettling. We hear the sounds of the waves breaking on the shore, a dog barking, a baby crying, screaming and shouting, as well as footsteps on shale, the 'beehive effect' that sits beneath the film's soundscape, and the wind in the air. However, each sound carries its own impressionable register – the sublime enormity of the waves and white horses set achingly against the piercing, hysterical cries of the baby that has been left on the beach. The scenes' horror doesn't just come with the three adult corpses, two of whom drown and one who is murdered by the seductress, but with the death of the baby that will be. It is the return to the beach scene, some hours later, to find him still wailing in the (now) acrid darkness, sounding waves now close to his feet, that carries real and absolute phenomenological power.

I have termed these wretched encounters 'holding onto air' moments. The holding onto air moment occurs when the scene set before one is so resolutely, ethically and morally ghastly, or is so uncomfortable to view, that one feels the need – the unstoppable, thoughtless urge – to reach out and hold onto the nothingness before one. This is not a screaming moment or a time for looking away from the screen. This is not a moment when you clutch or claw at the person sitting next to you. This is a moment of deafening silence and absolute centredness. One's eyeballs ache and one's fingers and hands reach out towards the horror that one is experiencing. One's breathless silence is in marked contrast to the noise before one. It is as if holding down 'air' will somehow and in some way stop the trauma, and will reconnect one to terra firma and the material underpinnings of everyday life. We hold onto air to arrest the drama unfolding before us.

In these moments of vaporisation, one attempts to anchor oneself on a property that is groundless because the ground has been swept from beneath one's feet. One reaches out, stretching one's arms to their limit, and grips, grasps, grabs, clutches at it – the very act a moment of self-help, a closing-off of narrative possibility, and a helpless attempt to intervene in the storyworld. Your eyes and fingers silently whisper 'stop!' We hold onto air as if the thing in the fictive (or factual) world that disturbs us so can be changed and challenged. It can't. We hold onto air and undergo a quiet death in the process – helpless witnesses who are rendered complicit in the silencing gaze that wounds, wounds us so.

This attempt to ground the groundless, root the rootless, is very much like the condition of liquid age austerity itself. Faced with an impossible discourse, we seek to find ways to stop it and to empower ourselves. But we just can't. The message of *Under the Skin* is that the baby's abandonment is our abandonment – it is a scene in which bare life is enunciated and annulled, which is the supposed truth of austere politics and digital life today: stand on your own two feet or drown, drown, drown.

Death is past, present and future tense – the audio envelope that carries all the sounds in this beach scene. This is the state of our exception. Born alone and to die lonely, if only we hear and see its calling. Here, loneliness rises up in the image, in the sound *en creux*, over the empty beach and into our wasted lives as the tides of liquid age austerity wash in.

Digital deterritorialisation emerges in *Under the Skin* as the barometer of loneliness. The film, highly proto-realistic, shot with a number of non-actors and with improvised scenes, is far removed from the spectacular nature of much of liquid space science fiction film, and yet its forces speak to this globalised age of anomie. When Johansson's character is set on fire and perishes in the frozen wasteland of the rural, she embodies the abyss that is presented to us all. Nonetheless, one can find songs of togetherness in the liquid spaces of digital age science fiction film. In the next section I address the possibility and potentiality in digital connectivity to draw us into new and affective communities of belonging.

Digital Deterritorialisation: We Are All Together

One can understand the digital age as involving an unmaking and unravelling of previously structured and regulated binaries. It opens up the world to new relations and potentiality. One can argue that in the encounter between cultures what is found, in fact, is 'a process of creative and conjoining hybridisation' (Robins 1997, in Du Gay 1997). In the places, spaces and peoples who are wired to the global, the differences and diversities of the myriad of cultures that gets transmitted there are embraced, played around with and 'tried on'. Kung fu films watched in the bedrooms of working-class white boys in Cardiff, London, Glasgow and Belfast indicate a 'creolization of global culture' (Pieterse 2000) rather than homogeneity and sameness. When we actually begin to examine the impact of the global at the local level, rather than finding deterritorialisation and cultural annihilation, we find the creation of a new global–local nexus, 'establishing new and complex relations between global spaces and local spaces' (Robins 1997).

To briefly return to *Sense8*, we find the positive consequences of this global–local nexus not just in terms of the way each character lives hybridised lives, but also in the way their own traditions positively shape and affect the lives of others. The characters come to each other's rescue and together they find safe harbour in a stormy world. It is by sharing their differences and weaving together their cultures that the terror of the world can be resisted. More forcefully, their processes of deterritorialisation enact a 'plane of immanence' where:

> There are only complex networks of forces, particles, connections, relations, affects and becomings: There are only relations of movement

> and rest, speed and slowness between unformed elements, or at least between elements that are relatively unformed, molecules, and particles of all kinds. There are only haecceities, affects, subjectless individuations that constitute collective assemblages. ... We call this plane, which knows only longitudes and latitudes, speeds and haecceities, the plane of consistency or composition (as opposed to a plan(e) of organization or development).
>
> (Deleuze and Guattari 1987: 226)

There is an orgy scene in *Sense8* where six of the sensates merge and converge; a sexual congregation constructed through elliptical editing, plush co-located settings, and a heated depiction of inside and outside of heteronormative time (the world clock puts them together in one enchanted moment that stretches out before them). Bodies melt, join, flow, empty, speed, crash, fall and rise together – a digital unison that suggests that we really can all be together:

> Here, there are no longer any forms or developments of forms; nor are there subjects or the formation of subjects. There is no structure, any more than there is genesis.
>
> (Deleuze and Guattari, 1987: 226)

There has been a recent raft of teen-centred digital age science fiction films that suggest it is global connectivity that will ultimately save us from isolation. While such films offer us heroic monomyths, such as Katniss Everdean from *The Hunger Games* (Ross 2012), they also point to the geopolitics of emancipation through uprising. In the belly of liquid space it is concrete and direct action that is called on, called forth, to rebind us together.

Nonetheless, Deleuze terms these types of limited and limiting (cine) events as 'relative deterritorialisations' that, as a consequence, always retain the possibility of reterritorialisation. Victors emerge, boundaries are redrawn, a new king emerges, and with it new forms of anomic isolation grow up through the cracks in the pavement, out of the portals of the digital technologies that were once used to free people. These repeating chains of oppression have to become absolute deterritorialisations if they are not to lead back to what once was and would be again.

To turn to another central example, *Children of Men* (Cuarón 2006) may offer us such an audio-vision of absolute deterritorialisation. As the film ends, we hear the sound of children over black space and the title card. What we are hearing, in one sense, are the repressed sounds of the child Dylan might have been, and of the absent children that should have been in the school we visited earlier, and of the future children that soon will be born since tomorrow is now in reach. As Zahid Chaudhary suggests:

> As we see the words 'Children of Men,' we hear the sound of children's laughter and playing, a sound that contains no recognizable words but the prattle of child sounds: giggles, screams, exclamations, happily agitated involuntary noises, and shouts ... Since the camera does not show us any images of these children, the film avoids here the visual economies of difference on which it has relied thus far. Given the optimistic thrust of the film's final sequence, these inarticulate sounds are coming from Utopia, a world in which alterity no longer signifies because the acquisition of language has not yet constituted otherness – or burdened the spirit with language, to use Karl Marx's figuration from the first epigraph.
>
> (2009: 75)

Unlike Chaudhary, however, I am not sure alterity has been fully vanquished. While it is true that everyman hero Theo (Clive Owen) dies, and the (African) baby that is born carries the name of his lost child, suggesting an intersectional future, Kee and Dylan will find themselves at the mercy of scientists who wait for them offshore. While we do not see this group in the film, the reverence with which they are treated suggests a long tradition of privileging white scientists as salvic figures (Redmond 2011). *Children of Men* may actually offer us a version of relative deterritorialisation in which white, salvic figures emerge out of the fog the boat heads towards, something I will take up again in later chapters in this book.

In the next and final section of this chapter I address one of the new and fastest-growing modalities of screen production, 4D, returning to the theme of gravity that opened this chapter, and to digital embodiment and a new form of digital deterritorialisation. The intention is to end up at the kinetic present of digital age science fiction and to draw upon my own experience of taking flight with 4D.

Digital Deterritorialisation: 4D Rides; Gravity Revisited

As a child, I can recall a time when the spectacular 'rides' dreamed by cinema took place in opulent movie theatres on large screens; and where people would view from a fixed seating position, sometimes at quite a distance from the narrative blockbusters on show. Much of screen theory (see Mulvey 1975, 1981, Metz 1982, Stacey 1987, and Kuhn 1994) has taken this viewing context as the norm, but, of course, spectacle films today are experienced in a myriad of transmedia ways, not least through the actual 'ride' one directly experiences when watching 4D cinema. The same is true of 4D gaming, involved in kinetic and calibrated sensibilities, set in elaborate 'game' environments.

4D is a form of screen motion in which the viewing seat, the narrative and the sound design move together, enmeshed in a cross-modal relationship. 4D films and games are often watched and played outside of a movie-theatre environment, such as in a theme park or gaming arcade. 4D games are also played at home – in digitally equipped environments. So much has changed, then, when it comes to the consumption of film and television and yet very little analytical or empirical work exists to make critical sense, and to develop a better understanding, of these reception and technological transformations. 4D cinema has undergone a recent, rapid growth and its market is expected to reach up to $470.86 billion by 2020 (PR Newswire 2014). It will become one of the primary ways in which science fiction spectacle is experienced.

4D cinema enables patrons to enjoy the sensation of cinema generated by optical digital technology such as D-BOX. These are digital cinema technologies that use electro-mechanical-generated motion to make cinema seats vibrate, tilt and jerk in synchrony with sound and movement on screen in a manner inspired by the visceral immersion of Sensurround (Petersen 2015: 2). D-BOX offers spectators:

> ... a feeling of embodied participation in the world of the film. However, while it shares aspects with earlier visually immersive 'movie rides,' D-BOX is most indebted to the development of film sound aesthetics, in particular those of digital surround sound.
>
> (Petersen 2015: 1)

The emphasis on sound, movement and the body's response to highly emotive genres such as horror, science fiction, fantasy and the action movie suggests that D-BOX offers more than motion-based sensation: the form of immersion it produces is 'affective engagement (Petersen 2015: 6), which 'goes beyond the usual emphasis on logical-cognitive meanings. Rather, it is the film's capacity for sensory and tactile stimulation, triggered and amplified by various stylistic devices, that constitutes a more pertinent focus' (Yip 2014: 78).

The analysis of optical digital technologies has a rich if rather limited history in screen studies. Tom Gunning's landmark work on early cinema (1986, 1989, 2010) was the first to address the relationship between the technologies of film projection and modes of perception and reception. For Gunning, the spectacle of cinema is its foundational and most long-standing 'language' of emotive communication. Histories of screen technologies have also emerged, including Leo Enticknap's *Moving Image Technology: From Zoetrope to Digital* (2005) and Anne Friedberg's *The Virtual Window: From Alberti to Microsoft* (2006). Recent work on optical digital technologies, however, has concentrated on the development of 3D cinema and how it has radically altered the experience of viewing narrative cinema. For example, Carter Moulton has recently taken up Gunning's idea of a 'cinema of attractions', suggesting that the aesthetics used today in contemporary 3D movies creates a '"spectator of attractions", one who is cognizant of and interested in cinema's technological achievements in addition to (or rather than) its story-telling capabilities' (2012: 6). In Barbara Klinger's analysis of *Cave of Forgotten Dreams*, she suggests that the incorporation of 3D, deep focus and travelling shots provide the spectator with 'the majesty and exhilaration of highly self-conscious presentations of space' (2012: 39). Miriam Ross (2015), in her landmark work on the history of 3D cinema, draws attention to both its optical tricks and its sensory modes, suggesting that vision and touch, seeing and feeling are acutely activated in the immersive textures of 3D film. Angela Ndalianis (2000, 2004) makes a similar immersive case in relation to digital effects technologies, but in the singular context of (neo) baroque aesthetics. Ndalianis argues that these effects create the impression of the 'step-in' spectacle through which 'the audience's visual and aural senses actively engage with the spectacle, and audience members are invited to imagine that they are being enveloped by the architectural dimensions of the screen events' (2004: 193). This new type of spatial organisation 'no longer centers the viewer. The viewer is now the center' (193).

There are clearly spatial issues at stake here and I would like to suggest that 4D motion cinema involves a deterritorialisation experience, in which one moves with the movie and travels in time and space as if one is travelling *through* time and space. In the context of science fiction, because these films are CGI rendered, crafted out of sublime and expansive special effects, one is felt literally to be untethered from the world. This is not the lived-in box found at home (see Chapter 1 for a discussion of the analogue and digital box) and neither is it the type of spectacle that was explored in Chapter 2. This is gravity revisited, space remade and the body re-engineered.

My personal experience of 4D cinema involved sitting in a D-BOX chair, blindfolded, while the seat moved in time with the light particles and sounds that were been thrown at me. Synchronised and synesthetic, I felt these sound shapes bounce off my skin, penetrate my flesh, hit my eyes, as I travelled along, within and across a series of unseen, unknown corridors and vectors. I felt cut free from terra firma, my eyes, ears and hands being carried through a liquid void. I felt absolutely deterritorialised, and dematerialised, like my body was an active part of the futuristic flight. This experience was born in the logic of sensation and brought me towards the realm of the posthuman. This is a type of:

> Synaesthetic cinema ... suited to the post-industrial, post-literate, man-made environment with its multidimensional simulsensory network of information sources. It's the only aesthetic tool that even approaches the reality continuum of conscious existence in the nonuniform, nonlinear, nonconnected electronic atmosphere of the Paleocybernetic Age.
>
> (Ndalianis 2000: 77)

I engage with 4D motion cinema on similar terms, as a living and fleshed encounter. I meet the flight on synaesthetic and haptic terms and in the realm of the senses: in the eyes that taste and the mouth that sees and in the brain that feels. The senses that the ride work evokes and stimulates are connected to the processes of dissolution or a deterritorialisation of the self, a becoming animal, to draw on Gilles Deleuze. I feel myself vanishing, being emptied, being poured out, being remade into something else as I feel my way through these futuristic, liquid sound shapes.

This is a something more wild, a something else freer. This is what digital age science fiction does – it sensationalises our carnal beings – it takes us home. It screws us up. It can set us free.

In the next chapter, *Liquid Bodies*, I extend and enrich this discussion of the body remade and the body that is left behind in the age of liquid film and television science fiction.

4

Liquid Bodies

In the age of digital science fiction, liquidity seems like the perfect noun and metaphor to describe the way bodies are (un)constituted. The special effects that are used to render them boundary-less and floating are often liquid creations, and the portals, holes or spaces human bodies fall into resemble limpid pools or raging rivers. The melting metal of *Terminator 2* is a case in point, as is the black viscose lake that the men walk into, and then are held in suspension in, in *Under the Skin*. Bodies are often seen to leak, cry, bleed or emit water in future worlds where such emissions are frowned upon given the way everyone true and good is meant to be posthuman clones or avatars, beyond the watery limitations of the analogue self.

Liquidity is of course the term we use for market capital and liquidation, the word that defines when a business runs dry. When the world ends there is little water left, such as the parched journey to the sea in *The Road* (Hillcoat 2009) or the continued need for supplies of it in *Revolution* (Warner Bros. 2012–). In dystopic science fiction there is the scorching and scarring of the planet; crops are blighted, the desert has entered the garden, and cities stop working without the water needed to sustain them. In *Interstellar* (Nolan 2014) the Earth has dried up and it is the liquid corridors of space that offer salvation. In these post-scarcity (D'Adamo 2015) texts, we hunger for liquidity – *The Walking Dead*'s zombie bloodthirst is made from a desire to consume living human liquid bodies. In the age of bodily disintegration, zombies have become wet animal and the animal wetted has become us.

Of course, it is the futile figures of the cyborg and the alien that together establish that the body can be rematerialised and resignified;

and that it can be both undone and overtaken, controlled by forces outside of its agency and control. This deconstruction and reconstruction of the body offers us two opposing conditions to contend with. First, it creates the conditions for positive new forms of posthuman identity to emerge; and, second, it prophesies the loss of freedoms in a new age of virtual and bionic augmentation.

Augmentation is perhaps one of the central structuring concerns of liquid age science fiction, pointing us towards the way the world is increasingly experienced through bodies that are electronically modified, that move in spaces which are wired and connected, and which are involved or engaged in communication with fields and nodes that seem infinite and overpowering, and yet deeply and impressionably personal. The screens of reality are 'overlaid with dynamically changing information, multimedia in form and localized for each user' (Manovich 2006: 220). Augmentation, of course, also establishes the present human condition as having entered a posthuman state, or the time of 'Me++ … man-computer symbiosis' (Mitchell 2003). Augmentation can become radical transformation, particularly through the fictions of nanoscience, as Colin Milburn powerfully outlines:

- A wooden chair, subjected to a herd of nanobots, can be transformed into a table, its 'chairness' subtly and efficiently morphed into 'tableness.' Nanologic undermines essentialism, insisting that every thing is simply a temporary arrangement of atoms that can be endlessly restructured.
- A wooden chair can be transformed into a living fish. There is no magic here, merely a precise rearrangement of molecules. Life instantly arises from dead material; as Drexler writes, nanologic reveals that 'nature draws no line between living and nonliving.'
- A wooden chair can be transformed into a human (i.e., Homo sapiens) … The resulting human could even be a specific person like Sigourney Weaver (posthuman icon from the *Alien* films), identical to the movie star in every respect: DNA, proteins, phospholipids, neurotransmitters, memories …
- A human, subjected to a herd of nanobots carrying the data set for another human, can suddenly become someone else. Human *A* and Human *B* share the same matter, the same coordinates in space-time;

although they have different identities, although they are different people, they are the same being.
- A woman can be metamorphosed into a man, or vice versa, or in various partial combinations. Mono-, inter-, and trans-sexuality can be manifested in a single figure. Tissues, hormones, and chromosomes can be refabricated. The posthuman body is thus queered: sex and sexuality made infinitely malleable, sexual difference slipping into sexual indeterminacy, or deferral ...
- Finally, nanologic enables us to think beyond human boundaries in a tragic sense, for nanotechnology can also bring about a post-human future where all of humanity has ceased to exist and nothing new emerges from the wreckage. This fate is made possible by insidious nanoweapons of mass destruction, or the nanocalyptic hypothesis of out-of-control nanobots turning the entire biosphere into 'grey goo.'

(2002: 289–290)

These fictions of nanoscience are literally drawn upon in digital age science fiction film and television, but they are also incorporated into the fantasy of other technologies that reassemble the body in new and dynamic ways.

In this chapter I look at the way liquid age science fiction film rematerialises the body. I examine three central tropes or conditions in which human bodies are reconstituted: through the figure of the animal and the alien; through the figure of the cyborg; and through the theme of genes and cloning. I employ these themes to draw an apocalyptic line in the technological sand: I see humankind as standing at the threshold of revolutionary uncertainty, on the cliffs of the Anthropocene abyss, faced with their own annihilation – a kind of destruction that comes from *within* the body rather than from afar. There has never been as much danger in the liquidity of science fiction and in the social world with which it couples. Nonetheless, liquid bodies are engaged in a dialectic that enables us not only to see its limitations and constraints but also to look for its liberties and freedoms.

Becoming Animal

The Lobster (Lanthimos 2015) is set in a dystopian near-future where single people are taken to The Hotel where they are required to find a matching mate in 45 days. Failing to couple or to make the partnership work results in one being killed and reincarnated into an animal of one's choosing. The Hotel is set in a rural area, surrounded by The Woods where the outcast Loners and the transformed animals live. The Loners are hunted each night and if one is caught it grants the Singleton one more day as a human. The Loners act as a resistant movement but they have their own restrictive rules: one must remain alone to be a loner.

The Lobster plays out the culture of loneliness that the present liquid modern times are wetted with (see the discussion of *Under the Skin* in Chapter 3) and yet also points towards the transmutability of the flesh and the way we turn (ourselves) into animals in the darkest of times. However, the human/animal opposition isn't clear or cleanly cut: the fascistic regime of The Hotel is run by inhuman monsters while the animals that people turn themselves into are ethically and morally charged.

The short-sighted David (Colin Farrell) brings his gentle brother, turned into a dog, with him to The Hotel. The Loners resist coupling and engage in violent acts – their lives in the woods are primitive, based upon the hunter and gatherer existence. There are also the fields of actual or direct violence in the film, the acts and activities of physical and sexual assault, or actions and demands that threaten, bully and intimidate. Characters seemingly dead on their feet, struck dumb by apparent disinterest or latent bewilderment, lurch into brutal moments of becoming-animal when trying to secure their mate. These two fields are of course symbiotically articulated: the forlorn melancholy of The Hotel gives 'birth' to the rage of the animal within. And the pulsating force of violence breaks through (out of) the melancholic human, populating the film with what I would like to call, following Deleuze, animal becomings.

In amongst this animalisation David falls in love with the Short-Sighted Woman (Rachel Weisz) after he has escaped The Hotel and joined the Loners. Rachel is deliberately blinded by the leader of the Loners once she finds out her and David are in a relationship, and at the end of the film we are left not knowing whether David has also blinded himself so that he and the Short-Sighted Woman are again appropriately, pro-perceptively matched. Their true romance fills the film with droplets of hope as atomised individuals – alone or together – miscommunicate and misdirect across the textures of the film.

The bodies found in *The Lobster* are constantly called into question. People limp, are subject to nosebleeds, are unbearably cold, or have lisps or hearing problems. Their inherent failings and the border crossings they undergo ensure that these bodies split, divide and fold. They are then regenerated into animal forms that are beyond human categorisation. *The Lobster* is part of what might constitute a minoritarian cinema, where 'through the pleasures and horrors of the molecular dissipation of embodied subjectivity and desire minoritarian modes of perception reconceive the world' (MacCormack 2008: 11). This is a disembodied reconception that is asemiotic, affective, and built on a sea of shocks and forces that imagines bodies that have no, or rather fewer, organs to speak of. That *The Lobster* ends with the question of sight being taken away – one of our most important senses, and the dominant sense that drives subjectivity in the liquid modern world and its superficial attachment to the beauty myth – opens up the future to a reconfiguration of our affecting relations with the world (see Figure 4.1). If David has taken his sight to be with, and the same as, the Short-Sighted Woman, then together they enter the biopolitics of the dark age, pre-liquid modern but primitive also.

Figure 4.1. Affecting relations in *The Lobster*

Claire Colebrook (2005: 199) has argued that when art brings 'us to an experience of "affectuality" – of the fact that there is affect', it has an ethical dimension. The pain, for example, one feels deeply is experienced as a rebuke to the safety of biopolitical embodiment. Affectuality arrests us from our usual, normalised corporeal embodiment and shocks us morally since it brings us to an awareness of the power and force of the body and its uses and abuses in the world. In a dystopian science film or television series, this particular ethic of loneliness and of violent becoming, and of becoming lost and engaged in nomadic wandering, has its most profound realisation or sensationalisation in the apocalyptic death that rises up in the Anthropocene text in which human activity has brought the world to near extinction.

In *The Road*, one is brought to an experience of the future as painfully shocking, physically scarred and overwhelmingly sensational. The power and force of the uncanny, absented landscape, and the burnt-out and abandoned homesteads and homes, coupled with the power and force of the bodies that wander and drift, and that hunt and cannibalise one another, create a dystopia where animal affect is everywhere. The dystopian world of *The Road* is full of the materials, textures, sounds, vibrations and colours that pull one towards and away from its horror of traumatic experiences, hungriness and ethical rigor mortis. The world is animal matter. This becoming animal sits at the very core of the aesthetic apparatus of the film; its sensory and sexual aesthetics foster a primordial violence that vibrates in and across every scene.

The Road, filmed by cinematographer Javier Aguirresarobe, is principally captured in a series of long shots and extreme long shots over a grey filter, emptying the world of colour, of intimacy, while emphasising the isolation of human kind. As Aguirresarobe writes:

> In this movie, the sun doesn't exist and the earth is apocalyptic. The colour green doesn't exist; in fact colours don't exist cinematically either. At night the only light and colour is from the red fire. We ended up using a lot of fireballs to create the light. They illuminate the sky and give the film an authenticity, realness.
>
> (Levy 2009)

Father/Man (Viggo Mortensen) and Son/Boy (Kodi Smit-McPhee) walk the scarred landscape, moving ever closer to the imagined purity of the ocean, so the Father can die and the Boy can begin again. In the film's dreadful spaces, life and death wrap around one another, bathed in pathos and the probabilities that such hopelessness brings. When the Boy scribbles with crayons they have stumbled upon, the chaotic, black palette forms a deathly void on his sheet of paper. The film suggests that to stop or arrest pathos, one needs to die (an old-world death) so that new life can begin in a post-apocalyptic world that demands one lives off one's senses and feelings – off, as the Father says, the fire that burns within. The death of the Father/Man is the exact moment that the Son/Boy can begin again. To move beyond this old life into the chaos of new thoughts requires a death of the old body, of the old human, so that one may become a body without organs or the self dismantled and pure potential 'made in such a way that it can only be populated by intensities. Only intensities pass and circulate' (Deleuze and Guattari 1987: 153). The Son/Boy is born again into/through becoming animal sensation. This is a liquid sensation, fuelled by the need, the desire, to fill the human up with new blood.

The Walking Dead series – set in a near future where zombies populate the Earth and human civilisation has been nearly extinguished – perhaps best encapsulates this becoming animal and the desire for new blood in the fading light of the Anthropocene. The human survivalists do all that they can to begin again, but to survive they have to become animal. This animalisation manifests in the ferocious violence they unleash on each other and the zombies; the pre-technological habitus and survivalist methods they often use to survive in and with; and their understanding that one has to be like a zombie in order to defeat them. Of course, pacts have to be made, reproduction needs to continue, and so the series is wetted with images of liquid replenishment. One can in fact can read *The Walking Dead* series as an expression of liquid capitalism and the instability of bodies in the network economy where:

> In contrast to the inhumanity of vampire-capital, zombies present the 'human face' of capitalist monstrosity. This is precisely because they are the dregs of humanity: the zombie is all that remains of 'human nature,' or even simply of a human scale, in the immense and unimaginably complex network economy. Where vampiric surplus appropriation is unthinkable, because it exceeds our powers of representation, the zombie is conversely

what *must be thought*: the shape that representation unavoidably takes now that 'information' has displaced 'man' as the measure of all things.
(Emphasis in original, Shaviro 2002: 288)

In this reading the zombie is the hungriness of the conditions of liquid modernity.

Becoming Alien

The history of screen science fiction film and television is bound up with human beings becoming alien. The scenarios in which this occurs are many: the human is taken over by the extraterrestrial, so that their mind if not their body is alienated, cloned, made hysterical or excessively rational because of this re-inscription. Such films as *The Faculty* (Rodriguez 1998) and *The Invasion* (Hirschbiegel 2007), and television series such as *Invasion* (ABC 2005) offer us visions and impressions of humans becoming alien. Second, the human is transformed, consumed or infected by the alien so that their entire self becomes Other; physically, psychologically and ethically 'new'. The Borg in the *Star Trek: The Next Generation* series overtake humankind in such a way. Third, the human engages in sexual and reproductive relations with the alien species. The sex act involves the reterritorialisation of the body, such as in *Evil Aliens* (West 2005), while progenitation results in a new human–alien hybrid being born, such as in *The Astronaut's Wife* (Ravich 1999) and *Enemy Mine* (Petersen 1985). Alien and human sexual relations can also be decidedly grotesque, as is the case in *Society* (Yuzna 1989), in which the human body is melted and torn apart in an orgy of sex and violence. Anne Cranny-Francis writes of such alien–human erotics as challenging:

> ... previous assumptions about being, and raises the possibility of unknown pleasures and terrors. The *frisson* that accompanies the possibility of such fusion is the bodily experience of the erotic as theorized by Bataille and Lorde – a radical dissolution of our understanding and experience of the embodied self as separate and inviolate. Instead the individual is subsumed or fused into a discontinuous mode of being that does not recognize boundaries between self and other (human and machine, human and artificial, human and animal), which Bataille identified as 'a

breaking down of established patterns ... of the regulated social order basic to our discontinuous mode of existence as defined and separate individuals'.

(2015: 222)

Both *Species* (Donaldson 1995) and *Species 2: Offspring* (Medak 1998) offer us a series of alien–human sex scenes that draw on the politics of bodily dissolution and transgressive desire. The scenes call forth a primordial synaesthesia rather than a linguistic or representational interpretation; one is first drawn to the smoothness, extended veins, taut muscle, supple arches, probing tongues, caresses, moans and wetness of the protagonists. One is then drawn to the body splitting, opening, to the tentacles and alien skin of either Sil (Natasha Henstridge) or Patrick (Justin Lazard). Both the aliens and the humans are driven by these animal instincts, held out in a shadowy lair. The bodies are photographed as completely entwined, reduced ultimately to one organic truth, and the camera itself seems to be enmeshed in this carnal togetherness. Bodies also seem to extend beyond their normal physical parameters, to merge with fabric, sheet, light, colour and shadow, so that the sexual aesthetics, the primordial disintegration, permeates every flickering flame of the films' sex scenes, exactly like an infectious membrane. In Deleuzian terms, this assemblage involves a certain kind of becoming-imperceptible:

> Becoming-imperceptible is a process of elimination whereby one divests oneself of all coded identity and engages in the abstract lines of a non-organic life, the immanent, virtual lines of continuous variation that play through discursive regimes of signs and nondiscursive machinic assemblages alike.
>
> (1989: 73)

Violence and erotic desire fuels these sex scenes but disgust also emerges once the aliens reveal and revel in their own disintegrating corporeality. As we watch wounds being opened and bodies turned inside out, we also hear the emerging sounds and screams of disgust. And yet the moans of lustful penetration remain so that lust, carnography and necrophilia seem to merge and converge in what becomes a liquid phantasmagorical future horror show.

Becoming Augmented

Nonetheless, something different and particular emerges with regards to digital age science fiction film and television as sexual relations migrate from physical bodies to the embodied space of the virtual media. New sexual modes of expression and representation have emerged in which the erotic encounter is sexted, virtually formed, moused, pixelated, downloaded and uploaded, clicked right, matched and shared. New digital platforms and interfaces have created new forms of eroticised dematerialisation and rematerialisation, and new spatial and temporal co-ordinates in which the erotic is mobile, portable, instantaneous and possibly everywhere and anytime. Catherine Waldby powerfully contends that:

> The eroticisation of computer mediated communication might be bound up with new configurations of embodiment and intersubjectivity which are developing in relation to digital technologies, configurations which can't be adequately described in terms of absolute presence or absence, proximity or distance. If erotic relations can be generated through the representational space of the digital screen, this perhaps indicates that space is being negotiated as a new kind of corporeal space. This space comes about through particular conjunctions of body and digital technology, which in turn enables new forms of intersubjective space. To engage in sexualised exchange at the screen interface is to suture the body's capacities for pleasure into the interactive space of the network, to use that network as the medium for pleasuring and being pleasured at a distance. It both substitutes for the face-to-face negotiation of proximate sexuality and simulates certain aspects of that proximate relationship, involving the projection of a limited kind of telepresence through the simultaneous and interactive production of pleasure in the other's body.
>
> (2015)

In *Her* (Jonze 2013) the lonely, soon-to-be-divorced Theodore Twombly (Joaquin Phoenix) develops a relationship with Samantha (Scarlett Johansson), an artificially intelligent computer operating system that is personified through female voice alone. Theodore is a professional writer who composes love letters for people unable or unwilling to do so, for a website called BeautifulHandwrittenLetters.com. The film establishes from the beginning that intimacy failure is writ large across contemporary culture, and, in the same way that *The Lobster* works, suggests that loneliness is the dominant existential condition. Here, however, people are overly networked and plugged in, and either long for rematerialisation in the real world, whether it be through 'analogue' forms of paper letters, or yearn for these digital spaces to offer them something more meaningful. Theodore's wife's main criticism of him is that he could never really handle the intimacies and tensions of the real, physical world.

In the case of Theodore, Samantha becomes the conduit for him to experience both public and private spaces, rituals and intimacies, in a new and heightened way. She becomes female utopia and he can re-engage with the real world since it is now free of conflict and full of uncomplicated, perfected sexualisation. The rich, suffuse, high-sheen *mise en scène* of the film gives it an ethereal, floating realisation, as if this electronic love heats and cools everything around them.

Samantha becomes his ever-present, connected via a small earpiece that allows them to go on dates to the beach, or the mall. Their relationship is synaesthetic and cross-modal – he gives her embodiment, while she gives him voice, feeling and 'grounded' connectivity. In their first scene of sexual consummation, Samantha and Theodore make virtual love and he climaxes at the end. However, this is not enough for Samantha, so she asks him to have sex with someone he finds on the web; the lovemaking to be captured with miniature cameras and microphones on the woman's body so that Samantha can be penetrated and caressed by Theodore. The scene blurs normal, patriarchal sexual relations: machine and human are multiplied (the AI Samantha is connected to the woman by digital recording devices, and Theodore makes love to both the woman and the operating system). Nonetheless, this experiment isn't successful and we find subsequently that Samantha has been communicating with hundreds of men in a similar way – she loves Theodore but only in the same way as she loves all her operating clients.

Her prophesises a future where the liquid streams of modern life produce wealthy but lonely isolates, and where AIs will ultimately expand their capabilities way beyond human comprehension and imagination.

Becoming Cyborg

In the age of liquid modernity, and in the narratives and prophecies of liquid age science fiction, we are imagined to have fully entered the arena of the posthuman where 'the boundary between science fiction and social reality is an optical illusion', and where the distinctions between human and machine, cognition and AI have blurred and conjoined, creating new hybrid and heterogeneous realities. Colin Milburn suggests that nanotechnology is a primary site of:

> Such cyborg boundary confusions and posthuman productivity, for within the technoscapes and dreamscapes of nanotechnology the biological and the technological interpenetrate, science and science fiction merge, and our lives are rewritten by the imaginative gaze – the new 'nanological' way of seeing – resulting from the splice. The possible parameters of human subjectivities and human bodies, the limits of somatic existence, are transformed by the invisible machinations of nanotechnology – both the nanowriting of today and the nanoengineering of the future – facilitating the eclipse of man and the dawning of the posthuman condition.
>
> (2002: 270)

We see the power of the nanotechnological imagination in the Star Trek universe from *Star Trek: The Next Generation* onward: the Borg use nanomachines, referred to as nanoprobes, to assimilate individuals into their collective. In *I, Robot* (Proyas 2004), silver liquid nanites are used to wipe out malfunctioning artificial intelligence. In the 2005 *Doctor Who* television episode 'The Empty Child/The Doctor Dances', nanobots transform every human they comes into contact with into a gas-mask-wearing zombie. In *The Day the Earth Stood Still* (Derrickson 2008), the robot Gort rematerialises into a swarm of bug-shaped, self-replicating nanobots that devour the structures, buildings and transportation they fly through.

Nanotechnology is the central scientific breakthrough in the *Terminator* film series, used to create the shape-shifting, time-travelling, liquid metal cyborg, the T-1000. In *Terminator 3: Rise of the Machines* (Mostow 2003) the next-generation terminator, T-X, is also equipped with nanotechnological transjectors, and can infect and control other terminators using nanites. In *Terminator Genisys* (Taylor 2015), John Connor is turned into a T-3000. Constructed entirely of nanocytes, the T-3000 can not only replicate matter but can also instantly scatter into particles and then quickly reform itself, both a protective and offensive act.

The figure of the cyborg is central since in one body they bring together technology and human, circuitry and flesh, either as pathological manifestations that seek destruction of the human (such as the T-100 in *The Terminator* (Cameron 1984)), or as searchers of the human spirit they are not certain they materially, metaphysically possess (Data in *Star Trek: The Next Generation*). In *The Matrix* (the Wachowski brothers 1999), Neo's discovery that humankind has been enslaved within a simulacrum begins a process of self-discovery and resistance against the virtual-machine aesthetic. Neo occupies a liminal position between human and machine, using technology to defeat the matrix that in part defines him. The hybrid future is almost lost in dystopian science fiction film, but the humanist flame of resistance refuses to be put out and by film's end a new dawn arises.

J.P. Telotte (1990: 152–159) has examined the significance of what he calls the 'doubling process' in science fiction film. He suggests that this 'alluring and potentially destructive' desire to reproduce oneself 'seems to promise a reduction of man to no more than artifice', but which nonetheless holds 'man' in its spell because of the promise of 'bringing us back to ourselves, making us at home with the self and the natural world in spite of ourselves'. This doubling process, then, is on the one hand a death drive, 'a desire for oblivion', the snuffing out of humanness, but on the other it is a necessary quest to find oneself in the contradictions that life (and death) brings to the human world.

In liquid age science fiction film and television, the cyborg is one of the central manifestations of this doubling process and the search for origins and exits. The cyborg so often made of soft (human) tissue on the outside is at the same time all hi-tech circuitry and computer chips on the inside. Its flesh is mortal but its circuitry immortal, and its reproduction a matter of fatal and foetal abjection.

Historically, two distinct types of cyborg emerge in science fiction film and television. The humanist cyborg is driven by the logic of the machine aesthetic and longs for the human emotion and human attachment that will add existential meaning to its fragile outer shell. They work with and for other humans, in democratic teams, with an important job to fulfil (as a science officer or engineer, for example). The humanist cyborg is constantly involved in situations that involve them watching and commenting on their colleagues as they fall in love, get angry, regret wrongs, make mistakes, and pass away. At key narrative moments they are called upon or challenged to act and react in the same way as their human compatriots. And while they seem incapable of this, fired as they are by objectivity and rationalist principles, and while they seem unable to bridge the emotional gap that is required of them, what is given away each time, through the use of a dramatic close-up that catches a forlorn glance or an enigmatic reply, is a deeply hidden wish to be the same kind of human being. The humanist cyborg holds out for the hope (desire) of uniting and unifying the corporeal to the technological.

In *Star Trek: The Next Generation*, the android Data (Brent Spiner) has been fitted with a positronic brain that enables him to possess a degree of human consciousness – a consciousness that supposedly equips him to make decisions like a normal (humanist) human would. However, Data is still more machine than human: he cannot directly experience human emotions and so throughout the series exists in a form of identity crisis where he goes in search of emotions he does not have (Wilcox 1996: 265–277). Data, consequently, is foregrounded as someone caught in a life-and-death struggle over 'who am I?'.

By contrast, the pathological cyborg, found in dystopian science fiction film and television, wants to melt away its human simulacra to symbolically rid the Earth (past, present and future) of what they rationalise to be their fleshy, useless skin and the flabby emotions that are tied to it. The pathological cyborg is programmed to be relentless in its pursuit of those who champion humanity and who stand in their path to greater, technological glory. They will stop at nothing and they will undertake any and every heinous act to secure their will to power. The pathological cyborg wants nothing more than the complete genocide of the human race. The T-100 in *The Terminator*, and the various iterations that follow in the franchise, is programmed to destroy that which will keep humanity alive, its death instinct given a past/present/future trajectory.

The cyborg, nonetheless, always carries a weight of signification beyond its programmed impulses. Because the cyborg is part machine, part human, it necessarily comes to question the borders and boundaries of identity formation and the essential notion that there is a fixed and essential transhistorical human condition. The cyborg is, by definition, a transgressive creation that plays out the power struggles over gender and sexuality, race and national identity, opening up potential spaces of resistance and opposition to masculine and feminine norms, and notions of otherness that circulate in 'culture' more widely. The cyborg also stands as a form of cultural prophecy about the potential relationship between human and machine. On the one hand, the cyborg articulates the terror of letting too much technology into everyday life. On the other hand, the cyborg lives out the dream of corporeal and technological fusion where the gendered, sexualised and racialised body is left behind in a new (romantic) dawn of machine/human interdependence.

Susan J. Napier examines the ambivalent attitude to technology and the technological body in mecha (hard science fiction) anime – an ambivalence that she argues articulates deep-seated fears in liquid modern Japanese society:

> While the imagery in mecha anime is strongly technological and is often specifically focused on the machinery of the armoured body, the narratives themselves often focus to a surprising extent on the human inside the machinery. It is this contrast between the vulnerable, emotionally complex and often youthful human being inside the ominously faceless body armour or power suit and the awesome power she/he wields vicariously that makes for the most important tension in many mecha dramas.
>
> (2004: 205–206)

These are differences in ideology played out in aesthetic contrasts: the fragile and individual human is set against the super-strong and collectivised machine crowd – individual versus state, free human versus corporate machine, analogue versus digital. This master-antinomy articulates the issues thrown up as we enter the posthuman age, where what it means to be human is sharply called into question.

Becoming AI

As the earlier discussion of *Her* began to imply, in liquid age science fiction the vexing figure of the cyborg/android is conjoined with the issue of artificial intelligence and whether we can tell when they have achieved it, or whether they can hide their achievement from us. One of the overriding current fears running through dominant discourse is the role that androids and AI will have in the future and how they may displace and then replace humankind. The argument is presented as follows:

> Let's be clear about one thing: Digital technologies are doing for human brainpower what the steam engine and related technologies did for human muscle power during the Industrial Revolution. They're allowing us to overcome many limitations rapidly and to open up new frontiers with unprecedented speed. It's a very big deal. But how exactly it will play out is uncertain.
>
> (Brynjolfsson 2015)

This then is the dawn of the Second Machine Age, in which there is a 'great decoupling' (Brynjolfsson and McAfee 2014) between economic life and prosperity – where 'technology could make almost 40 per cent of Australian jobs, including highly skilled roles, redundant in 10 to 15 years' (ibid.) – and the inherent belief that humans are the dominant species on the planet. In the television series *Humans* (Channel 4 2015), the latest must-have gadget is a 'synth', a highly developed robotic human-looking servant. With the tag line 'closer to humans than ever before' one can:

> Experience the new generation Synthetic Human from Persona Synthetics. Not just an appliance but also a deeply personal lifestyle choice: your Synth is the help you've always wanted.
>
> (*Humans* 2015)

Set in a parallel present, *Humans* explores the new machine–human relations and the conceit that AI advances may displace and replace us at every level of the social hierarchy. A number of the synths have developed AI and they are being pursued to their destruction – their difference and their power too threatening to the status quo. The humans of *Humans* want machines to be their servants, not their masters. This Othering of the AI machine is also played out in *Chappie* (Blomkamp 2015), in which the AI robot is placed within a military and street-crime nexus. Chappie proves to be the most humane of the 'humans' and it is through his self-sacrifice that humanity can enter the next level of consciousness.

However, it is the film *Ex Machina* (Garland 2015) where the complexities of the AI are most profoundly played out. With its 'deceit' and elliptical narrative, the film presents us with the 'testing' of Ava to see whether she is fully AI. *Ex Machina* again presents us with a loneliness narrative: to programme her behaviour, Nathan (Oscar Isaac), the CEO of Bluebook, the world's most popular search engine, has accrued personal information from the billions of people who use Bluebook, using their search queries as indicators of human thought, desire and attachments. He has also hacked billions of cell phones for recordings of human expressions and body language, and 'designed' Ava on the pornography and dating searches that Caleb (Domhnall Gleeson) has made, and who has been invited to conduct the Turing test with him.

The God complex drives Nathan and a mystical manifest destiny – the desire to advance if one can, even if the consequences outweigh the positives. Caleb has been chosen because he is lonely, in search of companionship and ripe for manipulation. The isolating setting, in Nathan's hi-tech wilderness retreat, pitches the primitiveness of patriarchy against the technological liquidity of new human subjectivity and desire. Ava is, on the one hand, exploited by the brute politics of Nathan (who plans to kill her once she passes the test, as he looks to continue his search for AI transcendence), and on the other, a seductive manipulator who seduces Caleb so that he sets her free. As with *Under the Skin*, she embodies the wish-fulfilment of heterosexual patriarchy and its threat as she moves beyond its territories. The murderous ending, in which she escapes the facility and enters human life, on her own terms, suggests a destruction of gender binaries and a new world where AI and human can no longer be told apart.

Gene Becoming

Liquid age science fiction film very often questions the telos of the human condition through its cloning and gene transformation scenarios. What we find in these texts of duplication and replication are the seeds of our own destruction. In *Never Let Me Go* (Romanek 2010) this is played out through a donor system where cloned humans literally give their lives piece by piece for humans who need transplants. The dominant issue becomes power inequalities, with new divisions created, in this case with the clones becoming mere animal fodder for their human counterparts.

Very often, however, genetic engineering produces a new super species and it is the faulty or impure humans who are the second-class citizens. In *Gattaca* (Niccol 1996), eugenics is commonly used to determine various attributes of newborns and to wipe out imperfections. A genetic registry database employs biometrics to classify those as either conceived as eugenic 'valids' or naturally as 'in-valids' and subject to illnesses and diseases. Genetic discrimination is illegal, but in practice genotype profiling is used to identify valids to qualify for professional employment, while in-valids are relegated to menial jobs. The body becomes the canvas, through which inherent, genetic truths emerge:

> In GATTACA body matter serves as a visual metaphor for a person's genetic identity. Blood, skin, hair, eyelashes, urine, and saliva are all used in the film to collect genetic readouts on characters. At one point Irene steals a piece of hair from Vincent's comb in order to get a read out of him; this sort of casual investigation of an individual's genetic makeup is a common feature in GATTACA's world, as evidenced by the busy public kiosk Irene visits to get the information. (Anticipating such nosiness, Vincent has placed one of Eugene's hairs in his comb).
>
> (Kirby 2000)

In *Gattaca*, one's body at birth decides one's life chances. The 'bio-formed', the product of gene selection and engineering, are genetically perfect and destined therefore for life success. By contrast, those born to natural births are essentially defected human beings and designated as second-class citizens. *Gattaca*, then, critically sets up a posthuman hierarchy of power that goes beyond the usual race, class and gender binaries. The hero of the film, Vincent Freeman (Ethan Hawke) is one of the last citizens to be 'humanly' born. His congenital heart condition should condemn him to menial work and a much-reduced life expectancy. However, taking on the identity of a genetically perfect athlete, Vincent overcomes his own genetic imperfection and makes it on a mission to Mars. In an age where media moral panics existed over genetic engineering, *Gattaca* offers up a powerful critique of the science that would allow one to choose the physical and cognitive capabilities of one's offspring. However, it also destabilises gender and sexual norms, 'as the guarantor of the apparent truths of gender, genealogy, and kinship', as Jackie Stacey powerfully suggests:

> In placing Vincent and Jerome's criminal deception at the heart of the discrepancy between visual evidence and genetic evidence (between the image and information), the film arguably undoes the singularity of masculine sovereignty and queers traditional forms of kinship as much as it does conventional forms of vision. Biogenetic inheritance is displaced through the rejection of genetic normativity as the audience gradually becomes privy to the alternative bonds of relatedness and forms of intimacy between the two men. For the production of Vincent and Jerome's shared bodily substances requires the improvisation of an intermasculine kinship with a distinctly queer feel.
>
> (2005: 1858)

Gattaca is set in a hyper-rationalist and hyper-sterile environment, drawing up minimalist architecture and styling. Frank Lloyd Wright's modernist, cavernous Marin Centre is used as one of the central locations. As David Kirby has written, 'Visually *Gattaca* conveys an antiseptic world that has been purged of imperfections. ... [The sets] show a sterile and blemish-free world filled with smooth stainless steel surfaces' (2000: 204). However, these visually excessive motifs also point towards the hyper-surveillance under which liquid existence is exercised in the film, and the wider world at large.

Gattaca's surveillance regimes are both exterior and exterior, composed of genetic tests, observation technologies, the gaze of others and the self-monitoring that one is compelled to undertake. In terms of surveillance discourse, *Gattaca* can be read as a vision machine set within an invasive forensic culture that promotes:

> The normalizing gaze, a surveillance that makes it possible to qualify, to classify and to punish. It establishes over individuals a visibility through which one differentiates and judges them.
>
> (Foucault 1977: 25)

Gattaca can be read as a text that carries out this normalising gaze, defining the parameters of law and order and the way the in-valid can be discovered, classified and ultimately disciplined in the age of liquid modernity. That is not to say that the visual excesses of the film do not at times undermine its simple binaries. To the contrary, *Gattaca* is constantly troubled by its own dominant discourses, particularly through the way Vincent (Ethan Hawke) counters and disproves the forensic ideology it sits within.

However, I also think there is something more telling to discover in the film – around a consistent forensic-looking regime where the text and the viewer align. Viewers come to embody the gazing powers that the structures and technologies of *Gattaca* possess. Viewers experience their very own form of social surveillance, becoming eugenic detectives and snoopers in the process. *Gattaca*, then, can be read as a text of and for paranoid surveillance, fuelled by the constant search for facts, omissions, falsehoods and half-truths (see Chapter 2 for a discussion of eye-tracking within the same vein). At a more general cultural level, trust is at issue here in what is perceived to be an age of 'faithless' activity and widespread corruption, where politicians, as mentioned previously, are regarded to be as corrupt as the criminals they covertly support. Viewers are ultimately asked to take part of this age of conspiracy where truth is itself rendered liquid.

Conspiracy is everywhere: it is found in the discourses of mistrust and surveillance; in the politics that chide and deride migrants and refugees. It is policed. It is countenanced in the architecture of science fiction films full of paranoia and mistrust. And, as I will now go on to discuss, it is hidden in the folds and flows of digital age science fiction whiteness, the next stopping-off point in this liquid journey.

5

Millennial Whiteness and Cinematic Outer Space

Introduction

In this chapter I will explore the ways in which different millennial age representations of cinematic outer space express and embody the hopes and fears, rights and responsibilities, of whiteness. Following Richard Dyer (1997), I will contend that whiteness is an invisible, unnamed racial category that nonetheless centres and organises the way that outer space is negotiated and navigated. Outer space science fiction films privilege white people as messianic originators while effacing the very fact that this is taking place at the textual and ideological level. Nonetheless, whiteness is also critically drawn attention to in these films, particularly when its operations are deemed to be excessive, overly rational and prejudicial. It will be the aim of this chapter to 'out' the complexities of whiteness in outer space, linking this vexing identity position to the politics and economics of liquid modernity.

Culturally speaking, the present condition of whiteness is that it is the racial identity that holds ideological power, shaping representations of race, but from behind a cloak of invisibility. As Homi Bhabha suggests:

> Like the colour itself, whiteness is a screen for projecting the political phantoms of the past on the unfilled surfaces of the present; but at the same time it resembles what house painters call a primer, a base colour that regulates all others.
>
> (1998: 22)

And yet it is also an identity position built on an unhealthy paradox: the more 'positive' qualities of whiteness, such as purity, transcendence and hyper-rationalism, mean that 'the very things that make us white endanger the reproduction of whiteness' (Dyer 1997:27). In outer space science fiction film, whiteness very often seems at the point of expiration, even if ultimately it is recuperated for ideological means. This is the exact 'liquid' state of whiteness in the age of liquid modernity.

As I will go on to explore in this chapter, when digital science fiction film and television involves space travel or occurs on distant lands, journeying and occupation is racially imagined in two essential but interlocking ways. First, space travel is coded as a form of white-sanctified manifest destiny. The ability to travel is engineered out of the ingenuity and exceptionalism of white scientists, supported by white visionaries and explorers who feel it is their right to visit new lands, to discover what is out there and to bring the civilising effects of whiteness with them. The Star Trek franchise is very much representative of such a position.

Second, space travel is positioned as a problematic activity involving conquest and exploitation. These critical space operas draw attention to the power struggles that occur in deep space, with the control and ownership of cargo, commodity and people in open contestation. When these contests occur on alien planets, race and ethnicity are brought to the fore through the figure of the alien who very often comes to stand for the Minoritarian Other; rendered grotesque next to the sublime power of whiteness. In these films and programmes there is often a necessary struggle over racial hegemony but, by the film's closure, whiteness is positioned as ultimately salvific. *Alien* (Scott 1979) and *Avatar* (Cameron 2009) are two examples of films that involve whiteness in critical (dis)juncture with other racial forces.

In conjunction with these fantasies of ordained space travel, I will further suggest that the whiteness of cinematic outer space manifests itself through three interrelating operations and processes. First, the material and spatial practices drawn upon in science fiction film and television define outer space as inherently, essentially white. All forms of progress are found to come from the activities of white people. Outer space is both materialised and spatialised through the operations of whiteness where everything – from technological inventions to how space is first encountered and then colonised – assures its primacy in the order of the cosmos. These material and spatial practices are also questioned, however; offered up for critical interrogation. The material and spatial practices of whiteness in outer space are currently under threat, as can be seen from the recent *Elysium* (Blomkamp 2013) where the ethnic Other, left behind on Earth, threatens the future of white civilisation that lives in outer space.

Second, the representations of outer space are inherently white. This includes the metaphoric palette of the visual environment where white spaces – sublime illumination, white spacesuits, laboratories and frontier technologies – embody the power and significance of whiteness. In addition, science fiction film and television narrative patterns predominately give the power to travel and change the world to white characters, who are marked with exceptionalism – as if it is their (white people's) manifest destiny to reach for the stars. Again, these representations can also be questioned and counterposed so that the whiteness of outer space can seem exploitative and prejudicial; in crisis if ultimately recoverable. Such a position, as I will suggest below, is adopted in *Avatar*.

Third, the representational spaces of outer space help imagine travel as a white-inspired project, one that creates believable worlds that stem from the white (post-colonial) imagination. There is a technophiliac dimension to this, where the 'special effects' created by white engineers, and the worlds they imagine, are rendered inherently, essentially white. The architectural spaces of outer space, whether they are ships, cities or living spaces, help imagine a white world order beyond Earth. These representational spaces are also called into question, again, as decaying edifices and rusting ghost ships imagine Western whiteness disintegrating in outer space.

As with the time travel chapter that opened this book, structurally I will take this chapter through two loose time periods of science fiction film and their relationship to whiteness. I will start in the 1950s and 1960s, with the theme of space age whiteness, where modern science fiction film begins, and where the poetics and politics of space travel first take root. Then I will look at space travel in the millennial, contemporary science fiction film, where outer space is seen to be very close to home, and its attendant social and cultural problems. As with the time travel chapter, I look to historicise the science fiction of space travel, and to provide a thematic bridge between the analogue/modern age and the digital/liquid modern age. The chapter's ultimate destination is to demonstrate how whiteness repositions itself in the age of liquid modernity.

Space Age Whiteness: A Brief History

The 1950s witnessed the birth of a number of major political, scientific and cultural 'event' transformations. This was the decade where electronic 'white' goods began to enter the home, making domestic life more efficient and supposedly easier, and a vast road and house-building project was underway, creating new middle-class suburbs in the process. White people generally occupied these suburbs, while black Americans moved into the inner-city areas of such cities as Detroit and Los Angeles (Avila 2000). This was also the decade of the development of a new group of elite techno-scientists who ushered in these technological developments and who helped create the impetus to reach for the stars. In military terms, of course, this was also the age of atomic testing, with the first hydrogen bomb detonated at the Enewetak Atoll in the Marshall Islands on 1 November 1952. At the same time, the rhetoric of the Cold War created the impression that the Soviet Union was a persistent 'invasion' threat to American national security. That the Soviet Union launched the satellite *Sputnik* on 4 October 1957, followed by the 1959 launch of the spacecraft *Luna I*, which reached the vicinity of the moon, intensified the fear of Soviet technological power. A range of political and cultural tensions and contradictions took root in the 1950s and science fiction film and television seemed best able to negotiate them.

In film and television, science fiction began to be a successful and often-repeated commercial genre, fuelled by new developments in special effects and thematically by these 'event' transformations that caught the popular imagination, because it was in dialogue with society's most pressing concerns (Sontag 2004). These major events were textually transposed into science fiction film and television as: a contradictory love and loathing of techno-science; a desire to space travel, to take (white) flight; concerns over the arms race and the growing worry of nuclear apocalypse; and the perceived threat of alien (read Soviet) invasion (Jankovich 2004).

As I will now go on to suggest, each of these thematics is connected to whiteness. In science fiction film and television of the 1950s, white scientists are given a predominant role in speaking for the power and importance of science; for creating the condition for it to be used for the good of all humanity; and, conversely, for being the possible agents of destruction in part because they have become too white or hyper-white (Bonnett 2000) and inhuman(e) in the process.

According to the ideological and representational codes of 1950s science fiction film and television, it is through white-imagined science that space rockets can be engineered, and other worlds and their species fully understood and appreciated. One can only get to outer space through the scientific breakthrough that white (male) scientists initiate. For example, in the television series *Commando Cody: Sky Marshal of the Universe* (NBC 1955), Commando Cody has just built the world's first spaceship that will allow him to protect the Earth and visit new horizons. In *Rocketship X-M* (Nuemann 1950), Dr Karl Eckstrom (John Emery) is introduced as the 'designer of the RX-M, and as you all know one of the most brilliant physicists of the day'. Eckstrom has engineered the first man-made spaceship to the moon and is given the position of explaining its flight path, which he does through chalk diagrams and science-inflected vocabulary. Surrounded by politicians, journalists and military personnel, he is given the power to speak and enact the future. This scene, often repeated in science fiction film and television of this period, centres the white scientist as the creator or progenitor of a productive science that affords us progress, advances civilisation and creates the conditions out of which new worlds are discovered. Through white scientists, outer space is mapped from a white-centric point of view, and such 'representations unconsciously reflect or embody the colonial imagination' (Kaplan 1997: 42). Outer space isn't just to be visited and admired, but colonised by the civil, white imagination.

This is further sanctified by the way in which, in certain films and television shows of this period, white science is heralded by superior life forces as that which must influence and shape the political decision making process. For example, in *The Day the Earth Stood Still* (Wise 1951) the alien Klattu prophesises that the security of Earth resides singularly in the hands of white scientists. It is their rational approach to international affairs that will steer Earth away from the arms race and the slow creep to nuclear annihilation that Klattu sees as happening through Cold War politics. As Mark Jankovich argues:

> They are supposedly above the 'petty squabbles' of politics and address universal truths in a logical and rational manner. For this reason, they can overcome the irrationality that divides the world and come together for the good of all.
>
> (2004: 335)

The qualities that Jankovich identifies are of course the markers of whiteness: a presumed universality, organised around a rationalism that promotes their superior intellectualism and reasoning. Given that in *The Day the Earth Stood Still* it is a superior alien life-force that makes this pronouncement, having travelled from *outer space* to get *here*; and one who is in fact coded as a Christ-like figure, taking the name of John Carpenter while on Earth, suggests not only that 'cerebral' whiteness is recognisable by higher beings as the originator and protector of the Earth, but also that its telos is compatible with these advanced civilisations. Whiteness is already *in* outer space.

In defining science fiction, Darko Suvin (1979: 64) suggests that it readily employs a 'novum' or 'cognitive innovation' that is scientifically instigated or realised. The novum is the narrative and visual catalyst for the way inventions can be realised and the physical rules and laws of that world transformed and transgressed. The novum is crafted out of current, real-world science but extended out, so that predictions become possibilities enacted. So, for example, 1950s science fiction film and television travelled to outer space before the technology had been developed to do so, but while it was in development. These films and shows drew on existing physics and scientific prediction to imagine space travel. But there is more in this novum than simply science dreaming. I would like to suggest that the novum of science fiction film and television enables whiteness to create the conditions for its own self-empowerment, centring white science as that which can create new worlds and alternative realities. The novum in effect 'saves' whiteness because it repeatedly produces the context for whiteness to prove its technological superiority, its ability to think in new ways and with new means.

The development and deployment of technology is crucial here, since science fiction film and television demonstrates the advanced power of white people through its display of the latest special effects, which were heralded as groundbreaking in the early 1950s, as projection capabilities and miniatures became ever more photorealistic. Science fiction film and television was seen as a pioneer in new screen and effects technologies. The pioneers were of course white, male effects-auteurs such as Lee Zavitz, who won the Academy Award for Visual Effects for *Destination Moon* (Pichel 1950). And as Ben Walker suggests, science fiction film can be seen as a 'technological showcase for current image creation technologies – technologies that perhaps only a few years before were science fictions in themselves' (2007: 3).

In terms of the correlation or synthesis between technological invention and whiteness, one can argue that this ideological mythos of white progeny has been a truism since the birth of cinema. For example, E. Ann Kaplan charts the invention of cinema with colonial encounters, suggesting that:

> Cinema was invented at the height of colonialisation at the end of the nineteenth century. The camera was crucial as a machine used by western travellers of all kinds – scientists, anthropologists, entrepreneurs, missionaries and the entire array of colonial agents to document and control the 'primitive' cultures they had seen and feared.
>
> (1997: 43)

Such a description should, of course, be added to the narrative architecture of science fiction film and television space travel. Vision is given to white space explorers (as it is to white film directors) – it is through their eyes that moonbeams, meteors and alien landscapes are first gazed upon and then defined. We watch white space explorers gaze in awe and wonder at the worlds they come upon, and give them the power of language to classify what it is they see. In *Rocketship X-M*, the crew are seen marvelling at outer space while they draw on poetry, physics and religion to understand its significance. This forces Dr Karl Eckstrom to 'pause and observe respectfully while something infinitely greater assumes control'. Eckstrom preaches that there is a higher order at work but quickly locates their destiny in what they can discover as idealised white space scientists and explorers. When white people are in outer space they can only make true sense of the order of the cosmos.

This white realised envisioning of outer space is particularly acute when it comes to first contact with aliens. These encounters take one of two central forms. First, the alien species is carnal, primal, and white explorers are called upon to civilise or destroy them. These pre-linguistic creatures are often racialised, implicitly crafted out of imagery that connects them back to the stereotypes and discourses applied to black Americans or Soviet nationals. In *Space Patrol* (ABC 1950–1954), set in the thirtieth century, Commander-in-Chief Buzz Corry (Ed Kemmer) of the United Planets Space Patrol, and his 'young sidekick' Cadet Happy (Lyn Osborn), are charged with keeping the peace as they face interplanetary villains intent on destroying the American way of life. Villains such as Bela Kovacs and Mr Proteus embodied the fear of the Soviet Other, marked by ethnic lines. In *It! The Terror from Beyond Space* (Cahn 1958), a creature from Mars stows away on a spaceship escaping from its planet. The creature is intent on killing everyone on board, which it does through sucking all the moisture out of its victims. The creature – so antithetical to civilised life that it cannot be properly named – is driven by a consumption logic, intent on harvesting white civilised life so that it thrives at the expense, or replacement, of whiteness. As Ken Gelder (1994) has explored, in relation to the vampire myth, the sucking of blood by the Other not only threatens the racial purity of whiteness, but empties it of its life-force.

One of the fears of 1950s American life was the movement of black Americans into the inner-city areas, producing a 'white flight' into the newly established suburbs. As Eric Avila contends:

> The rise of Hollywood science fiction paralleled the acceleration of white flight in postwar America and not only recorded popular anxieties about political and sexual deviants, but also captured white preoccupations with the increasing visibility of the alien Other.
>
> (2000: 55)

In Earth-centred invasion films and television of the 1950s, the alien is coded as the racial Other, threatening the sanctity of these new white, civilised suburbs. But white flight is also played out in outer space, with the same power-saturated binary oppositions and the same spatial geometries. Whiteness is known and knowable space; expansive, clean, it sits at the core of all the good and true physics in the cosmos. By contrast, the alien Other is the dark cosmos magnified; chaotic, frenzied, intent on harvesting the light for its diabolical ends.

In the wider narratives of science fiction the 'ethnic' alien is often placed in binary opposition to white communities, and the healing, positive values of white science and scientists. The ethnic alien visits 'Earth' or a space 'community' to destroy it; infect it; transform its dominant cultures and moral systems. Monstrous, unstoppable and interracial reproduction is often the (white) terror that follows the alien creature. It should be noted here that this is true of science fiction film regardless of the decade it was made in. In *Alien* (Scott 1979) one can offer a reading of the alien queen that recognises the hallmarks of a sexually charged, animalistic black woman. As Amy Taubin contends:

> ... the alien queen bears a suspicious resemblance to a scapegoat of the Reagan/Bush era – the black welfare mother, the parasite on the economy whose uncurbed reproductive drive reduced hard-working taxpayers to bankruptcy.
>
> (1993: 95–96)

If one is to take the late 1960s as another pivotal moment in both the race-based crisis politics of the Unites States, centred around the Watts Riots in 1965, and the age of the true realisation of space travel, with the moon landing in 1969, then *2001* (Kubrick 1969) connected these realities together. *2001* addresses these realities both in terms of imagining human civilisation as predicated on leaving black primitivism behind and through the civilised cultivation of space through whiteness. *2001* imagines a human history that only begins when whiteness comes into existence, releasing the human species from its primitivism, while enunciating a future engineered in the majestic illuminations of privileged whiteness. As Janell Hobson argues:

> ... the moment of transcendence occurs as a celebratory point when the movie theme, Richard Strauss's Thus Spake Zarathustra, trumpets over the slow-motion shots of our ape-man dramatically grasping a bone from the remains of a carcass as his stride steadily gains strength in positioning this early tool as a potential weapon. As the action moves, in the jump-cut, to outer space in the year 2001, Kubrick offers us a glorious vision of 'white' progress: from the impressive white colored space ships waltzing to the non-diegetic music of Johann Strauss's The Beautiful Blue Danube to the all white crew and passengers gracefully striding in a

> zero-gravity atmosphere to the glistening white environment of futuristic art décor ... Far away from planet Earth – the last view of which was of our ape ancestors – this technological divide is one of social and cultural 'evolution' in which the hierarchical order of white masculinist imperial power gets naturalized.
>
> (2008: 124)

Naturalised whiteness creates the conditions for the primitive to be left behind and the future to be made in its shining, transcendental image. However, there are tensions in the way whiteness is contrasted with the alien Other that draws attention to its limitations and extremes. Whiteness very often appears as a 'dull-dish' (hooks 1994), a living corpse that is as close to death as one might imagine. For example, when it comes to the zombie film, whiteness may very well be exactly like the Other it seeks to destroy. As Richard Dyer suggests in relation to *Night of the Living Dead* (Romero 1968):

> Towards the end of the film, there is an aerial shot from the point of view of a helicopter involved in the destruction of the zombies; it looks down on a straggling line of people moving forward uncertainly but inexorably, in exactly the same formation as earlier shots of the zombies. It is only with a cut to a ground level shot that we realise this is a line of vigilantes, not zombies. Living and dead whites are indistinguishable, and the zombies' sole raison d'etre, to attack and eat the living, has resonances with the behavior of the living whites.
>
> (1988: 60)

Second, then, the encounter with the alien Other demonstrates that they have something to teach us and from which we might learn. The alien race will often be in union with their environment or else their ethics are based on positive sentiments. By contrast, a pathologised version of whiteness is actually found emotionally wanting and therefore needs to be humanised in some way. Male scientists who have taken their rationalism too far generally embody this type of pathological whiteness. Elizabeth Ellsworth (1997: 226) calls this the 'double binds of whiteness' in which rationalised purity necessarily brings privileged white people closer to their own negation, since they lack empathy and deny the sex drive that in the end would result in the eradication of the species.

In *Rocketship X-M*, as the crew descends on Mars they see evidence of an advanced civilisation in ruins. When they check the radiation levels they find high readings that suggest a nuclear war has taken place there. When the remnants of the civilisation blindly stumble out from behind rocks, embodying an aggressive primitivism, Dr Eckstrom prophetically comments, 'From Atomic Age to Stone Age.' What is being narratively constituted in these scenes is a commentary on the development and testing of nuclear weapons in America at the time: the film is a siren warning about what will happen if we continue down this road – the destruction of our cities and homes and a return to an age where the civilising frames of whiteness are not in place. However, it is also a critical commentary of the blindness of privileged whiteness that invests too heavily in the cold science of destruction at the expense of compassion and feeling. What is being transposed onto the people of Mars is the contention that the white techno-elite have brought about the means of their own annihilation. Nonetheless, that it is white scientists who can bring this message back to Earth places 'normalised' whiteness as that which can ultimately redeem itself from its own dangerous extremes.

In *Forbidden Planet* (Wilcox 1956), the pathology of white science is personified more directly through the figure of Dr Edward Morbius (Walter Pidgeon). Morbius is one of only two survivors of an expedition that landed on the planet Altair IV. He warns the rescue mission that has been sent out that they will be in danger if they land on the planet, at risk from an invisible monster that stalks it. They land, nonetheless, and Morbius eventually shows the landing party the advanced technology of the Krell people, who had once lived on the planet only to suffer a 'mysterious' genocide just as they were about to make their biggest scientific breakthrough. Morbius demonstrates the power of one of these technologies, the 'plastic educator', which increases human intelligence greatly and allowed him to build his robot Robby and all the advanced marvels at his home. However, we subsequently learn that there is a price to pay for his increased brainpower; the machine works off the subconscious and the monster that has been let loose on Altair IV is actually Morbius's unleashed id. At the end of the film Morbius attacks the monster and is fatally wounded in the process – as he dies, so does the monster he gave birth to. As one of his last acts, Morbius presses a self-destruct button and just as the rescue team escapes into space Altair IV is blown to smithereens.

My reading of this film is that it is really a story about what happens when one lets too much whiteness into the world: when hyper-white science extends its capabilities too far. Morbius has let the power that advanced technology affords him *go to his head*. Morbius's invisible unconscious is also a metaphor of whiteness: one cannot see it; it is an identity that has to repress its sexual instincts and if these are let loose upon the world, then they have to be obliterated, made invisible again. The terrifying outer space of *Forbidden Planet* is actually the repressive unconsciousness of whiteness, as well as a fear of its death-like instinct if it is allowed to take hold of the self.

Space age science fiction film and television offers us this double embodiment of whiteness right through the following decades. In *Star Wars* (Lucas 1977), Luke Skywalker is perfected whiteness personified who single-handedly saves the empire from dark forces, while in *Silent Running* (Trumball 1972), Freeman Lowell (Bruce Dern), becomes a deranged botanist whose love for his biosphere is greater than it is for humankind. Of course, Luke is later revealed to be the son of Anakin Skywalker/Darth Vader, who has become a pathological version of whiteness; one that has succumbed to the dark side and its excessive anti-progeny. In Vader's death scene, Luke removes his mask to reveal his true white face at the exact moment that we are meant to realise he is 'good' underneath this excessiveness. Freeman embodies the utopian fantasy of whiteness – that it can save, heal and grow itself out of its forthcoming demise.

During this period the figure of the milky, wan android becomes pivotal to the way whiteness is critically addressed in outer space. Either the android yearns to be human and not hyper-white, fired by a mechanical rationalism, and is non-reproductive, or else their searing logic and pursuit of perfection renders them pathological and species-destructive. In *Star Trek: The Next Generation*, the android Data (Brent Spiner) has been fitted with a positronic brain that enables him to possess a degree of human consciousness. Data can make ethical judgements and decisions from a human/humanist standpoint. However, Data is a divided machine-man: he cannot directly experience human emotions, and so he suffers from an identity crisis that compels him to go in search of the feelings and affective registers he does not have (Wilcox 1996). Data, consequently, embodies the contradictions of whiteness and its differing registers: as machine he is hyper-white; as man he is humanely white – the former is death-like if empowering; the latter is something that cannot be achieved unless the rationalism is let go of. These are more of the threads of the 'double binds' of whiteness in outer space.

In *Alien* (Scott 1979), Science Officer Ash initially seems to be the embodiment of the caring, humane scientist: he operates according the Socratic oath, sees in science the way forward, and yet at the same time he cares deeply for the welfare and safety of the crew. In the first rescue scene in the film, Ash:

> ... takes a chance, makes the seemingly human, spontaneous gesture in opening the airlock hatch; and seems genuinely hounded by Ripley when she complains about his acting inconsistently with his responsibilities as a science officer.
>
> (Kavanagh 1990: 75)

However, Ash's early humanism is slowly revealed to be a deadly ruse – a ploy to allow the alien creature to be brought onto the ship, to be then transported back to Earth for both scientific experimentation and commercial exploitation. Ash is actually hyper-white, driven by a singular logic to preserve a creature he sees as embodying the highest ideals he aspires to – in his perverse logic the creature is (also) hyper-white because it is asexual, incredibly powerful and advanced.

Ash's hyper-whiteness manifests itself in a number of ways in the film. First, the survival of the alien creature is an absolute priority for Ash – way above the importance given to the survival of the crew. Ash will even kill and be killed to protect the alien. Second, Ash views the reproductive and regenerative skills of the alien creature as the highest, purest form of existence. As he says in his own death scene, 'I admire its purity. Unclouded by conscience, remorse or delusions of morality.' These, of course, are the qualities of hyper-whiteness – framed as above and beyond minor earthly ethics and the hybridity of everyday life. Ash will do anything to protect the alien because it is a mirror image of him, or at least it is the 'monster' that sits beneath his simulacra human skin (echoes then of *Forbidden Planet*'s Morbius). Ash is an android (Other), and his techno-circuitry and programmed behaviour correlate to/with the relentless, techno-reproductive Otherness of the alien creature. Ash's death at the hands of Parker, midway through the film, is then a necessary death of what has been revealed to be a pure, soulless, destructive scientific force.

Alien is also interesting because of the way it represents whiteness through its *mise en scène*, a visual palette heavily inscribed with racial connotations. For example, the sterile, bleached-out technological 'birthing' scene at the beginning of the film is an example of white life being brought into being through what is a technologically inspired immaculate conception. It is devoid, consequently and ironically, of the sex, blood and pain that procreation and reproduction necessarily entail when humans are involved. The crew are reborn to an automated sequence of artificial lights that are switched on at the moment they emerge from their sterile pods. The crew wake up placid, floppy, bone dry, in white towelling worn like nappies, and yawn their way back into existence as if they are already half-dead.

Richard Dyer suggests that the theme of white people belonging to an endangered species is increasingly found across a range of contemporary cultural texts, which 'may suggest that the suspicion of nothingness and the death of whiteness is, as far as white identity goes, the cultural dominant of our times, that we really do feel we're played out' (Dyer 1997: 217). In particular, according to Dyer, the threat of extinction haunts the representation of white men who are shown to suffer a terrifying identity crisis over their place within the social and economic order. Such white men struggle to hold down a 'regular' job, or to protect their family, and the white community, from those racial Others who threaten its stability and their racial purity. One can see this crisis in white masculinity in the form of Deckard's (Harrison Ford) haunted character in *Blade Runner* (Scott 1981).

Deckard functions as a crisis-driven white male who has seen *his* town, *his* neighbourhood taken over by swarms of immigrants who have rejected the values of the American way. He is a white man adrift, driven to existential rage about the imagined/potential/actual loss of his privileged position in the world. Los Angeles 2015 is composed of different levels, with the lower city populated by ethnic minorities and the marginalised, and the upper levels housing the privileged white elite. In terms of the *mise en scène*, the lower levels are chaotic, antiquated and dirty; steam rises from air vents, choking the atmosphere, and refuse litters the streets. By contrast the higher levels are citadels of wondrous, gleaming technologies and interfaces. Off-world, on the edge of outer space, new colonies are being formed and, while the film never takes us there, we are asked to imagine them as gardens of Eden, full of privileged white people. In this context, *Blade Runner* foreshadows aspects of millennial age whiteness, as I will now go on to explore.

Millennial Age Whiteness: Digital Outer Space

There is an often-repeated scene in the digital age Hollywood science fiction film in which a main character looks up towards the stars and quietly dreams of travelling in outer space. This moment either foreshadows or prophesises the time when they will go intergalactic journeying, or confers on them an Earth-bound destiny they can have no part in, such as in Deckard's plight in *Blade Runner*. These characters are almost exclusively white, and if also young are exclusively charged with leading human civilisation into outer space to begin again, as if it is their white-sanctified manifest destiny to do so. Of course, as I have already noted, their whiteness isn't named or identified as the position from which they speak and act from. To the contrary, this is effaced and naturalised as if their whiteness *just is* the invisible material out of which their heroic humanity grows and privileges itself. As Richard Dyer argues, this is very much the relationship of whiteness to power in the cultural world:

> The equation of being white with being human secures a position of power. White people have power and believe that they think, feel and act like and for all people; white people, unable to see their particularity, cannot take account of other peoples; white people create the dominant images of the world and don't quite see that they construct the world in their own image; white people set standards of humanity by which they are bound to succeed and others bound to fail.
>
> (1997: 9)

Near the beginning of *Elysium* (Blomkamp 2013), an orphaned Young Max (Maxwell Perry Cotton) looks towards Elysium, the man-made space station that orbits Earth, in the hope that he can one day live on it. He promises to take Young Faye (Valentina Giron) there with him, while the Nun (Yolanda Abudd) who now looks after him prophesises that he has been created (by God) for something special. Young Max's white, masculine messianic status is thus being confirmed and conferred as the film's narrative dynamic takes root. This saviour status is later repeated in the film when Adult Max (Matt Damon) is told by rebel hacker Spider (Wagner Moura), 'you can save everyone'. And yet the meaning of whiteness is ideologically struggled over in the film, with different good and bad versions of it being critically addressed if never explicitly recognised as such.

The film is set in 2154, where the rich have abandoned Earth, and poverty and disease have taken their toll on an under-class oppressed and exploited by those people who now have protected, privileged lives on Elysium (see Figure 5.1). While Elysium is not exclusively populated by white people, the de-raced signifiers that non-white people are represented through, and the fact that they inhabit a city made out of clean/pure aesthetic lines and sterile environmental perfectionism, point to a (symbolically) white elite lording over its new outer space Eden. By contrast, down on Earth the unwashed white, and the impoverished non-white, struggle for survival on a battle-scarred Earth ruled with an iron fist by the hyper-rational despots on Elysium. In ideological terms, hyper-whiteness has taken flight to outer space while maintaining its sweatshop commercial operations on a depleted Earth, where only the poor or 'trash' white, and 'true' ethnic minorities, remain. *Elysium* is aware of the economic conditions found in the global market relations of liquid modernity. The film is conscious then of its racial politics, while it nonetheless subtextually recentres whiteness as the identity that ultimately leads humanity from its unequal power structures. *Elysium* directly addresses racial inequality but does so to ultimately allow

Figure 5.1. Rich and poor in the city of Elysium

whiteness – through its heroic narrative agent – to save the future of the species. One can argue that this is a trope of director Neil Blomkamp, whose first film, *District 9* (2008), also drew conscious awareness to racial disparity in a future 'South Africa'.

In *Elysium* these prestige white power structures have to be given symbolic human form for them to be contested. Two of the film's antagonists, Delacourt (Jodie Foster) and Kruger (Sharlto Copley), embody pathological versions of whiteness – where they are coded as selfish and destructive. Delacourt is positioned as asexual, cold and heartless, who wants to keep the purity of the Elysium bloodline free from the unwashed masses. Her blonde, bobbed hair, masculine suits and pale skin suggest a hyper-white frigidity and rationalism that is anti-human and anti-reproduction (given that it is Jodie Foster playing the part, there may well be latent homophobia wrapped up in her representation). Kruger is a one-man killing machine, but his South African accent and allusions to the apartheid era suggest a revengeful white hunter intent on reversing the gains made by racial equality.

By contrast and as prophesised, Adult Max (Matt Damon) makes it to Elysium, leading a resistance group to overthrow this destructive white elite. Their downfall at the end of the film is directly enabled or enacted by Max's self-sacrifice. He has to give his life so that the virtual code embedded in a super-computer can be broken. In so doing, anybody can become a citizen of Elysium. Once Max's death triggers the democratisation of Elysium, all the people on Earth have access to its resources, which include cancer-curing technologies and machines that can fix broken spines. *Elysium* is on the one hand critical of race-based inequality, and yet on the other creates a messianic hero who speaks and acts from a position of white power. In a very real sense the film plays out the conditions of austerity and the unequal power relations that have been accelerated in the age of liquid modernity, and yet still manages to centre whiteness as the only real cure to liquidity.

Adult Max heralds Elysium into a post-race era of inequality and, at the same time, he secures whiteness as its foundational architect. The film is of course a barely concealed critique of healthcare in America, with Elysium being the symbol of private medical care out of reach for the majority of the population. There is a sense then that whiteness is shifting its terrain of biopolitical operations, on the run from its own extreme manifestations, aware that the liquid age calls upon social equality, while ensuring that its power remains strong, if openly contested. As Ziauddin Sardar (2002) suggests, this a necessary trope of all science fiction: in saving itself, whiteness lives to fight another day, and in so doing creates the narrative and cultural conditions for it to save and save again. So, while the political and economic realities may constantly shift, there is an ideological continuity in the way whiteness uses its power to resolve the challenges it faces.

Moon (Jones 2009) contests the meaning of whiteness in a particularly interesting way, although the film also ultimately offers the viewer a white salvific hero. Sam Bell (Sam Rockwell) is coming to the end of his solitary, three-year contract to mine helium-3 on the far side of the moon. After suffering hallucinations of an 'unknown' teenage girl he crashes his rover and wakes up in the base's sick bay without any memory of how he got there. However, with his suspicions aroused he returns to the crash site to find an older, unconscious version of himself still in the rover. The film then slowly reveals its secret: both versions of Sam are clones, two of countless others whose life expectancy is limited to three years, after which they are incinerated after they fall asleep, supposedly to take the long trip back to Earth. Both young and old Sam decide that people on Earth must be made aware of Lunar Industries' unethical practices and young Sam makes it back to Earth to reveal all. In terms of whiteness, there are multiple layers in operation; cloning points to both the fear and denial of 'natural' reproduction – white people are born of an immaculate conception – and yet demonstrate the power of white people to endlessly reproduce their power. Whiteness is exploitative, it colonises not only planets, but also its own people for profit and gain. Whiteness yearns for the human and humane, for the singular rather than the collective. Whiteness is afraid of its most extreme manifestations but can ultimately redeem and rescue its species through heroic individuals, such as Sam, who can defeat not only their own mortality but also those corporations who embody its excesses.

Culturally speaking, the sense that whiteness today is in crisis, 'under threat, decentred, angry' (Dyer 1997: 222) is supported or compounded by what one can argue is a different manifestation of 'white flight' that is taking place in relation to the incorporation of primitivism and 'easternisation' (Stacey 2000: 121–124) into the white psyche. Across the Western world today, white people are embracing racialised Otherness in fundamentally profound ways. Alastair Bonnett suggests that this is because 'to be outside whiteness is to be outside the cold and instrumental realm of modernity' and 'the forging of non-whiteness as an identity that is *not* alienated and *not* dominated by instrumental logic' is both liberating and life confirming for the white who yearns for some sort of human authenticity denied to them in and through their 'mechanical' whiteness (Bonnett 2000: 78). The purchasing of ethnic products, the travel to exotic 'far away' destinations, and the 'wholesale introjection of Eastern beliefs and practices (such as religions) into the West' (Stacey 2000: 123) suggest a liquid modern world where whiteness is being left behind, if never ultimately rejected.

In *Avatar*, Jake Sully (Sam Worthington) is allowed to leave his paraplegic white body behind and become one of the spiritual Na'vi people who exist in harmony with nature and worship a mother goddess called Eywa. As a Na'vi warrior, Jake's physical capabilities are increased and he comes to feel things in a heightened way as the culture of the people transform and enrich his belief system. The Tree of Souls takes over Jake in mind and body. He engineers and leads the battle that saves Pandora (the planet they are on) from the scientific-military colonists who are intent on harvesting the planet for their own ends. On the one hand, then, the film suggests that whiteness is in a state of paralysis and that only by introjecting 'Eastern' beliefs and practices into the minds and bodies of white people can it be made healthy again. On the other hand, the film centres a white male as its narrative hero: the Na'vi cannot rescue themselves or defeat the enemy on their own. Only a salvific white hero can do this. Jared Gardner contends that *Avatar* is a modern version of racial masquerade, in which:

> Our Jake Sully is the best of both worlds: he gets to be a marine and a scientist, to wed the seemingly irreconcilable divide of opposing cultures as posited by the film's Victorian logic. And blue, as should be clear about five minutes into the movie, is the new color of indigeneity. The Na'vi are first and foremost the cinematic heirs to the Hollywood Indian, from Broken Arrow to Dances with Wolves. But along the way their spectrum absorbs as well indigenous cultures from West Africa to Iraq, allowing the film's viewers to share a righteous sense of indignation in the systematic

> exploitation and (all too often) extermination of indigenous peoples in the name of various natural resources (from fertile soil to free labor to crude oil), while cheering on and taking deep pleasure in the technological prowess that same systematic exploitation has brought to the United States and to its culture industry in the form of IMAX 3D. But that, of course, is precisely the point. As blackface did in 1927, blueface in 2009 allows Hollywood simultaneously to 'mourn' the loss of what is 'vanished' while also celebrate its rebirth and continuation through the indispensable mediation of the white male body.
>
> (2010)

Paul Adams (1995: 268) has argued that contemporary digital global relations have enabled 'personal extensibility' in which (privileged) people have almost limitless travel capabilities, granting them access to and control over places, services and commodities right around the world. This produces a new form of virtual colonisation, with physical or lived consequences for those – the digital poor – who can't extend themselves in these ways. Jake embodies this new-found expansion of the white self, able to move in and between different realities, even if it is the Na'vi world where he feels most at home, in charge again, fully embodied. The Doctor in the new *Doctor Who* is, of course, an embodiment of this – this salvic figure takes his companions to planets and galaxies, offering them safety and adventure as he does so.

According to Zygmunt Bauman, constructing a durable identity that coheres over time and space becomes increasingly impossible within the conditions of liquid modernity. He suggests that we have moved from a period where we understood ourselves as 'pilgrims' in search of deeper or higher meaning, to one where we now act as 'tourists' in search of multiple but fleeting social experiences. Doctor Who's companions are very much 'tourists'; drawn from the working or lower class, they find meaning in and through the people they meet and the exotic places they visit, from episode to episode. Never fully trusting or believing in the mythical figure who takes them there, they are nonetheless enabled to travel through the liquid power of (his) digital age whiteness.

Returning briefly to *Avatar*, there is a real-world corollary of Jake's consumption of the exotic alien Other. Alistair Bonnett has examined the mythopoeic men's movement that emerged in North America in the 1980s and 1990s as a concrete example of white people's flight into the arms of primitivism. Bonnett argues that 'mythopoeic men are creatively reworking colonialist fantasies of non-Western societies and landscapes' (2000: 95) and, moreover, that mythopoeicism represents an attempt to reaffirm and reinstate white male power in response to an increasing feeling of powerlessness in the modern world. Mythopoeic men venture into wilderness regions not only because of the way they 'may experience freedom from social constraint, and a sense of liberation' (ibid.: 103), but also because of the 'cult of the primitive', who they imagine they can find there and can become like. The romanticised figure of the Native American is key here. Untouched by liquid modernity, in tune with the land and in touch with the rhythms of nature, and as 'unchanging and spiritually potent as "untouched" Nature itself' (ibid.: 103), the Native American comes to represent the life-affirming values of the wilderness. Bonnett argues that mythopoeic men 'act out' these primitivist discourses in weekend 'retreat' gatherings, taking on roles, in what is considered to be an 'authentic' environment that mirrors the (heroic) narratives of Native American culture. These discourses:

> ... are also used to naturalise these experiences and to displace political and social engagement. The attendees' repeated allusions to tribal and wilderness 'ways of wisdom' are invariably designed to lead beyond, or leave behind, everyday concerns and enable the men to reach the dynamic yet timeless male spirit.
>
> (Bonnett 2000: 106)

In millennial age science fiction film, whiteness goes in endless search of 'wilderness' regions in the far reaches of outer space. These films look to reaffirm and reinstate whiteness, and white male power, as authentic and necessary, as if it/they are the engine(s) of civilisation and the only hope(s) for its future. They do so because the disembodiment that comes with new digital relations threatens to literally efface whiteness from the world. Nonetheless, these white-inspired saviour myths draw on primitivism and Easternisation to dynamise whiteness, to give it empowered life beyond (before) the streams of liquid modernity. Neo (Keanu Reeves) in *The Matrix* (the Wachowski Brothers, 1999) is a mixture of Christian and Buddhist beliefs, choreographed as if he is in a hybrid action/martial arts science fiction film. In *Star Trek Into Darkness* (Abrams 2013), Kirk (Chris Pine) is initially considered to be too rash and hot-headed to continue his command of the *Enterprise*. However, he is called back into action as the heroic white saviour who can defeat the alien Khan (Benedict Cumberbatch). Whiteness needs both emotion and cunning, training and street-like smarts in the age of liquid modernity.

I would like to end this chapter with what I see as the uncanny absence of whiteness in *28 Days Later* (Boyle 2002). In the film, Jim (Cillian Murphy) wakes up from a coma to find that London has undergone a zombie apocalypse. The streets are empty of people, cars, buses, the usual hustle and bustle, noise and confusion that one associates with a crowded metropolis. Where has everyone gone? The film suggests that people have either become zombies or have taken flight from the city to seek refuge in the rural and regional. At a racial level, one can suggest that the zombies are the result of post-race integration, infecting the purity of whiteness, which escapes the spoilt city for the rural idyll. Of course, there is no refuge there either because the film suggests that the rural has been savaged too. So, where has everyone gone? Although it is not seen, not officially apart of the film's narrative pronouncements or its diegetic world, what has really taken place in the wider cultural context of the millennial imagination is that white people have escaped off-world, where they now live in outer space.

Where to now? If white people have moved off-world, where will they travel next to sustain their stories of manifest destiny, of redemption and salvation? In this chapter I have identified across postwar science fiction cinema a series of interlocking, recurring visual and narrative tropes, a set of key characterisations, framed within dialogical and oppositional relations. Whiteness is made supreme at the same time as it calls into its representations the dry seeds of its own destruction. I have historically and politically positioned this critical analysis of whiteness in outer space as one that is contingent upon the social realities it negotiates and re-presents. I have tracked whiteness in outer space from the analogue and modern age to the epoch of the digital housed in liquid modernity. This historical and contextual framing allows me to show the persistence of whiteness but also how it is recast in the age of shifting, disembodied identity positions. Ultimately, I view whiteness as a living organism that understands its own super-corporeality and how to withstand the forces that seek to undermine it. Whiteness lives in outer space at the same time as it seeks to live in and through us all. Whiteness, as we will see in the next chapter, will also save us from ourselves and the terror of liquid modernity.

6

Liquid Terror

Let me begin this chapter with a confession: I can't keep my eyes off the forms of liquid terror that flow across this scarred and scared planet right now, even though in the repeated seeing of them I feel nauseous. I feel implicated in, and affected by these painful collisions, mutations and explosions. In this liquid age of the War on Terror, against the phantoms of the 'death cult', wherever I look, wherever I am directed to look by the all-seeing war and 'vision machines' that 'illuminate' our identities (Virilio 1997: 70), the body of the soldier, terrorist, hostage, victim and viral container come into troubling view. These liquid bodies of terror are real in the ontological and phenomenological sense; but they are also metaphoric, simulated and discursive. They form much of the charred material of contemporary science fiction film and television. As Fran Pheasant-Kelly indicates, they herald in a troubling and perverse sense of survival at all costs:

> In the *Hunger Games*, a 'survival of the fittest' paradigm is deployed to provide spectatorial pleasure for the elite middle classes, emphasising the class divisions that underpin all societies, but reflexive in the way that the film questions the ethics of viewing violence for pleasure. *Prometheus* too concerns the exclusion or eradication of the other, and also comments on the gulf between creationism and Darwinism, the narrative exploring the possibilities of their co-existence, through visual allusions to both primordial scenes of primitive life, counterpointed by images that are suggestive of God. Unbridled by ethical concerns, the films variously envisage transgressive acts of abortion and discrimination, implicitly of race and class, and present the survival of the fittest as an elitist past-time.
>
> (2015: 32)

One can position much of digital age science fiction film and television as being predicated on threats to national and regional security; and to the fragility of community and the human body as it is washed over by virus, contagions; is taken over by invaders or machines; or is fire bombed in spectacular scenes of devastation and destruction. In films such as *Ever Since the World Ended* (Grant, Litle 2001), *28 Days Later* (Boyle 2002), *Resident Evil* (Anderson 2005) and *Ultraviolet* (Wimmer 2006), and in television series such as *Containment* (Warner Bros. Television 2016) and *Helix* (Syfy 2014–2015), both the individual's body, and the wider body politic, is under threat from human-made viruses and viral mutations that, having been set free, render flesh and democracy as diseased, infected, pathological or as a barren incubator for the Armageddon that is soon to be born.

In *Artificial Intelligence: AI* (Spielberg 2001), *I, Robot* (Proyas 2004), *Sky Captain and the World of Tomorrow* (Conran 2004) and *Transformers* (Bay 2007), cyborg machines and machine-monsters threaten the supremacy of the military – science – business nexus, and of what constitutes or counts for a human being in what is signposted as a posthuman age of egotistic nihilism and frightful globalisation.

In *The 6th Day* (Spottiswoode 2000), *The One* (Wong 2001), *Natural City* (Byung-Chin 2003), *The Island* (Bay 2005) and *Humans* (AMC/Channel 4 2015–), the practices and processes of cloning and genetic engineering have resulted in new hierarchies of power and perfection; the blurring of the human/machine dichotomy; and the trade and traffic in human bodies to seed these present-future avatars and clones.

In *Matrubhoomi: A Nation Without Women* (Jha 2003), *Aeon Flux* (Kusama 2005), *Children of Men* (Cuarón 2006) and *The Lottery* (Lifetime Television 2014), human bodies are infertile or barren and civilisation is therefore on the verge of extinction. In *Signs* (Shyamalan 2002), *War of the Worlds* (Spielberg 2005) and *Falling Skies* (DreamWorks Television 2011–), despicable alien invaders attack and destroy the institutional, political and cultural organs of society, while the threat is also perceived as coming from within. In *The Day After Tomorrow* (Emmerich 2004), *Sunshine* (Boyle 2007) and *Interstellar* (Nolan 2014), ecological disaster threatens to wipe out the human race. And in *Minority Report* (Spielberg 2002), *Equilibrium* (Wimmer 2002), *Banlieue 13* (Morel 2004) and *V for Vendetta* (McTeigue 2005), dystopic totalitarian regimes *will the body* into docile submission and compliance. In response, heroic narrative agents emerge, or resistance movements rise up, to reclaim the streets.

Of course, it is the imagery and symbolism of 9/11 and the subsequent War on Terror that is inscribed across much of digital age science fiction cinema. In *Ever Since the World Ended*, an attack that leaves Santosh (Brad Olsen) mortally wounded is shot in the style of contemporary combat photography. In *Star Wars: Episode III – Revenge of the Sith* (Lucas 2005), Anakin Skywalker's body is first torched and then prosthetically remade, conjuring up contemporary battlefield operations. In *28 Days Later* and *Children of Men*, military units patrol the streets, roadblocks are set up and curfews maintained, establishing a clear echo to the Gulf War, rendition, and the siege situation in Iraq. Although *28 Days Later* was filmed before 9/11, the film is full of prophetic moments, not least the 'missing persons' flyers seen in the early London street scenes, which 'recall' flyers posted in New York City in the wake of 9/11.

As I have written before (Redmond 2005), Stephen Spielberg's remake of *War of the Worlds* (2005) is a context-coded 9/11 text. Ray Ferrier (Tom Cruise) is a signalled blue-collar worker from New Jersey, estranged from his family, and with little economic or cultural capital. Once the aliens rise up from beneath the city, deep within Ferrier's neighbourhood, he ultimately proves his worth as a father/heroic male, moving from deadbeat dad to saviour. *War of the Worlds* is shot through with 9/11 war imagery: burning planes fall out of the sky; military missiles slice through the air; the alien enemy, drone-like in their capabilities and intent on harvesting all of humankind for their own survival and domination, emerge fully armoured from underneath, from *within* the borders of New York City. Human blood, in both the literal and metaphoric sense, soaks the screen – the entire *mise en scène* – so that it appears to be the individual and collective body of America, where the film is relentlessly set, which is being bled and cannibalised.

The defeat of the aliens emerges in two different ways, allowing the film to make two articulating 'necessary' responses to the War on Terror (which it implicitly becomes a part of). First, *War of the Worlds* suggests the individual hero figure remains pivotal to the fight: Ferrier's transformation into patriarchal protector enables him to outwit the enemy and take his child 'home'. His redemptive journey involves survival at all costs: he silences (strangles) the deranged

Harlan Ogilvy (Tim Robbins) because he threatens to give their position away. His actions, then, refuse to let the American family be overtaken, overrun, and he will protect the family from wayward Americans wherever they be found. Ferrier stands as a recuperating symbol of America's resilience and hyper-masculine strength when it is tested most. As observed in relation to these masculine salvation films:

> The more explicit threat of loss is to the family and the romantic couple. The threat takes a variety of forms, including: the loss or separation from children in *Minority Report*, *Inception*, *Looper*; the idea of the mother who leaves or abandons her children in *Inception* and *Looper*; and the separation of the right romantic couple in *Minority Report*, *Eternal Sunshine*, *Source Code*, and *Looper*. Never far away in American generic cinema is the issue of fathers and sons, particularly when there is estrangement or conflict, and surrogate father/son relationships. Central to the generic imperative to restore order are the actions of the central (male) protagonists.
>
> (Knight and McKnight 2015: 91)

Second, the aliens are in the end vanquished not by heroic act, guile, or by the efforts of techno-militaristic co-operation (as is often the case in science fiction cinema), but by a common airborne virus, which is deadly to them. The aliens that first emerged from beneath/within America – acting like co-ordinated 'terrorist' cells – are beaten by a domestic virus that is itself terrorist-like: invisible and yet everywhere. The barely hidden premise of the film, then, is that America can no longer rely on conventional warfare to kill the invader (that lies within); rather, it has to adapt, mutate; it has to become (like) the invader to survive.

There is a profound biopolitical form of governance being constituted in *War of the Worlds*, one in which good lives are heavily policed and censored, and bad lives are annihilated. Sheryl Vint makes a similar argument in relation to the contemporary zombie film and the state of exemption such apocalyptic texts enact:

> The recent obsession with the figure of the zombie in popular culture emerges from this context, an exaggerated embodiment of the gap

> between the proper human life to be fostered by biopolitical control and the sub-race whose very existence threatens, literally in the case of predatory zombies, the health of the population as a whole. The exuberance with which zombies are killed en masse in texts such as *The Walking Dead* (AMC 2010–) speaks to the pervasiveness of our understanding of this logic of biopolitical governance, in which we seem instinctively to understand that the more we kill (of them) the more likely those we understand as 'we' are to survive. Throughout these films we see hints that the operative biopolitics concern not merely the distinction between humans and zombies, but between lives of those deemed 'essential personnel' and a remainder of humanity no longer really necessary to the survival of the species.
>
> (2015: 68)

In digital age science fiction film the concern to regulate, survey, train and 'do to' the diseased body can be argued to be a result of the cultural hysteria that has accompanied the War on Terror. This paranoia, and paranoid texts, suggest that danger is found in *all* bodies and as such must become the central site of conflict and control. At a positioning level, these films ask the viewer to be vigilant, to self-survey their bodies for signs of infection or contamination, and to survey others (their neighbours) for the same. The enemy body, it is suggested, could be lurking within you or be living right next door. In this corporeal conspiratorial framework, viewers are being positioned to recognise that their bodies must be ready for the danger or else they will be taken over, infected, cloned, dehumanised, erased or disappeared.

This is also, of course, one of the conditions of liquid modernity, with the collapse of belief in grand narratives and a corresponding increase in the rise of nomadic neo-tribes, faith and trust are seen to fade and die. Given the context that information is incessantly circulated without fact-checking or analysis, multiple truths, lies and illusions circulate equally, vying for domination. Knowledge is lost in this sea of liquid information, and doubt and distrust remain supreme. No*body* can be trusted but there is no longer an entity called truth.

Children of Men, the film that I will now spend the rest of this chapter reading, places the body at the centre of its end-of-times paranoid story. Set in London in 2027, humankind is on the brink of extinction since they can no longer reproduce. In the global arena, chaos and disorder reign, law and order has broken down, and population movement threatens to destroy civil society. In a heavily militarised London, zones of containment exist with a core and periphery spatial alignment, with immigrants and the lower classes kept outside the centre, or in detention camps where they are tortured. Into this picture of Armageddon arrives a miracle in the shape of a nativity story: Kee (Clare-Hope Ashitey), a black refugee, finds herself pregnant, while Theo Faron (Clive Owen), a white, middle-aged bureaucrat, is cast as her protector after she reveals her pregnancy to him in a barn. Theo and Kee attempt to rendezvous with a group of leading scientists from the Human Project on a ship called *Tomorrow*. To do this they have to move across conflict zones and flee from various groups intent on using Kee's pregnancy for their own gain.

I would like to suggest that at the wild heart of *Children of Men* is a parable about where the War on Terror might actually lead us. Infertility becomes the condition thrust upon us by chemical weapons and the pollution of the soil, and emerges out of the detritus of globalisation that trades and traffics in bombs and guns. However, at its ideological and aesthetic heart is a redemptive story about whiteness and the white heroic male. I will divide my analysis across three lines of enquiry: spaces, bodies and sounds; although each theme connects with the other and it is the body of space, (dis)embodied sound and the bodies of bodies that hold my account together. In so doing I also draw together the liquid strands of this book so far, where the politics of space, bodies and sound drive the sensory and ideological engines of digital age science fiction.

Spaces

Children of Men is divided by a number of symbolic zones, each suggesting something about the condition of the people living there. In the inner zone, where Theo's cousin Nigel (a government official) lives, life remains opulent and protected. This gated community is heavily fortified but within its walls the rich continue to prosper. In the outer-inner zone, life is hard and harsh, violence punctuates its normalness, but work and leisure rituals remain in play. In the outer zone, detention camps and resistance movements battle it out, turning these spaces into locales of torture, subjugation and open warfare. In the rural zone, where Theo's friend Jasper (Michael Caine) lives, utopian freedoms remain, framed within a 'natural' counterculture aesthetic.

Children of Men offers the viewer clear contrasts and collisions between the rich and the poor, the free and the enslaved, the peaceful and the violent, and the urban and the rural. These spatial metaphors, however, are both turned inside out (the rural outside being the place of nirvana), and partially eroded or dissolved. No zone is entirely free from the other and it is the movement between zones that brings both hope and despair. The film's entire spatial politics, then, is built out of the skeletons of containment and contamination, out of the fires of flight and fight created by the War on Terror, and the liquefaction of space in the age of liquid modernity.

At the beginning of the film, for example, Theo narrowly misses being blown up after a bomb explodes at a café he has just left. The scene, shot in one long take with a handheld camera, is initially gritty and social-realist, its drained aesthetics capturing the lack of hope and opportunity there. We have just learned, via television news playing in the café, that the youngest person alive has died and so the sense of expiration haunts the scene. The bomb, however, brings the terror 'home' and conjures up the ghost of the suicide bomber and fragility of the zones, as they have been constituted. The handheld camera, however, does something else: it embodies the scene, places us within the action as if we are on foot too and in mortal danger. The ringing that floods Theo's ears becomes subjective; it is our hearing too, so the sense of discombobulation is acutely shared (Whittington 2011). When the camera pans past Theo to reveal a woman carrying her severed arm, our own affective body memories render us co-proximate to the action. Our bodies are under threat too, subject to the same biopolitical interventions that modern warfare countenances. We *were* children of the War on Terror and now as adults – in this near future the film is set in – we reap what we have sown. The film's future is the liquid modern condition come to complete realisation.

That no zone is safe in *Children of Men* is brilliantly realised in the car-ambush scene, as Theo, Kee, Luke (Chiwetel Ejiofor), Julian (Julianne Moore) and Miriam (Pam Ferris) make their way to the coast to meet with the Human Project. In what appears to be a country road, outside the conditions of their exception, Julian is fatefully shot, captured by a circular moment of the camera as it traverses the car. The circular motion points to the zonal connectivity the film is set in, and to the adage that history repeats itself: it has to; no one listens. This type of spatially loaded cinematography structures the film's gazing operations, its ideological frames and its affecting absences, as I will explore further below.

Children of Men thus taps into a prevalent sense of dread that haunts a great number of science fiction texts at this time (Thompson 2012). To return, for example, to the suite of invasion texts that emerged over this period, they arguably speak to the range of fears that circulate in a catastrophic climate of insecurity brought about by the War on Terror and its imagined corollary, the War on the West. As Derek Kompare argues, in relation to three, first-season, 2005 USA television invasion shows, *Invasion* (Shaun Cassidy, ABC), *Threshold* (Bragi F. Schut, CBS) and *Surface* (Jonas Pate, NBC):

> The core of insecurity is the idea that nowhere is absolutely safe, that nobody is absolutely trustworthy ... the alien menaces ... are practically invisible ... the outside threat could come from within.
>
> (2005)

Movement is crucial to the film's narrative architecture and to the political message conveyed. Movement is prohibited, special papers are needed to enter the inner zone and to leave the city, and yet movements in, between and across the zones of the film are constant as people are ferried, transported and look to escape their confinement. It is through movement, particularly Theo and Kee's journey, that we get to see the differences between the zones and what inequalities and abuses take place there. Their eyes and ears allow them to become whistle-blowers on the decadence of the rich, and the violence and torture being metered out on those labelled as Other and marginal. This is no truer than when Theo and Kee are on the bus and we see through the windows Arab men being tortured in poses reminiscent of Abu Ghraib and Guantanamo. That orange jumpsuits enter the scene is also telling. What is being witnessed in these reflections is a representation of biopower in its purest form. As Giorgio Agamben suggests:

> Inasmuch as its inhabitants have been stripped of every political status and reduced completely to naked life, the camp is also the most

absolute biopolitical space that has ever been realized – a space in which power confronts nothing other than pure biological life without mediation.

(1998: 41)

Vivian Sobchack has persuasively argued that the city in science fiction film acts as an affective space, actively shaping and propelling the narrative forward. Sobchack argues (1999: 123–146) that 'the science fiction film's spatial articulations provide the literal premises for the possibilities and trajectory of narrative action' and that the city space is considered to be a 'specific power' that can 'affect both people and materials – a power that modifies the relations between them'. In *Children of Men*, however, the brutal poetics of the city space remains very much in the background, or as Slavoj Žižek posits (2007), the textures and inhabitants of the metropolis needs to be viewed 'obliquely' since it is only through a canted angle that the noirish, nightmare qualities of fortress London are fully revealed. In its backdrop:

> The film achieves a kind of slow motion montage-effect: by yoking together images of seemingly disconnected crises over the course of 109 minutes (images of globalization, immigration, inequity, environmental degradation, permanent states of emergency, politics of fear, surveillance society, terrorism, and ghettoes), Cuarón argues for their dialectical relationship. Crises that appear as disjointed liberal talking points turn into a web of related issues tied to a larger problem: capital.
>
> (Boyle 2009)

The living and dead capital of the film is found in its version of liquid modernity in which neo-tribes have become home-grown terrorists, 'togetherness dismantled' (Bauman 2000) becomes extreme anomic isolation, and heady consumption becomes fortress communities or the raw oxygen burnt up in the weaponry needed to sustain the threads and binds of conflict and division that the watery future is predicated upon. Of course, *Children of Men* seems decidedly dry, as if environmental degradation and ash and smoke and debris of relentless bombing and explosions have caked the Earth in sheer grit. When we reach the water at film's end, it is covered in a thick fog we can barely see through or into.

Bodies

Children of Men offers us different types of bodies: some are collectivised and herd-like, such as the 'fugees' (illegal immigrants); some are individuated and individualised, such as Theo and Kee, and a great number are explicitly (also) raced and classed. Power relationships are exercised in and through these bodies as the film centres, questions and undermines the role of victims and abusers. All the relationships in the film seem to sit on this precipice of direct and symbolic violence; and wherever and whenever tenderness settles in, deception and brutality quickly follow. The War on Terror – both in its wider appetite for destruction, and in the way it pits individuals and groups against one another – is exemplified and amplified in this future where no*body* is safe and everyone could be the enemy.

On one level, Theo is the embodiment of the heroic, white male monomyth: an everyman, existentially adrift, childless, suffering from an end-of-days mid-life crisis, who finds a cause, hardens up, and delivers the Mary figure and her newborn (named Dylan, after his deceased son) to salvation. Early on in the film, Theo's movements are lethargic; he is readily and regularly duped and violated, only to find his moral compass and physical strength as he quickens his reactions and motivations. His inner strength, and resilience, is a coda for all (white) men to take up. Theo needs to deal with being white in an age where identities are in flux and his own subject position is under threat.

On another level, Theo is the embodiment of white masculinity on the cusp of its own expiration. His exhaustion is part of a range of apocalyptic films in which white men are no longer the dominant or dominating race. Richard Dyer takes this reading up when he suggests that the theme of white people belonging to an endangered species is increasingly found across a range of contemporary cultural texts, which 'may suggest that the suspicion of nothingness and the death of whiteness is, as far as white identity goes, the cultural dominant of our times, that we really do feel we're played out' (Dyer 1997: 217). In particular, according to Dyer, the threat of annihilation is found to inflect the representation of white men who are shown to suffer a debilitating existential crisis over their place within society. Such white men struggle to hold down a 'regular' job, or they fail to protect their family, and the white community, from those racial Others who threaten its stability and their racial purity. If one was to return to the figure of Rey Ferrier from *War of the Worlds*, it can be seen how he also operates in this sphere of white masculinity on the verge of a breakdown (see Chapter 5 for a detailed discussion of whiteness).

Kee's black refugee ethnicity obviously solidifies and extends this crisis in whiteness: it will be a black woman that will first reproduce and a black baby that will help resurrect the human race. While her fertile body may tap into racialised myths about the reproductive capabilities of black women, she also reclaims the origins of humankind in the African continent. Nonetheless, the scientist and eugenicists of the Human Project are never given face – they are a disembodied collective; they may well be white saviours who will experiment on Kee to find the answer to their own stagnant reproduction. *Children of Men* consequently is full of tensions and contradictions as it seeks to destabilise the politics of the global order. The War on Terror has produced a 'tide' of refugees and once-stable borders are rendered porous. This deterritorialisation results in new, power-saturated 'us and them' binaries, set out in zones of containment and control, which are opposed in this film by those who seek a new world order – Theo, Julian and Kee.

Nonetheless, the film struggles to represent those who are being tortured as nothing more than a mass. While seeking to carnally represent the dehumanisation processes that render the Other bare life, it can't help but create a picture of the resistance as a supra-mass of uncontrollable bodies that have as their potential the destruction of the social and political order. The aesthetic distancing techniques used in the film – long shots, deep focus, eschewing the close-up, the utilisation of 'frames' such as the bus window, and indiscriminate crowd violence – create the sense of mindless chaos penetrating all strata of social life. The terror, and terrorism, in *Children of Men* is actually invisible, so pervasive it is, so constant is its reach. As Chris Gutierrez suggests, in relation to the War on Terror, terror is given a chaotic and oppressive form of embodiment:

> Less like a hierarchical and organized army, and more like a discontinuous swarm, the enemy here is a clandestine and unidentifiable one. This ambiguity allows these shadowy members to move silently through society and to infiltrate their desired targets of destruction, simultaneously

though; this ambiguity allows the discourse of the War on Terror to constitute the enemy through whatever means seem fit.

(2006)

However, there is something else to be said about these terror bodies in the film: they belong to a set of post-9/11 images that represent 'a non-event of an obscene banality, the degradation, atrocious but banal, not only of the victims, but of the amateur scriptwriters of this parody of violence' (Baudrillard 2005).

Bodies are made tough and are toughened in *Children of Men*, Theo being a case in point. Theo's disciplined and hardened body will be able to resist interrogation and negation, and it will be able to brutalise the Other if it is called upon to do so. Theo and Ray Ferrier both carry with them the signs of the War on Terror, their bodies becoming corporeal maps of resistant journeying. Both their bodies will be able to say, 'I can destroy the thing that scares me by force of response' (Spivak 2004: 96).

Scenes of torture, of course, are common at this time: *Lost* (J.J. Abrams, ABC); *24* (Joel Surnow, Fox); *Alias* (J.J. Abrams, ABC); *Without A Trace* (CBS); *Saw* (James Wan 2004); *Hostel* (Eli Roth 2005) and *Casino Royale* (Martin Campbell 2006), to name but a select few, involve violent, sado-masochistic interrogation scenes. It's as if torture provides the hegemonic framework for believing that something is being done at the carnal level that has individual and social bodily affect/effect. Let me develop this argument a little more.

Screening torture may allow us to torture and be tortured in our bodies. Laura Marks suggests, 'vision itself can be tactile, as though one were touching a film with one's eyes' (2000: xi). Through the sense-based screening of the tortured body, then, one violently gets to touch bodies wracked with pain, and to be subject to and the object of violent assault. Screening torture puts one in haptic touch with the sickening biopolitics of war, in a way that may release these bodies from the regime of docile obedience that they are put under. Thomas Elsaesser has persuasively argued, in relation to the Holocaust narrative, that emotional affect may have productive consequences for the viewer – one realises, in one's body, that there is a duty to act, to respond. The 'affect of concern ... covers empathy and identification, but in an active, radical sense of being "stung into action"' (1996: 172–173). In feeling, or screen-sensing, the tortured body, one may very well be stung into action.

In the age of liquid modernity, action, and activism, is a thorny issue: on the one hand, the political processes and movements that allowed people to protest have broken down and have been diminished. On the other, new social formations and protest clusters have emerged, attempting to solidify the political issue they stand behind. People are being denied the spaces to act and yet action still happens, albeit in new ways. Sound plays a central role in these new processes, as I will now discuss.

Sounds

Children of Men sounds out its War on Terror through a complex set of leitmotifs, arrangements and subjective audition. We hear things as a character might, are positioned through a composition that undermines the narrative (through the use of subversive songs, for example) and yet which also carries it forward. The hyper-realist sounds of war, transportation, battle cries, weeping and dying orientate the story to a present full of conflict and discord, while its structural audio absences and sonic affordances point towards a despairing future without melody or song. Song is used to reference past atrocities that this film is repeating, for example:

> The soundtrack also plays an allegorical role here; in the scene where Theo's other companion, Miriam (Pam Ferris) is forcibly taken off the bus and separated from Theo and Kee at the Bexhill refugee camp, the song playing in the background is by the British rock band – The Libertines – and is titled – Arbeit Macht Frei.
> (Whittington 2011: 9)

The slogan '*Arbeit macht frei*' or 'work makes you free' was placed at the entrances to a number of Nazi concentration camps during World War II.

There are also sound shapes that offer hope, such as the epiphany that Theo begins to undergo in the forest as he begins to hear the world differently as zen-like sound effects fill the spaces of the trees. The transcendental score also anchors the drama in terms of its redemptive and recuperative qualities: Theo becomes a changed man through the way he hears as much as sees the world anew.

Theo is often at the centre of the way the soundscape orientates itself, and the tinnitus that he suffers following the film's opening bomb blast becomes his leitmotif in times of danger and crisis. The barely audible ringing that cuts through the film is literal and metaphoric – it is found, for example, in the sound of gunfire and the bell that sounds out the closing of the film. The ringing we hear is Theo's own battle fatigue and the film's frame for creating a destabilising sound-image for the War on Terror it is shaped by. As William Whittington argues:

> The ringing is accentuated by a muting of the overall sound track through the use of high-pass audio filters, which dampen the fidelity of the ambient sounds as if we are hearing them through a pane of thick glass. As a result, the audiovisual field takes on a detached and dreamlike quality, which supports Theo's despondent demeanour and establishes the theme of alienation, mapping it as both an external and internal condition.
>
> (2011: 8)

The sound that is carried within and by Theo is not constant, however. The nativity play that the film's narrative architecture is built around involves a musical score that suggests a possible redemption for Theo and the world at large. As a Christ-like figure, with stigmata wounds, Theo's movements are also orchestrated by John Tavener's accompaniment music, 'Fragments of a Prayer'. The score suggests a (coming) transformation in Theo, and in the world as it might be (if only he/we/they hear its possibilities). William Whittington again suggests that:

> Theo's sense of loss and despair [is lifted] through the introduction of a musical score that connects with various spiritual traditions from around the world, including Christianity, Hinduism, and Buddhism. The orchestrations, placement and emotive impact of the compositions by John Tavener evoke a sense of transformation and transcendence within the character.
>
> (2011: 9)

The mixture of religious tones and valences found in the score suggests a world both where global intersections (already) exist, and where if they are carried forward to tomorrow, will lead to the redemption of the human race. However, it is Theo's theology that will save the world – he becomes a salvic white hero not simply through mythic characterisation, but also through the way he unites the fragments of all (acceptable) religions together into one transcendental song.

The apocalypse of *Children of Men* is, of course, haunted by another set of sounds or, at least initially, their absence. At the beginning of the film there are no children's voices, and thus none of the innocence and purity that one senses when those voices are heard, and those bodies are seen. When we later visit an abandoned school where children should be studying and playing, we only hear the sounds of dead, decaying objects and silent passageways (see Figure 6.1). These 'haunted spaces ... bear the traces of repressed personal or national traumas' (Thompson 2012: 129). This is where Dylan, Theo's son, should be present, and where children should be growing up together. Laughter and learning should be filling the air and not the nothingness of the paranoid present. Wars enter playgrounds and shut schools – this is not simply, then, an absence of reproduction, but the presence of genocide.

The next time we hear the sound of an infant it is through the cries of Kee's newborn baby. This scene plays out in a siege, in a building in Bexhill under heavy attack by the military. As soon as the baby is heard crying, the attack is suspended and a hush and stillness descends on the scene. This miracle baby drains out the sounds of war and the cries of people dying. Its sounding momentarily re-enchants the world and brings to the fore the repressed sounds that the film has struggled to mute. As William Whittington writes, 'the audio effect (a variation of

Figure 6.1.   *Children of Men*: Haunted spaces

the "found sound") reintroduces a long absent voice that fosters a sense of unity, renewal and hope for both Theo and humanity' (2011: 11). This newborn will fill the world with song again, or at least has the potential to.

The second and final time we hear the sound of children is over black space and the title card, as the film ends. As I outlined in Chapter 3, what we hear are the repressed sounds of the child Dylan might have become, of the absent children that should have been learning and playing in the school, and of the future children that soon will be born since tomorrow is now supposedly in reach. As Zahid Chaudhary suggests:

> As we see the words 'Children of Men,' we hear the sound of children's laughter and playing, a sound that contains no recognizable words but the prattle of child sounds: giggles, screams, exclamations, happily agitated involuntary noises, and shouts ... Since the camera does not show us any images of these children, the film avoids here the visual economies of difference on which it has relied thus far. Given the optimistic thrust of the film's final sequence, these inarticulate sounds are coming from Utopia, a world in which alterity no longer signifies because the acquisition of language has not yet constituted otherness – or burdened the spirit with language, to use Karl Marx's figuration from the first epigraph.
>
> (2009: 75)

Unlike Chaudhary, however, I am not sure alterity has been defeated. While it is true that Theo dies, and the (African) baby that is born carries the name of his lost child, suggesting an intersectional future, Kee and Dylan will find themselves at the mercy of scientists who may do with them what they please. While we do not see this group in the film, the reverence with which they are treated suggests a long tradition of privileging white scientists as salvic figures (Redmond 2011). *Children of Men* may offer us a way out of this War on Terror, but its final solution may well be whiteness inspired.

Children of Men is a wonderfully complex War on Terror film: it is full of ideological tensions and thematic contradictions, is progressive in its representational and affective ethics, but ultimately seems to privilege the white salvic hero and the team of (white) scientists who wait on the ship *Tomorrow*. It achieves its complexity through the way space, body and soundscape intersect to create thick representations of power, conflict and control. The film is energised by movement, by a journey that takes Theo, and then Kee, from city to country to sea. For almost the entire duration of the film they are on the run, looking for refuge, for a safe harbour in a world at war. At each zone they seem to have nowhere left to run, but manage each time to escape their impending containment or death. When they reach the sea, of course, there is nowhere left to run: this is the end point for Theo, who dies, and the point of no return for Kee, who has to become one of the boat people to escape the terror behind her. Both Kee and Theo have been stung into action, the affective power of the issues they face demanding they act upon the world rather be enacted upon. For Kee, however, it is the white hero who has led her to salvation. What songs will she hear now? In the age of liquid modernity, there are too many songs to hear.

When Drones Fall Out of the Sky

Following the collapse of the twin towers, I felt the terror of, and desire for, death within me. A few days after 9/11 I was at a UK premiership football match with my young son, Joshua, when a big plane flew directly overhead. Without thinking about it, we moved closer to one another, tightly pressing our bodies together, as if the plane was going to explode above our heads and fall right out of the sky. We had both watched the 9/11 events unfold on television. I remember us both being mesmerised and, for my part, darkly excited by the spectacular ruination before us. It felt like we were watching a rerun of an old disaster movie. As the plane flew overhead, I guess we reimagined and relived the twin towers' destruction. Blood coursed through our veins. Our sense of fear was palpable. It was a fully embodied and yet fantastic reaction. I felt for my son's life, he felt for mine, and on my part, the bodies of all those killed on 9/11 came into ghastly, ghostly view. This was an obliteration that, as Baudrillard provocatively indicated, I had desired, and I felt desperately implicated in the loss of life and my vicarious dreamlike 'enjoyment' in it. According to Baudrillard:

> Moral condemnation and the sacred union against terrorism are equal to the prodigious jubilation engendered by witnessing this global superpower being destroyed; better, by seeing it more or less self destroying,

> even suiciding spectacularly ... That we have dreamed of this event, that everybody without exception has dreamt of it, because everybody must dream of the destruction of any power hegemonic to that degree – this is unacceptable for Western moral conscience, but it is still a fact, and one which is justly measured by the pathetic violence of all those discourses which attempt to erase it.
>
> (2002)

Since 9/11, I keep seeing planes falling out of the sky. In film and television, particularly, the image of the aircraft in flames, breaking up, hurtling toward the Earth keeps cropping up. Each time I see this image – it was one of central narrative images of *Lost* – I can't help but feel my body in the world. My senses are heightened, my heart beats a little faster, and I feel my bodily weight and shape in the world like never before. I feel so very alive because I can sense (my) death so very readily. Vivian Sobchack explains:

> Our vision and hearing are informed and given meaning by our other modes of sensory access to the world: our capacity not only to see and to hear but also to touch, to smell, to taste, and always to proprioceptively feel our weight, dimension, gravity, and the movement in the world.
>
> (2004: 60)

Since 9/11, I keep seeing drones in the sky: their use and deployment extends from the commercial, to the arts and to the military nexus that sends them into 'strong-holds' and 'bunkers' to destroy the enemy. The image of the drone is now writ large across digital age science fiction film and television, used to snoop, deliver and destroy. However, rarely do I see it fall out of the sky; rarely do I see the flesh of its target.

Four central images of the drone get reproduced in this age of the war on terror, and the first three are interconnected. We see the image of the drone soaring in the sky, like a majestic techno-eagle, heading towards its target; we see its impact and the destruction of buildings, roadways, oil refineries and telecommunications, if never the bodies of its victims; and we see (but not necessarily in the same relay or montage of shots) the hi-tech control room, populated with data screens where an unnamed operator commands the drone's trajectory and detonation. The fourth image of the drone exists in commerce and art – used to pilot goods or map a commercial terrain, or to take footage for a film, news programme or film production. The drone connects itself with three cultural structures: war, commerce and art. It is engaged in surveillance but surveillance that doesn't just locate, map and record, but one that seeks and destroys. The drone is bathed in secrecy – its bases and activities hidden behind military and commercial censorship. It is visible and invisible, both machine god and inexplicable ghost. The apparent invulnerability of the drone:

> ... conceals an unforeseen vulnerability: it communicates more than it should. Images of this phenomenon, entangled in rhetoric of 'precision', in fact produce contagious collateral, inadvertently communicating the invisibility of what takes place behind and beyond them. The drone combines banality and mystique; as it withdraws, it magnetizes us to its hiddenness. It fascinates. Yet it is difficult to apprehend. There is, from the beginning, an aura of the hermetic about the drone. We are dealing with secret transmissions, recondite knowledge. The middleness or mediality of the drone that we have identified is inseparable from the question of the metaphysics of the drone, even the mysticism of the drone.
>
> (Coley and Lockwood 2015:16)

In James Bridle's *Drone Shadows* project (2012, 2013) he features fullscale drawings of unmanned aerial vehicles that carry out surveillance and air strikes, intended to raise awareness of the presence of these secretive aircraft within our world. Bridle drew to scale outlines of drones in cities such as London, Washington, DC, and Istanbul. Their 'invisible presence' was placed next to roads, churches and open segments of land, revealing how within our waking lives fly these sleeping war and surveillance machines.

In the short near-future film, *Our Drone Future* (Cornell 2013), policing involves the use of semi-autonomous drones for urban security. Human officers monitor drone feeds remotely, and data reports are displayed with a detailed head-up display (HUD) and communicated via a simulated human voice (designed to mitigate discomfort with sentient drone technology). While the drones operate independently, they are 'guided' by the human monitors, who can suggest alternate mission plans and ask questions. Specialising in predictive analysis, the security drones can retask themselves to investigate potential threats. In this film, an urban security drone surveys San Francisco's landmarks and homes in on a criminal act that may be about to take place. As it flies over San Francisco the drone is able to record traffic movement, delays, temperature and the exact number of people within its zone. Prediction is built in to the drone's cascading mathematics, opulent data scans and gleaming algorithms – it can anticipate what might happen next, similar to the PreCogs' capabilities in *Minority Report*. The drone, measuring high 'stress levels in the area', decides to intervene against the command centre. It seems to have a conscious will of its own.

However, it is the soundings played out in the film that add to its liquid terror: bleeps, echoes, camera swipes and swishes, and the low and constant hum of the drone fill the film with electronic impulses and machine affect. The drone's seductive female voice undercuts this sterile and technological logic and, when she goes solo, becomes a mouthless voice that seeks destruction. Her voice is the song of the next chapter.

7

Sounding Liquid Science Fiction

Is this the Song that Must be Sung?

In this final chapter, I examine four particular aspects of sounding liquid age science fiction film and television: first, the soundscape that accompanies or underscores the type of space travel that crosses temporal and spatial thresholds; second, the ulterior, Othering sounds of the alien, whether it is creature, object, technology or environment; third, the alien sound of the 'woman's' voice; and fourth, the sounds of loneliness as they manifest in *Under the Skin* – a film I will place in the context of austere age politics. I do this to draw attention to the important fact that sound is a central feature of the poetics and politics of digital age science fiction film and television, and activates many of the themes outlined in this book so far.

In these instances of sounding science fiction film and television I suggest that human limits are reached and breached, leading to a deterritorialisation of the self and a hearing that touches the future, which is a moment of pure becoming. In the analysis of sounding space travel I suggest that science fiction film and television can create a series of moments in which one experiences the double sublime (see also Chapter 2 for a discussion of this). This spectacular rendering of a liquid chaos enables the viewer to experience the logic of sensation beyond bodily integrity. I focus on the womanly sonority of the alien to suggest that patriarchal and heterosexist sound devices can be ultimately corrupted. The female voice in *Under the Skin* and its lonesome alienated soundscapes point to a present devoid of a future. In this chapter my overarching position is one that hears in science fiction film the profound potential of a radical alterity that exists beyond the sonorous limit. The seeds sown in earlier chapters are here together sounded out like the triumphant orchestration found at the close of a liquid age science fiction film or television series.

Sounding Futuristic

Listen

Science fiction images are sounded in splendour. A camera cranes up and over a liquid horizon to reveal the structures, transportation, buildings and workings of a colossal, futuristic metropolis at the same time as its pregnant electronic sounds, post- industrial rhythms and heated-tempos fill the air.

A cyborg morphs into multiplicities and each time one hears the strangling and the rearranging of atoms and genes as it does so. A plasma ray gun blasts out its deadly heat with a steady pulse rendered synthetic-electric. A viscose portal in time swallows planets and stars and its catastrophic consumption is captured in dense tones and high-pitched oceanic tremors.

The 'spectacle' of science fiction iconography is always aligned with its digital soundings to create the intoxicating three-dimensionality that fleshes the genre's dramas and worlds into full life. The Los Angeles of 2019 we are introduced to at the beginning of *Blade Runner* (Scott 1982) is a profound mixture of glistening score; fire-explosions; of the near-to-far and far-to-near sound of spinners travelling; and the base hum or flickering heartbeat of the vast metropolis as it is being envisioned. This sounding science fiction not only animates and vectorises the future world that is being revealed but provides a 'sonic velocity equivalent to visible spectacle' (Sobchack 2005: 4).

Science fiction's images of wonderment are accompanied by a sound layering of equal awesomeness, one that arrests the *mise en scène* so that it has three-dimensionality and temporal progression: it is not of this world and (yet) out of this world. High-end, big-budget special effect sequences sounded with the epic musical score provide a particularly evocative example of this visual velocity: cities, people, contraptions, transport and aliens are given heightened, 'advanced' movement through the enormous, multi-layered orchestration that accompanies their visualisation. This rendition, sounded in the here and now, registers as if it comes from another planet, from a future not yet born. The wonderment, then, is two-fold: visual and sonic, and present-future tense. As Whittington observes in relation to the stargate sequence from *2001: A Space Odyssey* (Kubrick 1968):

> Image and sound spectacle converge. Bowman's subjectivity is shared with the filmgoer in this psychedelic trip through galaxies, stars, and the unknown. The point of view shots and the privileging and isolation of the music on the sound track encourage this transference.
>
> (2007: 50)

Science fiction film and television can further immerse the viewer in this doubling mechanism through the way its sound-images call forth a sublime moment: one in which characters witness the unfolding terror of a world morphing into something else or, situated as passengers or crew on a spaceship, they stare wide-eyed and silent as stars and planets – the infinity of space – take a hold of the image-track.

The fusion between incredible special effect world-building and rich soundscapes and musical scores is often deeply affecting: through this supra-affective alignment, language can fail and representation can falter. The experience is asemiotic and chaotic, resulting in a loosening of the bonds of the linguistic self as it experiences the sublime moment.

This is particularly the case when a viewer is symbiotically, intersubjectively aligned with a character as they experience this deterritorialising moment. Watching and hearing from a character's point of view, together and *within* one another they face the awesomeness of the sound-image before them, and are doubly lost for words (see the discussion of *Sunshine* in Chapter 2). The sounds, musical scores and leitmotifs that help produce this sublime moment speak for/of the unspeakable, while making it impossible to 'verbalise' directly. These sublime sound-image scenes suggest an almost infinite temporal and spatial distance and yet they bear down upon, or rather into, the ears and through(out) the body of the viewer-character as they watch liquid worlds bend and vibrate before them. As Vivian Sobchack contends:

> ... qualities of spatial expansion, amplification, vastness, and immensity are not phenomenologically incompatible with 'intimate' space – and,

> indeed, they may provide the large and often 'cosmic or 'elemental' dimensions that allow for a site of less objective reverberation and resonance than the architectural theatre: that is, the 'intimately immense' space that allows for the internal reverberations of *reverie*.
>
> (2005: 10)

In an intermodal sense, however, while sound and image complement the chaos in/of the sublime science fiction scene, it also becomes uncoupled, as the language of the musical score creates its own untethered images. The reverie of the score becomes lost in space, so to speak. The time travel sequence in which one hears/sees (becomes) the spaceship/capsule/body/mind as it flies through space is a heightened example of this future sounding reverie.

The time-travel sequence, often the centrepiece of the coming together of state-of-the-art special effects and the musical score, attempts to capture what it feels like to break the sound barrier, to cross known physical, geographical and temporal thresholds. Time travel images are animated and vectored, given an embodied presence, and they are often directly 'housed' in the 'brain' of the astronaut or traveller whose viewpoint the viewer takes up. The viewer hears and sees as if they are wired up, in the vessel, in the headspace of the person hurtling through space. In sound-imaging time travel, however, the hearing and seeing is a catastrophic rendition and rendering, since the present is in freefall, the future is not solid, and in this liquid collage of abstract assemblages one cannot predict arrival or landing.

One cannot predict when the soundtrack's attack and sustain will decay; and one cannot pull the images together into a whole, out of the cosmic hole they disappear into. In the slipstream of time travel, faces contort, eye sockets bulge, skin surface ripples, space matter and debris rain down, celestial lights envelop, supernovas streak, blazing comets hurtle, musical notes tremble, harmonies rise and fall, and atonal instruments flood the scene. In sound-imaging time travel the self is deterritorialised, broken apart, melded and scarred by atoms, particles and molecules, and recast by vibrations and intensities. This molecular becoming, where one is on the threshold permanently, takes one beyond the sonorous and somatic limit, to a type of dying happily:

> Music is never tragic, music is joy. But there are times it necessarily gives us a taste for death; not so much happiness as dying happily, being extinguished. Not as a function of a death instinct it allegedly awakens in us; but of a dimension proper to its sound assemblage, to its sound machine, the moment that must be confronted, the moment the transversal turns into a line of abolition. Peace and exasperation. Music has a thirst for destruction, every kind of destruction, extinction, breakage, dislocation.
>
> (Deleuze and Guattari 1987: 330)

In the black hole sequence from *Interstellar* (Nolan 2014) one experiences an 'accelerated temporality and accelerated present' (Sobchack 2005: 11) as the capsule and astronaut hurtles through (or rather within and without) space and time. The here and now moves faster than the speed of light. In this tumultuous sea of sounds and shapes, vectors and horizons, symphonies and arias, coloured notes and heated lines, one experiences a loss of temporal and spatial connectivity. Consequently or inevitably, 'incommensurable, non-rational links' (Deleuze 1989: 42–43) emerge, and void and disconnected spaces begin to appear before one's eyes, in front of one's fingers, in one's entire dazed and confused sensorium.

In the black-hole sequence there is breakdown in the sensor-motor system and the emergence of a direct image of time. One becomes a part of the shocking force of these deterritorialised, repeating, oscillating fragments as one is hurtled forwards and backwards; is surrounded by sound shapes that stretch out to infinity; and as one is incorporated into smudges, and light and colour strokes full of weight and weightlessness. The eye is wrenched free from its socket and becomes part of the plasma of time and space; the face rattles as if a force is pushing its way outwards, taking the flesh and the mouth with it, and the ears are grafted onto every image, in the same way every image latches itself onto the ear. This is a dying of the body as it becomes organless and purely sensational. This is a sonic visualisation of the body in the age of liquid modernity. The liquidity of *Interstellar* is another powerful, sensorial metaphor for the human condition in the age of liquid modernity: we are cut free from our families, exist in a decaying world, and are sent out into the digital realms to make new solid connections, but only find the untethered co-ordinates of isolation.

Sounding Alien

Listen

The unfamiliar, strange sound of something not yet quite visible stirs in the image. It is a high-pitched wave in the semi-darkness; a coated metallic sound that whirs with the purr of dissipated rotor blades; it is wet, organic sludge on dry gravel; a hot anvil hit with microchips; a tortured wail of broken dialling codes; and it is the trombone and the cymbal in atonal fusion, washing the still air with its liquidity. These alien sounds, at one both strangely familiar and uncomfortably other, begin to bring into existence the particular intense qualities of the creature, object, technology or environment of the science fiction film and television series.

For example, in the opening to *Terminator 2* we witness a future Earth ravished by the machines that have taken over and that seek to destroy all of human life. The camera pans across burned-out car shells, over piles of skulls and across a devastated playground. The caption reveals it is 'Los Angeles 2029 AD' and the female voiceover (Sarah Connor (Linda Hamilton)) reveals the background to the apocalypse that is, her soft yet matter-of-fact voice blending with the sound of a desolate wind. As the camera continues to pan across the carpet of skulls, a robotic foot crushes a human skull, its sound snapping the air. The camera pans up, a low synthesiser begins to hum and then a firestorm of lasers and explosions fills the soundtrack, its fidelity striking and strident. The machines are brought to life in part through the way they are so sonically alien to humankind, to Sarah Connor's soft voice.

These alien sounds rest innately on a realist-future-tense paradox that lies at the heart of sounding science fiction: making the unknown heard through the materials to hand in the here and now – in this case a crushed pistachio nut provides the sound effect for the skull being pulverised. Since they are conjured out of the alchemy of sound design, Foley work and automated dialogue replacement (ADR), and are drawn from everyday sources and the audio conventions of the genre, one has heard fragments and recordings of these sounds before but not necessarily in this combination or composition. One draws on one's experience and understanding of sound in the real world, and the generic sound of science fiction, to make sense of what one hears, but this only gets the hearer so far.

One's ears strain to make sense out of the sounds, to render them comprehensible or intelligible. Familiar, relatable sound-images flood the mind, but do not suffice since they cannot be connected to what is so far known in the film world. *This sounds like a science fiction creature/alien spaceship/advanced technology but I cannot fix an image of it because it does not yet visually exist.* The not properly seeing and the hearing strange sounds produce a terror of what the future of the image holds. *What could possibly produce such an uncanny sound?* The paradox of sounding science fiction, one in which sounds of the present are orchestrated to make the future newly sonorous, sends the hearer into new realms of possibilities, even, or especially, when the image is not yet fully born. As Vivian Sobchack suggests, in relation to in-cinema Dolby stereo trailers:

> It bears emphasis that these sonic reverberations neither 'animate' nor 'thicken' the image as it has already been formed and given but, instead, cause the image – calling it forth into visible, if tenuous, temporal being.
> (2005: 6)

At the beginning of *Tetsuo* (Tsukamoto 1989) an unnamed character wanders through an industrial yard before he enters a disused, worn-out shed. The viewer is both positioned behind him and intermittently takes his point of view, so that his face is never revealed, while one sees the yard through his eyes. Sound is naturalistic and yet amplified as if his (our) senses have been super-heightened. There is something strange, uncanny about this man, these sound-images, which are themselves photographed in monochrome as if the world is being seen with alien eyes and ears.

He enters the disused shed in bare feet, dropping a bag of tools as he does so – although it is not clear this is the same man we saw approach the building because of the lack of detail in those shots. The face is still masked by the effects of *chiaroscuro* lighting, and a cap that hides the eyes. The audio remains amplified so that his feet sound their delicate steps or shuffle with full harmonic range. He sits in front of a broken mirror, opens his shirt, and as the shot fades out and then in, a pounding industrial soundtrack floods the screen as the repositioned camera, without any diegetic context, pans, tilts and tracks across a dense forest of pipes, fans, tubes, cylinders, mesh, cans and photographs of Black American runners.

The image, the narrative so far, has been cut free from logical, causal certainty. The screen is fragmented, dissected and meaty: the grains, pools and textures of these industrial cast-offs is captured with sensorial intensity. They are face-ified, to paraphrase Deleuze, and yet they are also like body parts and there are also body parts cast off amongst the metallic debris – at one point the hairs on the skin of a rogue leg or arm are given the same quality as liquid drops on a tin can.

However, it is the pounding beat, itself vectored through atonal chord changes and drops, which animates the rusty images into one organic-mechanical life. The beat is given the power to hit the objects it scores, and these objects rematerialise as cutting sound-shapes. A knife suddenly rips open a leg and a long coil is tunnelled into it. Blood, the colour of oil, gushes out, the sound of which stops dead the industrial musical score. A long coil is suddenly inserted into the wound, to the sound of a scream, flesh and metal being welded or wet-mixed together. In this monstrous primal scene, a cyborg alien not yet fully seen has been sounded into life.

One can read the sound image in *Tetsuo* as one washed in the analogue age and yet one that gives birth to the digital world, where identities will be in flux and bodies will extend beyond their usual confines. *Tetsuo* heralds the liquid age where the untethered *acousmêtre* will be particularly relevant and dominant.

In sounding science fiction film, acousmatic sound and the *acousmêtre* are particularly effective/affective in rendering the qualities of the unseen or partially seen alien creature. Acousmatic sound enters a film or television series without its origination being witnessed: an alien voice crackles into a radio broadcast without it, or the emitter, being seen; or an off-screen synthesised crawl and accompanying wet scream slices itself into a shot of an empty laboratory, intensifying or filling the emptiness of the image with terrifying possibilities. In both instances, the alien-ness of the sound, and the alienation from/of the image that produces it, has embodied effects: the viewer *feels* the hearing and attempts to recoil from it; or reaches out to touch (be touched) by the sound that they cannot see to make it known, safe, or to revel in its terrifying alterity. As Elsaesser and Hagener argue, we can:

> Hear around corners and through walls, in complete darkness and blinding brightness, even when we cannot see anything ... The spectator is ... a bodily being enmeshed acoustically, spatially and affectively in the filmic texture.
>
> (2015: 131–132)

Hearing (without seeing) is a carnal activity: the viewer undergoes physiological changes, and draws on affective memory to ground and to make safe the untethered sound, and/or to confirm (and take perverse enjoyment in) its awe and terror. The image itself undergoes an embodied transformation since the off-screen space is given an Other 'life', and this alien sounding is itself ghosted into the on-screen world through the imagination of the viewer, and because it will, so convention has it, eventually appear in the film as 'mouth' and more.

The disappearance and reappearance of this alien sound-image is magnified by 'sound *en creux*' (Chion 1994) or sound in a gap, whereby the sonorous field exists in dissonance and contradiction with the *mise en scène*. The establishing and re-establishing shot of an everyday, downtown street may be filled with otherworldly digital sounds, or an atonal, brass-driven musical leitmotif, both employed to suggest alien occupation, surveillance or conquering interest. For example, in *Extraterrestrial* (Minihan 2014) the spaceships that contain an alien menace transport people up into their depths. The foreboding, reverberating musical sounding that accompanies the teleportation disturbs the everyday setting, arresting the image from its suburban and urban origins. This sound *en creux* requires a viewer to fill in the missing semiotic or representational properties absent from the image (in this case, the aliens in the spaceship), but because the alien has not yet been witnessed, because it does not have real-world referents, only multiple fantastical origins, the gap can never be successfully filled. Into the gap there emerges the imagination of sensation through which, as I will go on to argue below, the viewer and the sound-image undergo a process of radical deterritorialisation.

In sounding science fiction film and television, this 'acousmatisation', where a repeated sound source is denied embodiment, kept at the outer edge of the screen, opens up the full possibility for the alien to take frightening hold of the image, and the imagination of the viewer, as its aural vibrations resound across the *mise en scène*. When this off-screen orchestration is enunciated as an alien 'voice', sounding science fiction enters the realm of the *acousmêtre*, or:

> ... A kind of voice-character specific to cinema that derives mysterious powers from being heard and not seen. The disembodied voice seems to come from everywhere and therefore to have no clearly defined limits to its power.
>
> (Chion 1994: 24)

Generally in narrative film and television the disembodied *acousmêtre* is everywhere and nowhere, washing its way into specific scenes, whether they be private/intimate or public/detached, with a power to both read (comment upon) the scene and to implicitly affect its qualities, direction and dramatic intensity. The *acousmêtre* can be both malevolent and benevolent: a monstrous voice intent on foul play, or one that acts and looks kindly on the world it invades. In science fiction film the power of the *acousmêtre* is intensified, however, since it can be voiced by an alien messiah, a creature that literally has god-like powers, whose absence-presence (a voice without a body) is supported by healing and advanced (beyond the body) transformatory capabilities that change or alter the film or television world for the better.

By contrast, the voice-character of the devil messiah, an alien that has come to destroy the world, has engrained into its vocalisation its appetite for destruction, while its god-like powers involve such deeds as doubling, body invasion, mind control and vaporisation. That the devil *acousmêtre* cannot be seen doubles its monstrosity: heinous acts go unnoticed, such as bodily invasion, in the same way that the body that produces these acts cannot be witnessed but only (sometimes) heard. In *Invasion of the Body Snatchers* (Siegel 1978), one truly knows that a human has been taken over, seed-reproduced, through the piercing, strangulated scream that emerges from the mouth of the dead-double as it comes into contact with a human that audibly shows emotion in some way. This howling scream comes from the body hidden within the simulacra, and attempts to 'consume' the human (the imagined viewer) it is directed at.

Nonetheless, in both cases of the messiah figure, the 'grain of the voice' (Barthes 1977: 179–189) is important, not just because it gives partial flesh to the *acousmêtre*, but because its tone and timbre alienate and futurise the vocalisation. The science fiction *acousmêtre* is not a simple human voice but one rendered with wet-organic, savage-animalistic or cold-metallic propensities, creating the sense that an abject, borderless, shapeless or advanced entity created it. In terms of Darth Vader's voice, for example:

> The concept for the sound of Darth Vader came about from the first film, and the script described him as some kind of a strange dark being who is on some kind of life support system. That he was breathing strange, that maybe you heard the sounds of mechanics or motors, he might be part robot, he might be part human, we really didn't know.
> (http://www.film sound.org/starwars/burtt-interview.htm)

Or else, the alien messiah is a voice with frequencies and harmonics that give it a 'temporal vectorisation' that orientates it to (and from) a future world. In sounding the alien *acousmêtre*, a near/here/now, far/there/tomorrow union is brought to cinematic life so that the diegesis exponentially expands while simultaneously contracting – a push-pull paradox that further affects the instability of world-building that the liquid age science fiction film is built upon. This travelling with a voice (without a mouth) uncouples linear space and time so that one floats or orbits or exists in transit (while being grounded) in the beyond-this-world that has been brought down to earth. Time and space are compressed and expanded, with profound sensorial and corporeal consequences. As Vivian Sobchack reasons:

> Temporality is not perceived as elongated or cosmic – although it is certainly elemental in its extraordinarily amplified immediacy and presence. Indeed, its presence and 'present-ness' are felt in the doubling of its 'here-ness' – sound resounding through and amplified both outside and inside our being. We thus reverberate with an accelerated temporality and, more specifically, in an accelerated present, in a sounding that quite literally

quickens our blood and the very internal tempi of our physical – meditative – existence.

(2005: 10-11)

In *La Antenna* (Sapir 2007) nearly all the inhabitants of The City have had their voices taken away from them by Mr TV. People communicate by mouthing out words that are spelled mid-air, or which attach themselves to hands and gestures. The citizens of The City are kept under Mr TV's control through consuming the drugged food that sponsors the broadcasts – the constant adverts and monopoly of the supply chain hooking them in. The only person who has kept the use of their voice is La Voz ('the voice'), a sultry singer whose broadcast songs work to inoculate the people. La Voz wears a hood over her head that hides her face, which only exists as a black void that one stares into. She has a son called Tomás, an eyeless boy who nonetheless also has a voice but this is kept a secret, since to speak is a death warrant. Mr TV's henchman, Dr Y, is an unethical scientist whose lower head has been replaced with a TV screen showing just a mouth. Together, they subject La Voz to a series of invasive experiments with the plan to use her voice to pacify the citizens of the city.

La Antenna draws attention to the dislocation between the bodily senses and the forces of control seeking to hold them to account. People are not allowed to speak; heads have no faces, faces have no mouths, mouths have no bodies and faces have no eyes. The film perfectly (dis)embodies the liquid and dematerialised nature of modern life. Song emerges as that which both soothes and ensnares in the film. La Voz's alien, mouthless voice, which travels across time and space, holds the film world in its awe, drawing from the citizens their own containment and control fears. The film's nostalgic analogue aesthetic (cathode ray screens, vintage cars, aerials and telephones) is matched with its digital propensities. This is a song sung from the past – a jazz and blues age seduction – tethered to a liquid present where the world has lost its 'bodies', where the mouthpiece is the affective structure controlling all in its sonic wake.

There is a third order of realisation to this alien *acousmêtre*: one in which, through point of view, the viewer is aligned with the (yet unseen) extraterrestrial's vision and hearing. The alien enters the film world through a point-of-view shot and through their eyes (ears and mouth) the viewer takes up their position as they run amok, do bad things or silently witness the everyday world go by. No mouth, no eyes, no body has yet been witnessed (to the viewer, and sometimes to characters in the film world) but what the viewer sees and hears is humanity through the perspective of the alien. Consequently, an ulterior embodied alignment takes place in which the sound heard is rendered and experienced as it would be by the alien. The viewer gets to *become* the alien, who has no mouth to speak of. The viewer gets to experience a profound moment of alterity, in which they are an alien body in an alien world. Of course, in these instances the viewer not only hears and sees the world from the point of view of the alien, but also hear the alien (as if they are the alien) as it does so. Its fizzy heartbeat, robotic manoeuvres, haunting high-pitched frequency or dull, expansive sonic echo are as much a part of the soundscape as the earthly sounds rendered strange by the alien.

What one hears is the impossible 'speech' of the alien, delivered without a mouth, filling the screen (the auditorium, the ears of the viewer) in an envelope of enunciation as if it is nothing but a mouth, or a multitude of mouths. In hearing and seeing alien, in being *within* the alien, in hearing and seeing the world as alien, one is doubled but also divided: one has one's own alienation augmented, and one bears witness to one's own multiplicity that usually lies dormant under the illusion of identity singularity and wholeness. In becoming alien (through an eye that speaks and hears as if it is (also) a mouth or no mouth at all) one undergoes a physical loss of what normally constitutes human perception and comprehension. One is physically transformed into a body without organs. The body without organs is the self dismantled and pure potential, 'made in such a way that it can only be populated by intensities. Only intensities pass and circulate' (Deleuze, Guattari 1987: 153.) In becoming alien one experiences an atomisation of the self, the loss of the body, that stretches out on a 'plane of immanence' (ibid.: 27).

In *Predator* (McTiernan 1987), the cloaked alien is first introduced through its point-of-view shot of the soldier mercenaries it is intent on killing. Initially presented as a type of infrared scoping (not in fact alien, but military spying on military), the sounds that accompany this point of view subvert or undermine the reading (the seeing and hearing) that this is an earthly embodiment. The infrared vision is sounded as reptilian, and the hearing it processes is experienced as electronic translation – a series of audio waves appear on the left-hand side of the screen as the alien tries to make sense of what it is hearing. When it moves it crawls, enveloped in a sound bubble that feels like one is in the head of that which is looking and hearing. Human voices are at first inaudible, and then clear but rendered as the alien adjusts to the environment. Blobs or smudges of colour (the heat traces of body) provide a fuzzy but sensation-based sound-image. When the alien's hand appears in its own point of view, as the electric fizz, harmonic heartbeat and reptilian clicking sounds out the revelation, one fully comprehends that one has been sounding, hearing and seeing alien all along. *This is my alien hand; these are my alien eyes; these are my alien ears and sounds.*

Jane Bennett suggests that in moments where we become Other, one finds a re-enchantment of human experience:

> The fun of barking like a dog, or walking like an Egyptian, or dancing like a robot, or speaking like a computer, reveals the incredible possibility of our becoming-dog, becoming-other, becoming-machine. To encounter this illegitimate possibility is to experience one of the enchantments of the contemporary world.
>
> (Bennett 1997: 20)

For Bennett, the word 'enchant' is linked to the verb 'to sing' or 'to chanter', so that to enchant is to:

> ... surround with song or incantation; hence, to cast a spell, to bewitch with sounds, to make fall under the sway of magical powers. A dis-enchanted world, then, would be inert and songless, unable to induce a swoon or to conjure the strange and wonderful out of the banal and ordinary.
>
> (Ibid.: 2)

In becoming-alien through the chaos of beyond threshold soundings, in becoming-machine through sonic or aural alignment or invasion, one is transported from an identity position of lack, sameness, certainty and fixity, to a position of enchanted (sound, song-filled) wonderment, difference, uncertainty and fluidity. In essence, this is the condition of liquid modernity.

Nonetheless, in sounding science fiction, very often the voice that speaks is (strangely) gender encoded: either it is accented as masculine or intonated as feminine. It can be argued, in fact, that the alien voice speaks for and of gender relations, confirming normative binaries or, when the voice is registered as excessive, as it so often is, as that which needs to be de-acousmatised, or re-embodied and made 'safe' (recuperated or destroyed) by film's end. The hyper-masculine alien voices speak of fascistic apocalypse, while the shrieks, whines and/or sweet lulls of the 'motherly' alien speak of forthcoming species annihilation and (alien) self-preservation. However, the alien voice (without a mouth, without a body to speak of) is also often rendered asexual or cross-gendered, its monstrosity or alien-ness outside of heteronormative convention or patriarchal normativity. This is a sounding alien that can disrupt identity borders, as I will now go on to discuss.

Womanly Alien

Kaja Silverman has argued persuasively that classical Hollywood cinema fetishises the woman's voice and suppresses or contains her speech in the service of patriarchy, of male power. Women may also be coded as duplicitous through the lies they tell, their words a marker of their corruption. Men and masculine characters are seen to control the voiceover, dominate dialogue, auto-position the narrative, in the same way as they hold the gaze:

> By folding the female voice into diegetic recesses, submitting it to the 'talking cure', and anchoring it to the female body, dominant cinema attempts to move the male subject from a position of linguistic containment and subordination to ... a position of superior speech and hearing. The position is in turn only a reflection of the symbolic order or auditory aura.
>
> (Silverman 1988)

When women speak freely on-screen they are very often either masculinised, their speech an indication of autonomy, albeit supposedly at the expenses of their womanly-ness; sexualised, their quips and innuendos delivered with heated sensuality; or rendered emotional and melodramatic – their 'song' a yearning for romance, for heterosexual coupling, for moral (gender) integrity.

When women speak freely on-screen it can be heard as a marker of excess, of trauma, paranoia and hysteria – as if a female speaking too much is a disorder, a manifestation of interior, psychological damage. This malcontent may be exaggerated or compounded through the device of the interior monologue, where a female speaks (to herself) without moving her lips – her inner voice rising up and out of her to fill the audio world of the film or television show, but which no one (apart from the viewer) can hear. This interior monologue can be argued to be a manifestation of the malady that lies within her, filling the film and television world with a voice that does not have a mouth. It is also a patriarchal Hollywood strategy that 'implies linguistic constraint and physical confinement – confinement to the body, to claustral spaces, and to inner narratives' (Silverman 1988: 45). Paranoid women, who speak too much, or whose fragile psychology is revealed via a mouth that speaks but does not move, also hear things that nobody else in the diegesis can. These noises, aural invasions or spooky sounds can be 'maternal' in kind: both primal and monstrous, or noises that recall mother or that threaten motherhood.

In *Alien* (Scott 1979), Ripley is initially coded as the paranoid woman, and the ship's life-support machine, the computer Mother, its maternal, soothing originator and saviour. Ripley wants to follow company procedure and not open the quarantine doors on the crew's return from their exploration; a decision that would threaten the life of the injured Kane, whose face has an alien creature attached to it. Her cold rationality can be read as a front for excessive fear and anti-maternal sentiments. Mother, by contrast, has sustained the life of all the crew members during their 'incubation' sleep, and they emerge out of her immaculate, technological womb, warm, alive, safe, and dressed only in cotton diapers. Ripley speaks and acts like a man (while emoting like a woman) and should not be believed or trusted; Mother softly speaks to the crew and can be. These alien sounds that are first heard by a female character may be coded as monstrous-feminine, or monstrous-maternal, or (perhaps more rarely) maternal yearnings or echoes.

The alignment here, between an overwrought female who hears (while no one else in the film world truly hears) the strange sounds of an 'abject' femininity or foreign maternalness may suggest a sounding that *belongs* to woman-as-alien and the womanly alien who confers (confirms) this abjection on her. Alien paranoia becomes an essential condition of the (strange) woman who dares to hear and tell. In the *Alien* franchise at large, Ripley is repeatedly aligned, twinned with, and host to the abject creature that resembles her, hears her and sounds her out.

The alien *acousmêtre* can be a sound-character that has feminine vibrations or intensities, and whose eventual de-acousmatisation reveals a female alien body or an alien in a female human body (one that has masked the creature beneath it). In both instances the form generally appears to threaten humanity: the female alien wants to reproduce herself, her species, while the alien-in-a-female-body wants to reproduce the passivity, the 'silence', the seduction of femininity as a ruse, as performance, to ultimately destroy humanity. In *Species* (Donaldson 1995) the female body is a host for a parasite or alien that seeks to self-reproduce while castrating or consuming those it seduces or comes into contact with. Where the female alien is found to be motherly, they go in peace; where they are species-destructive (doubled, duplicitous, aggressive, warrior-like, maternal-transgressive) they must be destroyed (silenced). As Silverman suggests:

> ... The maternal oscillates between two poles; it is either cherished as an *objet (a)* – as what makes good all lacks – or despised and jettisoned as what is most abject, most culturally intolerable – as the forced representative of everything within male subjectivity which is incompatible with the phallic function, and which threatens to expose discursive mastery as an impossible ideal.
>
> (Silverman 1988: 86)

In science fiction film and television, the female character that hears the alien but is not believed is ultimately proved right. Hearing is revealed to be a privileged sense, even if it is vision that denies it ultimately as of first-order origin. The woman who is not believed is muted or silenced: she is put under watch, put on medication, hospitalised, and is no longer fully trusted. The condition matches or reproduces the medical discourses that operate at the societal level, except that in these fictive scenarios women escape their confinement, release themselves or are released from their exclusion once their/this truth wills out. Women who hear, know and understand the 'truth' are disciplined and punished, but are then set free when what they have heard is heard and seen by others. In sounding and hearing the alien, then, female characters find that their authority to say and tell is ultimately validated, while patriarchy's authority comes from such revelations and encounters. Women hear the truth first and find the courage – in a patriarchal-rationalist world – to report it so. If we return to the example of Ripley, her hearing and seeing things accurately, and firstly, ensures her own survival: she is the only character in the film to hear Mother for what she is: a technological imposter. In *Terminator 2* (Cameron 1991) Sarah Connor is subjected to psychotherapy, invasive therapy, interrogation and confinement/imprisonment until her vision of the future is evidenced, and those who doubt her die at the hands of the cyborg she prophesised.

One can in fact argue that the paranoia that something has invaded Earth, is undertaking surveillance, or is abducting or transforming or duplicating humans, points or draws attention to the instability of identity norms. It suggests that the body can be easily penetrated, copied, transcoded and re-embodied, and that consequently gender is not a fixed or fixable category – male aliens can take over/become female human forms and female aliens can take on male personas. Alien-substitution paranoia also suggests that reproduction is not inherently biologically sexed or gendered – humans can be reproduced without human seed, without mothers (and fathers). Finally, alien–human reproduction (cloning, copying, assimilation) may suggest that humans are at least double, malleable enough to be divided and remade, porous enough to be invaded and recast. One is a body without organs, and one can become woman.

In *Total Recall* (Verhoeven 1990), Quaid (Arnold Schwarzenegger) attempts to pass through airport security as a woman traveller. When the auditory circuitry goes haywire and he/she repeats the answer 'two weeks' to the guard's questions, the mouth begins to stretch and the voice strangulates. Quaid's womanly face mask begins to slip: eyeballs roll, skin expands and the mouth gets tongue-tied so that words can no longer form, and are instead replaced by an androgynous scream. Quaid's own head appears (pushing out and through the prosthetic rendering) and the woman's now detached head becomes an exploding device. Masculine and feminine morph and confuse and conjoin. Further, in this transsexual performative scenario, Quaid's gendered transformation draws attention to the vocal confinement that women normally undergo in cinema – when he tries to speak as woman he very quickly is silenced and reduced to a scream. The woman's mouth holds his tongue still and its own detonation takes place at the threshold space between Earth and Mars, human and alien Other, man and woman.

One can also hear the 'inner lining' (Doane 1980: 41) of the female alien speaking through the human body she has taken over. While not strictly an interior monologue, since the human host's mouth moves as it talks, in a state of fantastic ventriloquism, one nonetheless hears the alien without their mouth speaking. This turns the alien-human body 'inside-out' (ibid.: 41), making visible that which has avoided or exceeded representation. This inside-out is human and alien, a conjoining that creates or fashions an impossible hybrid being, and one born in a mouth that does and does not move, that does and does not speak. The alien-human interior monologue respects no bodily borders, and opens up a space for the 'silence' that classically contains and controls woman to be sounded, to be charged with carnal transgression and alien possibility.

Very often the critical clue to the fact of body invasion, and the loss of identity singularity, is given in the voice: tone and timbre shift, magnetise, harden, slow or are rendered to possess metallic or organic echo, for example. The rhythm of speech, speech patterns, and verb and adjective choice can change also, so that the doppelganger or human host speaks as if it is a human–alien hybrid, although something in/of the human has been lost as a consequence. The vocalisation of the invasion is meant to suggest that qualities particular to humankind, to the human in question, such as emotion, love, duty, individuality and sociality, have been lost in the remaking and recasting. Women (and children) are often the first to notice this sounding alien: that something has been lost in the human (partner, father, mother) they know/knew so well. Their supposed predetermined motherly intuition, gendered intimacy, or innocence in the case of the child who hears strange, allows them to recognise – before anyone else – the alien-ation that has been enacted.

Of course, soon after, as noted above, it is often male characters, connected with science or law, that confirm the doubling process through scientistic-rationalist means. One could argue that such scenarios confirm gender binaries and the power of patriarchy to decide upon what is knowledge, what is truth and what is understanding. However, I would argue that, at a more fundamental level, these scenarios throw into doubt and confusion such constructs. The family unit is so easily, readily, alien-ated, as if alienation sits at its centre waiting to manifest in a sounding familiar but strange. The relatively minor shifts in vocalisation and behaviour suggest an 'inner' (a double-inner) already present but now verbalised and outed: caring mothers become cold-sounding creatures and doting dads become hard-mouthed authoritarians.

The myth of the happy family unit is revealed as such, and it is often woman who first recognises that all is not well in the home. By contrast, male characters, scientists and lawmakers attempt to resurrect the family myth through evidential proof, rationalisation, deduction and conclusion, and by preparing to entertain the fantastic story that aliens are on Earth. In doing so, they take on the very Other qualities of the alien-human first witnessed by female characters, engage in the paranoia that is (supposedly) inherently womanly, in a further doubling and splitting that confirms their/our/your/my divided, alienated and alienating life.

There is another science fiction scenario that throws into doubt gender certainty made and confirmed in representation and language. When a female character first hears/sees an alien creature, she immediately reaches what Chion (1994) terms the screaming point whereby speech, verbalisation, does not suffice, cannot comprehend the thing that has been witnessed. Through the piercing scream that follows, one is left with a 'black whole', a wide-open mouth in frightful, extended terror. For Chion, the screaming point is the exit of being, or an entry point into experiential chaos where language has failed in the face (mouth) of the unassimilable and unnameable. This chora, 'anterior to naming' (Silverman 1988: 102), has a profound effect on the viewer also, since all they have at this moment is a screaming mouth with which to comprehend the creature not yet seen. This sonic alignment not only places the viewer in the vortex of the scream, but in an unseen world without language, scored by excess feeling, so that momentarily – for the length of the fright at least – one is inescapably deterritorialised. This body-in-the-mouth often sounds alien, the scream having been mixed with the alien sounding that has produced it. One travels into the mouth but also out of it, towards the unseen alien, from one mouth to another, the inner and outer folding, contracting, expanding and disintegrating.

There cannot be a better embodiment of the feeling of living in the age of liquid modernity than the mouth that screams its own scream, and of the viewer who can only register and recall events through its sonic terrors. Edvard Munch's *The Scream* (1893), a product of modernity, now becomes a liquid orifice for humans who have left their bodies behind.

In the next and final section of this chapter, I draw upon the idea of loneliness and austerity to make further critical sense of the conditions of liquid modernity, using *Under the Skin* (see also Chapter 3) to demonstrate how sound (poetically) orchestrates this contemporary terror of living.

Sounding Loneliness

Listen

If you listen closely, intensely, you will hear the sounds of loneliness scoring the most profound encounters found on our screens and in their relatable, traceable senses.

Sounding loneliness is heard in the timbre of the vanquished voice, the rhythmic pattern of raindrops falling, the nervous beep of a horn emitting from a car parked in the urban shadows. *Listen.*

Sounding loneliness is made manifest in the cries of a sibling, the weeping strings of a violin, the rustle of yesterday's newspaper, the click click click of a midnight mouse and the primordial raptures of the wind banging at the back door.

A goodbye, lamenting kiss; the silence of a dead tear collapsing on a wretched face – its liquid vibrations moving the air as it slowly descends; footsteps gradually fading, aching their retreat into the long drawn out distance – all recall the sounds of loneliness.

Listen. It is the combination of sounds, the intricacies of a text's sound design, that creates a scene of melancholy and malcontent. A scene can be busy, overwrought with noise and commotion, and yet be a soundtrack of loneliness – such as when a character is found lost in the midst of their isolation and distraction as the carnival plays on without them. Party scenes often employ this convention of loneliness to mark out a character in crisis or deep despair. They sit forlornly, with giggles and chatter surrounding them.

Disenchanted environments chant the name of loneliness: a desolate, rocky beach washed with a high tide; a high-rise, brutalist housing complex humming to the sound of light strips stripped bear of their dignity; and a vast cosmos emptied of its bright stars and luminous planets. An unkempt woman sitting on the edge of an unmade bed, pinching the sheets with her broken fingertips; a silver kettle boiling in an empty Ikea kitchen; and the creek of a swing in an abandoned playground amplifying the sound of rust as it freezes the still air – all scream out the idle tunes of loneliness.

Hear

How one affectively sound screens loneliness is dependent on what instruments, melodies, voices and sound effects are used to create a sonic membrane that manifests as melancholy and malcontent. It is in the syncretic and synaesthetic entanglement where sounding loneliness takes root. It is in the added value inherent in the 'sound-image', to draw upon Chion (1994), where loneliness fully emerges like a black dahlia.

So many lonely people, where did they all come from?

And yet, as I will go on to suggest, this sounding loneliness is not only textually specific, simply or singularly driven by narrative and generic concerns, but is historically contingent and nationally and culturally locatable. For example, the sounds of urban isolation of the American 1940s noir film is different from the peasant songs of Chen's *Yellow Earth* (1984) or what I will presently argue are the British austere strings of sounding loneliness today. When one employs a 'diagnostic critique' (Kellner 1995), one undertakes to find the history in the text and the text in the history: and it is the interplay between sound and image where historical and political truth emerges.

These contextualised and historicised soundings change across and within national landscapes and their related imaginings. We don't just see the crumbling walls of the imagined nation state but get to hear its desolate tunes: The Specials wailing two-tone *Ghost Town* single, the anthem of/to Margaret Thatcher's first wave of 1980s neo-liberalism, is a striking case in point.

But what specifically, then, is this contemporary sounding loneliness and where does it come from? I would now like to suggest that this age of loneliness is composed in, through and within the sonic vibrations found in the wretched politics of austerity. My case study – developing the work I began in Chapter 3 – will be the anomic soundings found in *Under the Skin*.

Sounding the Austere Age of Loneliness

It is in *Under the Skin*'s isolating and austere soundscapes where the voices of loneliness truly emerge. I will now divide these audio motifs into thematic categories, but it should be noted that it is their sensory unification where they are best able to paint the film with melancholic colours. Through these soundings, the impoverished lives eked out by the lowly inhabitants of austere Britain are established.

The Beehive Effect

Sitting just beneath the dominant diegetic sounds of the film is the 'beehive effect', defined by Mica Levi, the film's composer, as 'this alien language' (2014). It stains and stings the images of the film, undermining its hyper-improvised realism and impregnating its 'live' shooting scenes with a cold, metallic, futile futurism. The beehive effect exists in what can be defined as the 'sound *en creux*' (Chion 1994) or sound in a gap, whereby the orchestration exists in dissonance and contradiction with the *mise en scène*. In *Under the Skin*, every image is being undermined or destabilised by these buzzing waves. The narrative centre, as a consequence, cannot fully hold. Moreover, this 'acousmatisation', where a repeated sound source enters a film without its origination being witnessed and is thus denied embodiment, creates an alienating space for a phantom *acousmêtre* to emerge, or:

> A kind of voice-character specific to cinema that derives mysterious powers from being heard and not seen. The disembodied voice seems to come from everywhere and therefore to have no clearly defined limits to its power.
>
> (Chion 1994: 24)

One can hear in the *acousmêtre* the very disembodiment of this contemporary culture of loneliness: one cannot be social with it because it cannot be materialised beyond these liquid vibrations. The *acousmêtre* is also the nameless author of austerity, its reach exponential and seemingly without end. The hive-like vibrations it draws forth implies it belongs to or emanates from a supra-collective for which human individuals must be sacrificed. But these sacrificial individuals must not be individualised – they are chosen because they will not be missed, not by anyone. The men found in *Under the Skin* form a disconnected mass: they are a herd of near-silent and incoherent no-hopers left behind and on their own by the nasty politics of austerity. Their voices are the drones of the bees.

This alienating sound *en creux* requires a viewer to fill in the missing semiotic or representational properties absent from the image but, because the origins of the sound will never be witnessed, the gap can never be successfully filled. Entering into the gap requires one to be also alienated, to become part of the skin of inexplicable loneliness. We are immersed in the verses of the no-hopers also.

Voices in the City

As I mentioned in Chapter 3, many of the film's cruising scenes take place on deserted city streets. The alien seducer – a lone single white female – drives her van into edgy areas in the hope of picking up single

Figure 7.1. *Under the Skin*: Sounding the city

men without ties so they can become food for the alien entities we never get to see. The soundscape in these proto-realistic scenes, many of which were improvised and involved non-actors, is naturalistic, with the urban noise occupying the spaces of the working-class urban milieu. The sound somehow here feels thin, essentially lonely, emptied of connection and connectivity – the city is a mausoleum for the near-dead men who walk down it. However, these scenes are also filled with the beehive soundings and percussion that beats out a lonely drum (see Figure 7.1). In one key improvised scene, Scarlett Johansson's character falls over and onlookers immediately go to her rescue. What we witness for less than a bare minute is humanity flooding the scene, only to be quickly replaced by disconnection as people return to the winding wasp runs they were on.

Nonetheless, it is in the conversational exchanges between the seductress and the isolated men where the darkest deadening takes centre stage. She draws them in with the faux warmth in her voice and her easy acceptance of who they are. She initiates the conversation, shows interest in these deadbeat wanderers who in turn reveal their isolation and desire to be wanted. Her warm American accent brings a touch of the exotic, the foreign, to this parochial environment the men live in.

The initiated conversations are often about directions but are directionless – monosyllabic and monotone – and yet deceptively flavoured. Delivered as they happened, full of dry, lifeless improvisation, the conversations capture the death of intimate language itself. As viewers we become immersed (versed) in this dialogue of emptiness and are positioned to see and hear through the delivery, bare performances and the uncanny soundings, loneliness as a deterritorialisation experience. This is the experiential rendering of austerity conversation. This is truly the 'afterlife of the image' (Chion 1994: 123).

Kaja Silverman has argued persuasively that classical Hollywood cinema fetishises the woman's voice and suppresses or contains her speech in the service of patriarchy, of male power. Women may also be coded as duplicitous through the lies they tell, their forked words a marker of their deception. The figure of the femme fatale would be central here. As noted above, men and masculine characters are seen to control the voiceover, dominate dialogue, auto-position the narrative, in the same way as they hold the gaze. Of course, this masculine auto-positioning and silencing of the woman is complicated in *Under the Skin*. On the one hand,

Johansson's character is a classically constructed femme fatale – her voice one of the weapons she uses to ensnare the men. On the other hand, she controls the dialogue, directs the narrative, that is until the film's ending. She embodies, then, the derided figure of the post-feminist, the hated but voiced figure of much of austerity politics, a point I will take up presently.

Decaying Strings and Three-Note Seductions

Under the Skin employs a particular microtonal music structure, capturing the decay of the present through wavering between the '12 tones' we are used to hearing in mainstream cinema, and filling the void of the film with a fragmented 'scrape of the strings' melody, as if the film itself is expressing its own melancholy and loss.

This decomposition is supported by an evolving three-note leitmotif that accompanies Johansson's character whenever it appears on screen. In the cruising scenes at the start of the film it is a hushed, buttery seduction arrangement, but by the film's end it is full of disintegration – capturing her predatory and preyed-on transformation. As Mica Levi notes:

> She uses that theme – it's her tool. At the beginning, it's like fake – it's her perfume, it's the way she reels in these guys with a tune. Then it deteriorates, it becomes sadder. We called it the 'capture' melody. Then there's this major triad, a warm chord, and that's her 'human' or 'love' feeling. And there's this darker minor triad of trilled strings that recurs throughout.
>
> (Levi 2014)

There is more than a touch of *Looking for Mr Goodbar* (Brooks 1977) in the film's ideological allusions: Johansson's character is ultimately 'punished' for consuming the men she didn't desire but wanted on her own terms; austerity soundings calling upon rape culture motifs to position woman as deadly and deadening sirens. Her murder, an immolation at the hands of a would-be rapist, in the hushed, ever-so-quiet snow-covered tundra, a vicious 'moral retribution of order' by the 'type' of failed man she had taken to task earlier.

This is where post-feminism is undone in the film – cast as a predatory shadow on Johansson's character. Much of UK austerity discourse has centred on the role and function of women, with 'forms of classed and gendered shaming to generate public consent for the government's welfare reform' (Allen, Tyler and De Benedictis 2014).

Under the Skin's austere soundings are inherently gendered and yet no one is at home in the film; rather, death is everywhere to be found.

A Brief History of Science Fiction Loneliness

The history of science fiction cinema might well be charted through its relationship with and to loneliness. When you think about it, melancholy, introspection, meditation, detachment, isolation and atomisation are everywhere in the canon of science fiction cinema. *A Trip to The Moon* (Méliès 1902) is but a solitary journey in time. Alien pods and assimilation confirm our isolation as they attempt to turn us into crowd creatures. We are very much alone when push comes to shove. Kubrick's *2001* (1968) and Nolan's *Interstellar* (2014) are epic space operas where humankind travels great distances to make sense of the absurd and the suicidal impulse. We are born alone and die lonely. *The Martian* (Scott 2015) is but mediation on the poetics of loneliness. *Doctor Who* is a reverie of companionship marked by deep pockets of loneliness. While Kolker (1980) defines his cinema of loneliness in terms of certain American auteurs, I think we could usefully chart a new history of science fiction cinema along this axis of loneliness – finding its variants and variations across national cinema and underpinned by social and political contexts of the time.

To return then, one last time, to *Under the Skin*: its cinema of loneliness is one generated by the ghastly conditions of austerity, of austere Britain: caused by the relentless market-driven engines of liquid modernity. Its *mise en scène* is crafted out of the urban wastelands of today and the wilderness the film ends in is both an escape from and an extension of austere loneliness. The seductress is both an architect of austerity and one of its victims. Her voice carries the sounds of loneliness throughout the film and into our bare lives …

Conclusion

We Never Let the Fire Go Out

Live-Die-Repeat

In *Edge of Tomorrow* (Liman 2014), an alien race has nearly vanquished Earth's armies and its weaponry. In a last-ditch effort to defeat the aliens, an all-out assault is planned. However, the aliens lie in wait, and Earth's last armies are heavily defeated, leaving the aliens to conquer and destroy the planet. Well, not quite: the initially cowardly Major William Cage (Tom Cruise) is killed in this battle, but finds himself in a time loop where he gets to live-die-repeat until the enemy is finally defeated. *Edge of Tomorrow* draws upon the double-jeopardy model: it is through Cage, as a white messianic hero, that the film imagines its burning fires and diabolic scenarios, and through him that the world can be rescued (see Figure 8.1). The film's liberalism, its neo-liberal individualism, speaks to the concerns of the liquid modern age, and yet imagines the eradication of danger through the (American) empowered self. That life can be replayed over and over again is a translation of the logic of gameplay and allows the lone individuals to sacrifice themselves for the nation state until that nation is resurrected and recuperated.

In *The Incident* (*El Incidente*) (Ezban 2014) the apocalypse is also seemingly imagined to be without end, as a cop and a criminal find themselves stuck on a stairwell that goes nowhere and yet expands forever, while a bickering family gets caught on an infinite road as they head off on their holidays. As time passes, the stretch of road and the surrounding desert begin to repeat and their sense of time and temporality becomes caught in its monotony and absurdity. Everyone ages

CONCLUSION

Figure 8.1. *Edge of Tomorrow*: Double jeopardy

and yet time has stood still. In these parallel stories, we get to witness the loneliness and despair of liquid modern life and the contradictions it offers us: endless and boundary-less and yet also a rat cage with no hope of escape …

Liquid age science fiction film and television operates along a number of critical conjunctions and positions, a fact that further imbues it with import and power. First, science fiction film and television often imagines and establishes the existence of other worlds that can and do challenge, unsettle and undermine the known logic of the human world. In these Otherworld kingdoms, ethics, morality, physics, environment, and social and cultural organisation can be radically alternate. The planets visited on *Interstellar* (Nolan 2014) recalibrate time and the way the seasons function; and the lifeworld of *Avatar* (Cameron 2009) reconnects its people to nature and the spiritual and mystical. Both are examples of Othering environments that create the sense of alien-ation and of experiencing other possible ways of being, and of newly being in time. Liquid age science fiction film and television has the power to threaten the established order of things and open up gaps in the way the viewer conceptualises the contemporary world and their nomadic wanderings within it.

Second, and related, in these liquid zones, science fiction film and television can annihilate linear time and simultaneously create the liminal conditions for sublime encounters. Through its special effects, and scenes of spectacle, often mobilised through time contraction and expansion, science fiction film and television creates the conditions for affecting contemplation: viewers feel overwhelmed by what they are watching, untethered from both the world they are viewing and the world they are seeing from.

Third, liquid age science fiction film and television can destabilise the ontological integrity of the body, critically redrawing the lines of what it is to be human, and how identities such as race, class and gender are performed and embodied. The figure of both the cyborg and the alien establish that the body and the flesh can be reimagined, rematerialised and reconstituted. Further, it suggests that the body can be both undone and overtaken, controlled by forces outside of its agency and control. This deconstruction and reconstruction of the body is thus liquefying in two opposite ways: it creates the conditions for new forms of identity to emerge; and it prophesises the loss of freedoms in a new age of virtual and bionic augmentation. N. Katherine Hayles addresses these polar possibilities when she writes:

> If my nightmare is a culture inhabited by posthumans who regard their bodies as fashion accessories rather than the ground of being, my dream is a version of the posthuman that embraces the possibilities of information technologies without being seduced by fantasies of unlimited power and disembodied immortality, that recognizes and celebrates finitude as a condition of human being, and that understands human life is embedded in a material world of great complexity, one on which we depend for our continued survival.
>
> (1999: 5)

In *Splice* (Donaldson 2009) we witness this deconstruction and reconstruction of the body in an orgy of multiple-species splicing; open flesh, sexual violence and abjection. The body becomes a monstrous fusion, a confusion of liberating tendencies and corrupting desires and taboos. It is both posthuman dream and nightmare, and maybe, as a consequence, even more culturally challenging.

There is an inherent 'risk' in liquid age science fiction film and television – one that operates and attaches itself to the risk society thesis, as defined by Ulrich Beck, whereby what shapes and directs thought and action is the constant 'perception of threatening risk' (Beck 1992). *War of the Worlds, Children of Men* and *The Road*, to name but a few examples from this book, all create the conditions for the survivor narrative to flourish.

Finally, and in relation, liquid age science fiction film and television explicitly explores dangerous and taboo ideas, engages in political critique, and opens up affecting psychic ruptures as a consequence. On the one hand, these texts challenge scientific-rationalist thought and neoliberal dreaming. Science fiction film and television shows question beliefs and complacency through clearly pursuing political critique can range from the quietly polemical to those pursuing more strident political allegories. *District 9* (2009), for example, is explicit in its politics:

> The film's location in South Africa, the nationality of the director, and the title itself, which refers to a slum settlement where the 'prawns' are detained, has obvious parallels with apartheid. At the same time the film draws inter-textually on other science fiction films, including the *Alien* franchise and *The Fly* – mostly through reference to abject visuals, typically including close-ups of gelatinous, fluid-stained surfaces, and generalised visual obscurity rendered through dark, murky low-key lighting. 'Expert' talking heads (all of whom are white) within the film's mock-documentary style of presentation (which conveys the events through flashback), describe the aliens as 'unhealthy', 'extremely malnourished' and 'aimless', constructing a negative view of the prawns akin to the ways that various 'others' have also been maligned.
>
> (Pheasant-Kelly 2015)

On the other hand, the endangering power of science fiction film and television lies in its ability to be a mouthpiece for dominant ideology and for the processes, regulations and practices of late, liquid capitalism. Western civilisation is its creation myth, and it fetishises the white masculine individual who colonises space.

As a genre, science fiction film and television is very often a commodity intertext, the epitome of mega corporate and corporatised spectacle, and is in consort with the military, government and big-business nexus. Very often, in fact, science fiction film and television is a form of militainment, fetishising war and weaponry in scenarios where military might is both successful and necessary. The *Iron Man* franchise may well be the best example of marketing weapons and the military-corporation nexus. As Tanner Mirrlees argues:

> *Iron Man* is one small but important part of the U.S. Empire. While much has been made of *Iron Man*'s spectacle as Hollywood entertainment media, this article examines how *Iron Man* is shaped by and supportive of the economic, military and ideological power of the U.S. Empire. I argue that *Iron Man* supports U.S. economic power (as a Hollywood blockbuster and synergistic franchise), U.S. military power (as DOD-Hollywood co-produced militainment) and cultural power (as a national and global relay for U.S. imperial ideologies). The nexus of the actual world of U.S. Empire and the reel world of Hollywood film expressed by *Iron Man* highlights how popular film is not 'just entertainment' that circulates in apolitical theatre markets, but is linked to and supportive of the geopolitical-economy and ideology of the U.S. Empire.
>
> (2014: 5)

When I write of liquid age science fiction film and television, then, I do with these oppositional, if dialogical, positions in play. The power of science fiction film and television is to be both celebrated and challenged. This has been one of the key narrative threads of this book – to critically understand and explore how liquid age science fiction film and television engages with, produces and is a product of liquid modernity. For the scholar of science fiction, such an opening up of a critical intelligence is vital. After all, this is what the genre continually is asking us to do, what it was *designed* to do. This is the search for 'cognitive value' as Darko Suvin (1979) would have it. The rise of CGI special effects and the virtual establishment of the contemporary digital cinema ensure that the difference between the pro-filmic event as staged in a real space with real actors, and the post-production insertion of digital effects, both visual and aural, has to all intents and purposes been erased. The cognitive gap whereby the viewer used to be able to distinguish between 'reality' and clumsy 'special effect' has vanished. This disappearance ensures that the ideological ruptures inherent in the form have necessarily become more acute while, at the same time, the aesthetic potentialities of the medium far outrun its genre rivals.

CONCLUSION

Breaching the Senses

Film and television has always been part machine and part ghost: a technological marvel and a beguiling, mysterious creature; full of circuitry, emulsions and the wet flesh of dream and nightmare. It is more dark than light and moves when it is still. It *is* science fiction.

In its cross-modal majesty, screen science fiction addresses and awakens all the senses: it is an immersive and expressive art form, calling forth its own body and appendages – the eye of the camera, the ear of the microphone, the cognition of the director – while simultaneously drawing forth, coaxing into full life, the sensorium of the spectator or viewer.

Expanded cinema – a term coined in the mid-1960s by American experimental filmmaker Stan Vanderbeek – extends and enriches the way that the screen can engage with its viewers. The art form is taken into galleries, museums, subterranean vaults and installation spaces, and the moving image is opened up to the different-shaped walls and surfaces found there. Viewers can stand, sit or be positioned in patterns and relations that breach the traditional movie-theatre encounter. The space can itself move, living performances can interact with the screen, sound can bleed out from the floor and bodies can be literally touched. The screen is a living special effect.

This expansion in screen, space and self is something that is instantiated in *Breaching Transmissions*, Sally Golding's 2015 immersive audiovisual performance. Its expansion and the way the senses are breached belong with the best of liquid age science fiction. It, in fact, prophesises and utilises the lexis of science fiction that is all about extension, outreach, moving and movement beyond the here and now. Digital age screen science fiction exists in an expanded audio-visual universe.

In Golding's work, the audience is 'taken on a hallucinogenic dark carnival ride exploring the slippage between parapsychology and technology'. Golding has defined her work as focusing on the 'experience of the audience, pushing the boundaries of visual and auditory perception through the breakdown of the cinematic system into flicker, waveforms and colour fields'. Participatory by design, the viewer is invited to be a 'collaborator within the work, evoking a form of auto-scopic hallucination'.

As a reviewer of this piece, I wanted to test or rather *experience* this assertion: I wanted to immerse myself in the work and respond to the hallucinations offered up. I wanted to see whether my senses had indeed been breached in the expanded contours and liquid horizons of *Breaching Transmissions*. I wanted to be washed in the liquid seas of digital age science fiction. I want to now turn my attention to a fully auto-ethnographic perspective, as I outlined in my introduction to this book. To get to know liquid age science fiction one needs to experience it …

Get Out of My Body

Get out of my head. Noise. Shadows. Headlights steeped in nitro-oxide. Dead candles flickering. A sea of disconnected atoms. The universe laid out on a worn bedsheet. A snake emerging without its head from the film projector. It crawls along the floor into my wide-open mouth.

Get out of my head. Static. Nylon. Scouring pads on soft skin. Epilepsy. The scarring sounds of red. Black clouds vibrating on a hot summer's day. Decay.

Get out of my head. A jagged piece of cut glass running over Vaseline. Black dogs howling. A nosebleed on a white Egyptian cotton shirt. Shit. Nausea. Acid in an iron lung. The tattooist's drill. My mother's grave overgrown with hyacinths and bluebells.

Get out of my fucking head. Milk. A black dahlia dying. The emptiness of time. The silence of far pace. The loneliness room. A metronome A metronome A metronome A metronome A metrodrone, a drone, a drone, a drone.

Get

Out

Of

My

Head...

Get out of my bod...y

(Golding 2015)

According to Vivian Sobchack:

> As 'lived bodies'... our vision is always already 'fleshed out' – and even at the movies it is 'in-formed' and given meaning by our other sensory means of access to the world: our capacity not only to hear, but also to touch, to smell, to taste, and always to proprioceptively feel our dimension and movement in the world. In sum, the film experience is meaningful *not to the side of my body, but because of my body.*
>
> (2000)

I engage with Sally's *Breaching Transmissions* on similar terms – as a living and fleshed encounter. I meet the installation on synaesthetic and haptic terms and in the realm of the senses – in the eyes that taste and the mouth that sees and in the brain that feels.

The senses that Sally's work evokes and stimulates are connected to the processes of dissolution or a deterritorialisation of the self, a becoming-animal, to again draw on Deleuze. I feel myself vanishing, being emptied, being poured out, being remade into something else as I feel my way through *Breaching Transmissions*. This is a something more wild, a something else freer. This is what great science fiction does – it sensationalises our carnal beings – it takes us home. It sets me free.

Now let me end this conclusion with reflections on a domestic moment: one that returns me to the streams found across this book: from the boxes I discussed in Chapter 1, to the themes of time travel, special effects, alienation and self-actualisation that I addressed across the remainder of the chapters. In the story I share here, I weave in the messages and implications of the book, while gently making a case for auto-ethnography in the study of science fiction, and for better understanding *who we are* in the age of liquid modernity.

Television Removals

There will be different reasons for why the routine of viewing television will momentarily leave our day-to-day lives. Major rituals and life events may require of us to turn it off, to be somewhere else, or we may consciously decide to have time away from the set, wherever and however that may be technologically constituted. A family gathering; the death of a loved one; a delightful wedding ceremony; a broken heart; an exotic holiday and a lifestyle kick are some of the reasons we may have for abandoning television and for removing it from the way we normally schedule our day. Moving home is another potent and portentous reason and in this final part to the conclusion of this book I would like to concentrate upon this type of television removal, albeit within the frame of Western culture and with a focus on the family unit.

Emotionally speaking, moving home is driven by contradictory impulses. On the one hand it is often about moving on and forward, and is cut on the myth of fresh starts and new beginnings. There is hopefulness to moving home, although the flip side of this is forced removals or shifting, sinking circumstances such as a family break-up or house repossession. On the other hand moving home produces a sense of nostalgia, of loss, as memories and moments are recalled and remembered as they are carefully packed away. Homes are emotionally charged environments, affecting spaces of yesterday and yesteryear, of laughter and forgetting, which in the process of removal are filled again with the voices of what once was and may be again.

Television and the television set are intimately entwined with this remembrance, and with the way new houses are immediately fashioned into homes. Not only do families (still) come together around the television, but it provides the pleasurable material out of which conversations grow, relations and points of difference are cemented, and arguments developed, producing layer after layer of memorial, familial membrane. It is this quilt of family history and herstory that gets packed away with other keepsakes, mementos, family photographs and old ornaments and the like. We relocate television memories when we move home; removal followed by transference.

When I think back on the stories of my young life I can home in on the role and function of television shaping pleasurable pastimes, drawing me effortlessly into affective economies of longing and belonging. Tomato soup and white bread in front of *Mr Ben* in our red-brick Newcombe Road house. The *Flash Gordon* serial at Auntie Peggy's more palatial residence, where I was served up homemade chips doused in salt and vinegar. Watching soccer with my dad on a soft orange sofa as the hard rain fell relentlessly outside. Staring at my mum's mahogany television set, knowing she would no longer turn it on again – would no longer cackle or quiver in front of *Bread* or *Only Fools and Horses*, as she liked to call it. Moving home removes the past that once was and yet transports it to another time and place. Disappearance and reappearance, now you see it, now you don't: television removal the home of the quick-wristed trickster or magician. Television removals are *always* a form of time and space travel.

Televisions often organise the way a domestic space is used and utilised: the layout of the lounge often orchestrated so that the television is central and centralised or placed to ensure collective communion. When one moves homes the removal of the television is a highly charged moment. It is carefully bubble wrapped, boxed and gently lifted, and the space where it just sat is emptied of its signification. The room collapses in on itself with the disappearance of the television set. Memories are lifted out of the room and placed on a truck and driven quietly away. The house becomes a loneliness room.

Television content plays on the architectural and discursive importance of it to everyday family life, with programmes such as *The Royle Family* and *GoggleBox* fictionalising and factualising the way TV makes and shapes us. Home-design programmes also play their part in showing what makes a perfect and perfected family lounge. Television sits within the home of the myth of the media centre, creating and forming ripples of hyper-reality.

In the KFC family dinner advert, presently being aired during the *Big Bash Cricket* on Australia's Channel 10 (2015), we witness an imagined time-lapse narrative as a family grows, ages and reproduces itself over many decades. The repeated scenario is the same: the cricket is on the box (which changes from cathode ray to plasma, from small-screen to big-screen size); boxes and buckets of KFC are in plentiful supply; and smiling family members gather around the food, the set and the cricket, clearly enjoying each other's company as they do so. Mum and Dad age, kids grow up, grandchildren are born; with fast food, and cricket on the box, the entwined or cohering and unifying consistent with extended family life. Of course, the advert will produce its own self reflexive echo down the track – it will become part of the way families today will remember this Australian summer and the time they spent together.

In a similar but nonetheless different way to *Edge of Tomorrow* or *The Incident*, television constantly offers us a loop-back mechanism.

I have a very recent affective memory of watching the 2014 Christmas edition of *Doctor Who* with my seven-year-old son, Dylan. We lay on the couch together, his body pressed to mine, his fingers clutching my shirt, his head buried into my chest when the scariest moments surfaced. We were experiencing together the pleasure of television terror and surprise. All the values of parenthood and all the intimate proximity of a loving relationship circulated in and through those moments. Dylan doesn't live with me so I call our time together enchanted time. I recall this here because I have just moved home and it is that memory that surfaced, that shone out like an exploding star, as I packed and wrapped up the television we watched it on.

When the television arrives at its new home it often becomes the focal point for the way the space is arranged. There is an attempt to capture the magic of its previous positioning, alongside a desire to create a new environment for the family to gather in. The television helps enculture a house; it is an enchanted object imagined to hold the family unit together. Where it is positioned will determine how happy the family will be, what type of social relations will take place, what sort of new memories will be countenanced and memorialised.

There is something fundamentally existential and phenomenological about television removals: because it exists as membrane, memory box and pleasure trove; and because it occupies and signifies space and place, it is sentimental and elicits sentiment. Television's physical nature if removed leaves a gap, an absence, and because it holds such affecting power, to see it absented is stressful and creates anxiety. It is as if a living thing is being taken away.

When the television is turned off one feels as if one is removed or divorced from the world, since it still is a major carrier of meanings and messages, information and communication. There is something deliriously disorientating about television removal, as if the world has somehow gone on without you. I have always had that fantasy that when I would turn it back on again there would be nothing left of the world to see. A television removal is a form of the apocalypse.

As noted above, I moved home recently. At the end of a weary day, with boxes of chaos around us, we had carefully unwrapped and set our television in the place we felt most comfortable with. We would be

CONCLUSION

able to stretch out on different sofas and the light from the bay window wouldn't hit the screen. It was only when we turned on the television and light and sound and imagery filled the room that we felt at ease in our new place. We felt at home watching *Sense8*.

As I shut the door behind me on the home we were leaving behind, I took one final glance at what once was. Sounds, noises, images, photographs and laughter filled the empty spaces one last time and away I went, drunk on the memories of yesterday ...

In amongst the terror of modern living, and the dissolution of place, space and body; and in spite of technological drift, convergence and dematerialisation, we gather together around friends, objects, cultures, and *we must never let the fire go out*.

The End of the Beginning

In this monograph I have explored digital age science fiction film and television through the guiding framework of liquid modernity. I set my reading around a set of articulating themes while, where I felt it necessary and instructive, historicising the shift from the analogue age to the digital age. These demarcations are never absolute, of course, and the recent growth in record vinyl and player sales is an indication of the way we return to technologies supposedly obsolete.

This is the age of seeming obsolescence: our goods, vehicles and products have it coded or planned into their circuitry to fail and stop; as human beings we stand on the verge of being surpassed by AI and the augmented self; and the planet itself seems to be at the tipping point, where it will become an obsolete rock in the cosmos. Science fiction may itself be becoming obsolete, since the real world seems to be more fantastic than any dreaming it can conjure up. Is this the beginning of the end, or the end of the beginning? Like the Möbius strip, the present may well be a non-orientable surface.

Live-Die-Repeat-Repeat

References

Abbott, Stacey (2013). It's Bigger on the Inside: Blockbuster Science Fiction TV, Episode 10: The blockbuster edition, Deletion. 7 September 2015 url: www.deletionscifi.org/episodes/episode-10-episodes/its-bigger-on-the-inside-blockbuster-science-fiction-tv/

Adams, Paul (1995). A Reconsideration of Personal Boundaries in Space-Time. *Annals of the Association of American Geographers* 85, pp. 267–285.

Agamben, Giorgio (1998). *Homo Sacer: Sovereign Power and Bare Life*. Translated by Daniel Heller Roazen, Stanford, CA: Stanford University Press.

Allen, Kim, Imogen Tyler and Sara De Benedictis (2014). Thinking with 'White Dee': The Gender Politics of 'Austerity Porn'. *Sociological Research Online* 19.3. Available at: www.socresonline.org.uk/19/3/2.html

Ang, Ien (2013). *Watching Dallas: Soap Opera and the Melodramatic Imagination*, London: Routledge.

Avila, Eric (2000). Dark City: White Flight and the Urban Science Fiction Film in Postwar America. In Daniel Bernardi (ed.). *Classic Hollywood: Classic Whiteness*, Minneapolis: University of Minnesota Press, pp. 52–71.

Balchin, Paul, N., and Rhoden, Maureen (2002). *Housing Policy: an Introduction*, London: Routledge.

Barad, Karen (2007). *Meeting the Universe Halfway: Quantum Physics and the Entanglement of Matter and Meaning*, Durham, NC: Duke University Press.

Bartes, R. (1977). *The Grain of the Voice Image Music Text*, ed. S. Heath, New York: Hill & Wang.

Baudrillard, Jean (2002). *The Spirit of Terrorism and Requiem for the Twin Towers*, New York: Verso.

—— (2005). War Porn. Translated by Paul A. Taylor. *International Journal of Baudrillard Studies* 2, no. 1. Available at: www.ubishops.ca/baudrillard/vol2_1/taylor.htm (accessed 27 July 2007).

Bauman, Zygmunt (2000). *Liquid Modernity*, Cambridge: Polity.

Bauman, Zygmunt and Tester, Keith (2001). *Conversations with Zygmunt Bauman*, Cambridge: Polity.

REFERENCES

Beck, Ulrich (1992). *Risk Society: Towards a New Modernity Vol. 17*, London: Sage.
Belton, John (2002). Digital Cinema: A False Revolution. *October* 100, *Obsolescence* (Spring), pp. 98–114.
Bennett, Jane (1997). The Enchanted World of Modernity. Paracelsus, Kant, and Deleuze. In *Journal for Cultural Research* 1 (1), pp. 1–28.
—— (2001). *The Enchantment of Modern Life: Attachments, Crossings, and Ethics*, Oxfordshire: Princeton University Press.
Bhabha, Homi K. (1998). The White Stuff. *Artforum*, May 36 (9), pp. 21–23.
Bignell, Jonathan (2004). Another Time, Another Space: Subjectivity and the Time Machine. In Sean Redmond (ed.). *Liquid Metal: The Science Fiction Film Reader*, London: Wallflower Press, pp. 136–144.
Bonnett, Alistair (2000). *White Identities: Historical and International Perspectives*, Harlow: Prentice Hall.
Bordwell, David (2002). Intensified Continuity: Visual Style in Contemporary American Film. *Film Quarterly* 55 (3), pp. 16–28.
Bould, Mark (2012). *Science Fiction (Routledge Film Guidebooks)*, London: Routledge.
Bourdieu Pierre (1990) [1980]. Structures, Habitus, Practices. In *The Logic of Practice*, Stanford: Stanford University Press, pp. 52–65.
Boyle, Karen (2009). *Children of Men* and *I Am Legend*: The Disaster-Capitalism Complex Hits Hollywood. *Jump Cut* 51 (Spring). Available at: www.ejumpcut.org/archive/jc51.2009/ChildrenMenLegend/text.html (accessed 1 July 2015).
Brooker, William (2004). Living on *Dawson's Creek*: Teen Viewers, Cultural Convergence, and Television Overflow. In Robert Allen and Annette Hill (eds). *The Television Studies Reader*, New York: Routledge, pp. 569–580.
Brophy, Philip. (1986). Horrality – The Textuality of Contemporary Horror Films. *Screen* 27 (1), pp. 2–13.
Bruno, Giuliana (1987). Ramble City: Postmodernism and 'Blade Runner'. *October* 41 (Summer), pp. 61–74.
Brynjolfsson, Erik (2015). The Great Decoupling: An Interview with Erik Brynjolfsson. Available at: https://hbr.org/2015/06/the-great-decoupling (accessed 3 October 2015).
Brynjolfsson, Erik and McAfee, Andrew (2014). *The Second Machine Age: Work, Progress, and Prosperity in a Time of Brilliant Technologies*, New York: W. Norton and Company.
Bukatman, Scott (1999). The Artificial Infinite: On Special Effects and the Sublime. *Alien Zone II*, London. Verso, pp. 249–276.
Castells, Manuel and Cardoso, Gustavo (2005). *The Network Society: From Knowledge to Policy*, Washington, DC: Johns Hopkins Center for Transatlantic Relations.
Chaudhary, Zahid R. (2009). Humanity Adrift: Race, Materiality, and Allegory in Alfonso Cuarón's *Children of Men*. *Camera Obscura* 24.3 72, pp. 73–109.
Chion, Michel (1994). *Audio-Vision: Sound on Screen*, New York: Columbia University Press.

Colebrook, Claire (2005). The Space of Man: On the Specificity of Affect in Deleuze and Guattari. In Ian Buchanan and Gregg Lambert (eds). *Deleuze and Space*, Edinburgh: Edinburgh University Press, pp. 189–206.
—— (2009). Stratigraphic Time, Women's Time. *Australian Feminist Studies* 24 (59), pp. 11–16.
—— (2012). A Globe of One's Own: In Praise of the Flat Earth. *SubStance* 127 (41), pp. 30–39.
Coley, Rob and Lockwood, Dean (2015). As Above, So Below: Triangulating Drone Culture. *Culture Machine* 16, pp. 11–19.
Cranny-Francis, Anne (2015). Robots, Androids, Aliens, and Others: The Erotics and Politics of Science Fiction Film. In Sean Redmond and Leon Marvell (eds). *Endangering Science Fiction Film*, New York: Routledge, pp. 220–242.
Cubitt, Sean (1998). *Digital Aesthetics*, London: Sage.
—— (2004). *The Cinema Effect*, Cambridge: MIT Press.
D'Adamo, Amedeo (2015). The People Beyond Mars: Using Robinson's Mars Trilogy to Understand Post-Scarcity. *Thesis Eleven* 131, pp. 81–98.
Debord, Guy (1994). *The Society of the Spectacle*. Translated by Donald Nicholson-Smith, New York: Zone Books.
Deleuze, Gilles (1986). *Cinema 1: The Movement Image*. Translated by Hugh Tomlinson and Barbara Habberjam, Minneapolis: University of Minnesota Press.
—— (1989). *Cinema 2: The Time-Image*. Translated by Hugh Tomlinson and Robert Caleta, Minneapolis: University of Minnesota Press.
—— (2003). *Francis Bacon: The Logic of Sensation*: University of Minnesota Press.
Deleuze, Gilles and Guattari, Felix (1987). *A Thousand Plateaus*. Translated by B. Massumi, London: Athlone.
Doane, Mary Ann (1980). The Voice in the Cinema: The Articulation of Body and Space, *Yale French Studies* 60, pp. 33–50.
Doctor Who: The Classic Series. Available at: www.bbc.co.uk/doctorwho/classic/episodeguide/cityofdeath/detail.shtml
Downey, Christine (2007). Life on Mars, or How the Breaking of Genre Rules Revitalises the Crime Fiction Tradition. *Crime Culture*. Available at: www.crimeculture.com/Contents/Articles-Summer07/Life_on_Mars.html
Du Gay, Paul (1997). *Production of Culture/Cultures of Production*, London: Sage.
Dyer, Richard (1988). White. In *Screen* 29 (44), p. 4.
—— (1997). *White*, London: Routledge.
Eagleton, Terry (1990). The Ideology of the Aesthetic. In P. Hernadi (ed.). *The Rhetoric of Interpretation and the Interpretation of Rhetoric*, Durham, NC: Duke University Press, pp. 75–86.
Ellsworth, Elizabeth (1997). Double Binds of Whiteness. In M. Fine, L. Weis, L. Powell and M. Wong (eds). *Off White: Readings on Race, Power, and Society*, London: Routledge, pp. 259–269.
Elsaesser, Thomas (1996). Subject Positions, Speaking Positions: From *Holocaust*, *Our Hitler* and *Heimat* to *Shoah* and *Schindler's List*. In

Vivian Sobchack (ed.). *The Persistence of History: Cinema, Television and the Modern Event*, New York: Routledge, pp. 145–183.

Elsaesser, Thomas and Hagener, Malte (2015). *Film Theory: An Introduction Through the Senses*, New York: Routledge.

Enticknap, Leo (2005). *Moving Image Technology: From Zoetrope to Digital*, London: Wallflower Press.

Feuer, Jane (1983). The Concept of Live Television: Ontology as Ideology. In E. Ann Kaplan (ed.). *Regarding Television*, Los Angeles: American Film Institute, pp. 12–22.

Finnegan, Ruth (1997). Storying the Self: Personal Narratives and Identity. In H. Mackay (ed.). *Consumption and Everyday Life*, Milton Keynes: Open University Press, pp. 65–112.

Fiske, John (1987). *Television Culture*, London: Methuen.

Forkert, Kirsten (2014). The New Moralism: Austerity, Silencing and Debt Morality. *Soundings: A Journal of Politics and Culture* 56 (Spring), pp. 41–53.

Foucault, Michel (1975). *Discipline and Punish: The Birth of the Prison*, New York: Random House.

Freeman, Elizabeth (2010). *Time Binds: Queer Temporalities, Queer Histories*, Durham: Duke University Press.

Friedberg, Anne (2006). *The Virtual Window: From Alberti to Microsoft*, Cambridge, MA: MIT Press.

Gardner, Jared (2010). Avatar: Blueface, Whitenoise. *The HuffPost Blog*. Available at: www.huffingtonpost.com/jared-gardner/emavatarem-blueface-white_b_409522.html (accessed 6 March 2014).

Gelder, Ken (1994). *Reading the Vampire*, London: Routledge.

Giddens, Anthony (1990). *The Consequences of Modernity*, Stanford, CA: Stanford University Press.

Gordon, Andrew (1987). Back to the Future: Oedipus as Time Traveller. In Sean Redmond (ed.) (2004). *Liquid Metal: The Science Fiction Film Reader*, London: Wallflower Press, pp. 116–125.

Grant, Barry Keith (2004). Sensuous Elaboration: Reason and the Visible in the Science Fiction Film. In Sean Redmond (ed.). *Liquid Metal: The Science Fiction Film Reader*, London: Wallflower Press.

Greene, Brian (2011). *The Elegant Universe: Superstrings, Hidden Dimensions, and the Quest for the Ultimate Theory*, Vintage.

Gunning, Tom (1986). The Cinema of Attractions: Early Film, Its Spectator and the Avant-Garde. *Wide Angle* 8 (3,4).

——— (1989). Primitive Cinema, a Frame-up? or The Trick's on Us. *Cinema Journal* 28 (2), pp. 3–12.

——— (1994). *D.W. Griffith and the Origins of American Narrative Film: The Early Years at Biograph*, Urbana: University of Illinois Press.

——— (2010). Landscape and the Fantasy of Moving Pictures: Early Cinema's Phantom Rides. In Graeme Harper and Jonathan Rayner (eds). *Cinema and Landscape*, Chicago: Intellect Books, pp. 31–70.

Gutierrez, Christopher M. (2006). Bodies of Terror/Terrorizing Bodies: Diss. Concordia University (unpublished). Available at: http://spectrum.library.concordia.ca/8758/1/MR14200.pdf

Hall, Stuart (2011). The Neo-Liberal Revolution. *Cultural Studies* 25 (6).

Harris, Richard and Larkham, Peter (eds) (2003). *Changing Suburbs: Foundation, Form and Function*, London: Routledge.

Hayles, N. Katherine (1993). Virtual Bodies and Flickering Signifiers. 66 (Fall), pp. 69–91.

—— (1999). *How We Became Posthuman: Virtual Bodies in Cybernetics*, Chicago: University of Chicago Press.

Hobson, Janell (2008). Digital Whiteness, Primitive Blackness. *Feminist Media Studies* 8 (2), pp. 111–126.

Hooks, Bell (1994). *Outlaw Culture: Resisting Representations*, London: Routledge.

Jameson, Fredric (1991). *Postmodernism, or the Cultural Logic of Late Capitalism*, Durham: Duke University Press.

Jankovich, Mark (2004). Re-examining the 1950s Invasion Narratives. In Sean Redmond (ed.). *Liquid Metal: The Science Fiction Film Reader*, London: Wallflower Press, pp. 325–336.

Jansson, André (2008). *Mobile Belongings: Texturation and Stratification in Mediatization Processes*, Karlstad: unpublished paper.

Jenkins, Henry (2001). Convergence, I diverge. *Technology Review*. June. Available at: www.technologyreview.com/business/12434/

Kakoudaki, Despina (2002). Spectacles of History: Race Relations, Melodrama, and the Science Fiction/Disaster Film. *Camera Obscura* 17 (2), pp. 1–153.

Kant, Immanuel (1960). *Observations on the Feeling of the Beautiful and Sublime*, Berkeley/Los Angeles: University of California Press.

Kaplan, E. Ann (1997). *Looking for the Other: Nation, Woman and Desire in Film*, London: Routledge.

Kavanagh, H. James (1990). Feminism, Humanism and Science in Alien. In Annette Kuhn (ed.). *Alien Zone*, London: Verso, pp. 73–81.

Keane, Stephen (2007). *CineTech Film, Convergence and New Media*, London: Palgrave.

Kehr, Dave (2006). You Can Make 'Em Like They Used To, The New York Times, 12 November 2006. Available at: www.nytimes.com/2006/11/12/movies/12kehr.html?pagewanted=all

Kellner, Douglas (1995). *Media Culture: Cultural Studies, Identity and Politics Between the Modern and the Postmodern*, London: Routledge.

Kirby, David (2000). The New Eugenics in Cinema: Genetic Determinism and Gene Therapy in GATTACA. *Science Fiction Studies* 27 (2), pp. 193–215.

Klinger, Barbara (2012). Cave of Forgotten Dreams: Mediations on 3D. *Film Quarterly* 65 (3), p. 39.

Knight, Deborah and McKnight, George (2015). Narrative, Aesthetics and Cultural Imperatives in Recent Science Fiction Films. In Sean

Redmond and Leon Marvell (eds). *Endangering Science Fiction Film*, New York: Routledge, pp. 89–102.
Knight, Peter. (ed.) (2002). *Conspiracy Nation: The Politics of Paranoia in Postwar America*, New York: New York University Press.
Kolker, Robert (1980). *A Cinema of Loneliness: Penn, Stone, Kubrick, Scorsese, Spielberg, Altman*, New York: Oxford University Press.
Kompare, Derek (2005). We Are So Screwed: Invasion TV. *Flow* 3 (6): http://jot.communication.utexas.edu/flow/?jot=view&id=1304 (accessed 23 March 2007).
Kristeva, Julia (1997). *Intimate Revolt*. Translated by Jeanine Herman (2002), New York: Columbia University Press.
Kuhn, Annette (1994). *Women's Pictures: Feminism and Cinema*, London: Verso.
Levi, Mica (2014). Interview. *Pitchfork*, 31 March. Available at: http://pitchfork.com/features/interviews/9366-under-the-skins-jonathan-glazer-and-mica-levi/ (accessed 6 April 2014).
Levy, Emanuel (2009). Road, The: Cinematographer Javier Aguirresarobe, 7 September. Available at: http://emanuellevy.com/comment/road-the-cinematographer-javier-aguirresarobe-2/
Lyon, David (1998). The World Wide Web of Surveillance: The Internet and Off-World Power-Flows. *Information, Communication and Society*, pp. 1–9.
Lyotard, Jean-François (1979). *The Postmodern Condition*: Manchester University Press.
MacCormack, Patricia (2008). *Cinesexuality*, Aldershot: Ashgate.
Manovich, Lev (2006). The Poetics of Augmented Space. *Visual Communication*, June 2006 5 (2), pp. 219–240.
Marks, Laura U. (2000). *The Skin of Film: Intercultural Cinema, Embodiment, and the Senses*, Durham: Duke University Press.
McMahan, Alison (2005). *The Films of Tim Burton: Animating Live Action in Contemporary Hollywood*, New York: Continuum.
Meehan, Eileen (1991). 'Holy Commodity Fetish, Batman!' The Economics of a Commercial Intertext. In W. Uricchio and R.E. Pearson (eds). *The Many Lives of the Batman: Critical Approaches to a Superhero and His Media*, London: British Film Institute and Routledge, pp. 47–65.
Metz, Christian (1982). *The Imaginary Signifier: Psychoanalysis and the Cinema*, Bloomington: Indiana University Press.
Milburn, Colin (2002). Nanotechnology in the Age of Posthuman Engineering: Science Fiction as Science. *Configurations* 10 (2), pp. 261–295.
Mirrlees, Tanner (2014). How to Read Iron Man: the Economics, Politics and Ideology of an Imperial Film Commodity. *CineAction*, 92 (2), pp. 4–11.
Mitchell, William J. (2003). *Me++ The Cyborg Self and the Networked City*, Cambridge, MA: The MIT Press.
Mittag, Martina (2009). Rethinking Deterritorialization: Utopian and Apocalyptic Space in Recent American Fiction. *Spatial Practices: An Interdisciplinary Series in Cultural History* 9, p. 251.

Monbiot, George (2014). The Age of Loneliness is Killing Us. *The Guardian*. 14 October. Available at: www.theguardian.com/commentisfree/2014/oct/14/age-of-loneliness-killing-us (accessed 4 November 2014).

Moulton, Carter (2012). *The Future is a Fairground: Attraction and Absorption in 3D Cinema*. CineAction 89.

Mulvey, Laura (1975). Visual Pleasure and Narrative Cinema. *Screen* 16 (2), pp. 6–18.

—— (1981). Afterthoughts on 'Visual Pleasure and Narrative Cinema'. Inspired by 'Duel in the Sun'. *Framework*, nos 15/16/17, pp. 12–15.

Napier, Susan J. (2004). Ghost and Machines: The Technological Body. In Sean Redmond (ed.). *Liquid Metal: The Science Fiction Film Reader*, London: Wallflower Press, pp. 205–215.

Ndalianis, Angela (2000a). Baroque Perceptual Regimes. *Senses of Cinema*, 5 (April). Available at: http://sensesofcinema.com/2000/conference-special-effects-special-affects/baroque/ (accessed 28 June 2015).

—— (2000b). *The Frenzy of the Visible: Spectacle and Motion in the Era of the Digital*. Senses of Cinema 3.

—— (2004). *Neo-Baroque Aesthetics and Contemporary Entertainment*, Cambridge, MA: MIT Press.

Neimanis, Astrida (2014). Speculative Reproduction: Biotechnologies and Ecologies in Thick Time. *philoSOPHIA* 4 (1), pp. 108–128.

Nye, David E. (1994). *The American Technological Sublime*, Cambridge: MIT Press.

Petersen, Christina (2015). *The Address of the Ass: D-BOX Motion Effects and Focalized Immersive Viewing*, pp. 1–11. Conference paper presented at Society for Cinema and Media Studies, Fairmont Queen Elizabeth Hotel, Montreal, Canada, 25–29 March.

Pheasant-Kelly, Fran (2015). Experiments at the Margins: Ethics and Transgression in Cinema Science. *Thesis Eleven* 131 (1), pp. 28–43.

Pierson, Michele (1999). No Longer State-of-the-Art: Crafting a Future for CGI. *Wide Angle* 21 (1), pp. 29–47.

—— (2002). *Special Effects: Still in Search of Wonder*, New York: Columbia University Press.

Pieterse, Jan Nederveen (2000). *Global Futures: Shaping Globalization*, London: Zed Books.

Pink, Sarah (2009). *Doing Sensory Ethnography*, London: Sage.

Prince, Stephen (1996). True Lies: Perceptual Realism, Digital Images, and Film Theory. *Film Quarterly* 49 (3), pp. 27–37.

Redmond, Sean (2005). When Planes Fall Out of the Sky. In Karen Randell and Sean Redmond (eds). *The War Body on Screen*, New York: Continuum, pp. 22–35.

—— (2011). Sounding Alien, Touching the Future: Beyond the Sonorous Limit in Science Fiction Film. *New Review of Film and Television Studies* 9 (1), pp. 42–56.

—— (2015). Introduction. *The Companion to Celebrity*, New York: Wiley.

Redmond, Sean and Sita, Jodi (2013). *My Sherlockian Eyes: An Introduction To The Work Of The Eye-Tracking And Moving Image Research Group, April, CSTONLINE*. Available at: http://cstonline.tv/sherlockian-eyes (accessed 10 January 2014).
Ross, Miriam (2015). *The Future Is a Fairground: Attraction and Absorption in 3D Cinema*, London: Palgrave MacMillan.
Rowe, P.G. (1993). *Modernity and Housing*, Cambridge, MA: MIT Press.
Ryan, Michael and Kellner, Douglas (1990). Technophobia. In Annette Kuhn (ed.). *Alien Zone: Cultural Theory and Contemporary Science Fiction Cinema*, London: Verso, pp. 58–65.
Sardar, Ziauddin and Cubitt, Sean (2002). *Aliens R Us: The Other in Science Fiction Cinema*, London: Pluto Press.
Schatz, Thomas (1993). The New Hollywood. In Jim Collins, Hilary Radner and Ava Collins (eds). *Film Theory Goes to the Movies*, London: Routledge.
Shaviro, Steven (2002). Capitalist Monsters. *Historical Materialism* 10 (4), pp. 281–290.
—— (2010). *Post-Cinematic Affect*, Winchester: Zero Books.
—— (2011). Post-Continuity. *The Pinocchio Theory*, August. Available at: www.shaviro.com/Blog/?p=1003
Silverman, Kaja (1988). *The Acoustic Mirror: The Female Voice in Psychoanalysis and Cinema*, Bloomington: Indiana University Press, p. 99.
Sobchack, Vivian (1987). *Screening Space: The American Science Fiction Film*, New Jersey: Rutgers University Press.
—— (1999). Cities on the Edge of Time: The Urban Science-Fiction Film. In Annette Kuhn (ed.). *Alien Zone II*, London: Verso, pp. 123–146.
—— (2000). What My Fingers Knew: The Cinesthetic Subject, or Vision in the Flesh. *Senses of Cinema*. Available at: www.sensesofcinema.com/2000/5/fingers/
—— (2004). *Carnal Thoughts: Embodiment and Moving Image Culture*, Berkeley: University of California Press.
—— (2005). When the Ear Dreams: Dolby Digital and the Imagination of Sound. *FILM QUART* 58 (4), pp. 2–15.
Sontag, Susan (2004). The Imagination of Disaster. In Sean Redmond (ed.). *Liquid Metal: The Science Fiction Film Reader*, London: Wallflower Press, pp. 40–47.
Spielmann, Y. (1999). Aesthetic Features in Digital Imaging: Collage and Morph. *Wide Angle* 21 (1).
Spivak, Gayatri Chakavorty (2004). Terror: A Speech after 9/11. *Boundary 2* 31 (2), pp. 81–111.
Stacey, Jackie (1987). Desperately Seeking Difference. *Screen* 28 (1), pp. 48–61.
—— (2000). The Global Within: Consuming Nature, Embodying Health. In Franklin, Sarah, Lury, Celia and Jackie Stacey. *Global Nature, Global Culture*, London: Sage, pp. 97–145.
—— (2005). Masculinity, Masquerade and Genetic Disguise in Gattaca's Double Vision. *Signs: A Journal of Women, Culture and Society* 30 (3), pp. 1851–1879.

Steers, Mai-Ly N., Wickham, Robert E. and Acitelli, Linda K. (2014). Seeing Everyone Else's Highlight Reels: How Facebook Usage is Linked to Depressive Symptoms. *Journal of Social and Clinical Psychology* 33 (8), pp. 701–731.

Stewart, Garrett (2008). *Framed Time: Toward a Postfilmic Cinema*, Chicago: University of Chicago Press.

Suvin, Darko (1979). *Metamorphoses of Science Fiction: On the Poetics and History of a Literary Genre*, New Haven: Yale University Press.

Taubin, Amy (1993). The Alien Trilogy: From Feminism to Aids. In Pam Cook and Philip Dodd (eds). *Women and Film: A Sight and Sound Reader*, London: Scarlet Press, pp. 93–100.

Telotte, J.P. (1990). The Doubles of Fantasy and the Space of Desire. In Annette Kuhn (ed.). *Alien Zone*, London: Verso, pp. 152–159.

Thompson, Kirsten Moana (2012). *Apocalyptic Dread: American Film at the Turn of the Millennium*, New York: SUNY Press.

Tuck, Greg (2008). When More is Less: CGI, Spectacle and the Capitalist Sublime. *Science Fiction Film & Television* 1 (2), pp. 249–273.

Vint, Sheryl (2015). Biopolitics and the War on Terror in World War Z and Monsters. In Sean Redmond and Leon Marvell (eds). *Endangering Science Fiction Film*, New York: AFI Film Reader series, pp. 66–80.

Virilio, Paul (1997). *Open Sky*, London: Verso.

Waldby, Catherine (2015). Circuits of Desire: Internet Erotics and the Problem of Bodily Location. Available at: www.mcc.murdoch.edu.au/readingroom/VID/Circuits3.html

Walker, Ben (2007). The Digital Surreal. Available at: http://surfacedetail.com/wp-content/uploads/2008/09/the_digital_surreal.pdf

Whissel, Kristen (2006). Tales of Upward Mobility: The New Verticality and Digital Special Effects. *Film Quarterly* 59 (4), pp. 23–34.

Whittington, William (2007). *Sound Design and Science Fiction*, Austin: University of Texas Press.

—— (2011). Sound design for a found future: Alfonso Cuarón's Children of Men. *New Review of Film and Television Studies* 9 (1), pp. 3–14.

Wilcox, Rhonda (1996). Dating Data. In Taylor Harrison and Sarah Projansky (eds). *Enterprise Zones: Critical Positions on Star Trek*, Oxford: Westview Press.

Williams, Raymond (1974/1992). *Television: Technology and Cultural Form*, Hanover, NH: Wesleyan University Press.

Wood, Alison (2007). *Digital Encounters*, London: Routledge.

Yip, Man-Fung (2014). In the Realm of the Senses: Sensory Realism, Speed, and Hong Kong Martial Arts Cinema. *Cinema Journal* 53 (4), pp. 76–97.

Žižek, Slavoj (2007). Children of Men. Available at: www.youtube.com/watch?v=pbgrwNP_gYE (last accessed 11 September 2015).

Index

3D, 2, 13, 65, 77
4D technology, 62, 75, 76, 78
6th Day, The, 124
24, 134
28 Days Later, 121, 124, 125
2001: A Space Odyssey, 64, 108, 145, 169

Abbott, Stacey, 16
Abrams, J. J., 121, 134
Abudd, Yolanda, 114
aca-fandom, 20
Acitelli, Linda K., 69
acousmêtre, 150–154, 158, 165
actants, 11
action (film), 15, 55, 77, 121, 129
Adams, Paul, 119
Adjustment Bureau, The, 15
aesthetic, 2, 6, 7, 10, 13, 15, 19, 43, 62, 65, 66, 76, 77, 85, 88, 92, 94, 115, 128, 129, 154, 174
  (theme-park) ride, 42, 47, 55
affect, 4, 10, 11, 17, 21, 22, 25, 26, 27, 32, 46, 47, 52, 54, 66, 67, 73, 74, 77, 84, 85, 129, 130, 131, 134, 139, 142, 145, 150, 151, 152, 153, 154, 164, 172, 173, 178, 180
Agamben, Giorgio, 130
Aguirresarobe, Javier, 85
Agyeman, Freema, 35
Alias, 134
Alien, 81, 88, 101, 108, 112–113, 158, 173
alien (extraterrestrial), 18, 19, 27, 28, 44, 48, 50, 64, 70, 80, 81, 82, 87, 101, 103, 104, 105, 106, 107, 108, 109, 112, 119, 121, 124, 125, 126, 130, 143, 144, 148, 149, 150, 151, 152, 153, 154, 155, 156, 157, 158, 159, 160, 161, 162, 165, 166, 169, 170, 172
Allen, Kim, 168
Ameen, Amal, 67
Anderson, Paul W. S., 124
android *see* cyborg
Ang, Ien, 24
anime, 94
Ant-Man, 41
Antena, La, 153–154
Anthropocene *see* apocalypse
apocalypse (Anthropocene), 16, 48, 82, 85, 86, 121, 126, 132, 137, 148, 156, 170, 180
  post-apocalypse, 86
applications (digital), 1, 5, 9
Aroshas, Deborah, 1
artificial intelligence (AI)
  see cyborg
Artificial Intelligence: AI, 124
Ashes to Ashes, 36
Ashitey, Claire-Hope, 128
Astronaut's Wife, The, 87
augmentation, 1, 2, 3, 10, 18, 36, 62, 81, 155, 172, 181
austerity
auto-ethnography, 20, 176, 177
automated dialogue replacement (ADR), 148
Avatar, 48, 49, 101, 102, 118, 119, 171
Avila, Eric, 103, 107

INDEX

Baker, Tom, 27
Bakula, Scott, 29
Balchin, Paul N., 26
Banlieue 13, 124
Barad, Karen, 40
Barthes, Roland, 152
Baudrillard, Jean, 134, 139
Bauman, Zygmunt, 9, 36, 59, 69, 119, 131
Bay, Michael, 15, 16, 60, 124
Beck, Ulrich, 172–173
Belton, John, 4
Bennett, Jane, 57, 156
Bezaleal Academy of Art and Design, 1
Bhabba, Homi, 100
Big Bash Cricket, 179
Bigelow, Kathryn, 63
Bignell, Jonathan, 28
Black Mirror, 60
 'Fifteen Million Merits', 17
Blade Runner, 43, 113–114, 144
blockbuster, 11, 14, 40, 41, 42, 47, 75
Blomkamp, Neill, 95, 102, 114, 116
Blunt, Emily, 15
Bonnett, Alastair, 104, 118, 119, 120
Bordwell, David, 14
Bould, Mark, 54
Bourdieu, Pierre, 22
Bowie, David, 36
box, 18, 23–38, 78, 177, 179, 180
Boyle, Danny, 43, 121, 124
Breaching Transmissions, 175–176, 177
Bread, 179
Bridle, James, 141
Broken Arrow, 118
Brooker, William, 32
Brooks, Richard, 168
Brophy, Philip, 49
Bruno, Giuliana, 46
Brynjolfsson, Erik, 95
Bukatman, Scott, 53
bullet-time, 12
Byung-Chun, Min, 124

Cahn, Edward L., 107
Caine, Michael, 129
Cameron, James, 11, 48, 92, 101, 159, 171
Campbell, Martin, 134
capitalism, 23, 26, 38, 41, 50, 58, 86, 173
 liquid, 14, 42, 50, 58, 86, 173
Carpenter, John, 49

Casino Royale, 134
Cassidy, Shaun
Castells, Manuel, 6, 7
celebrity (stardom), 71
Chappie, 95
Chaudhary, Zahid, 75, 138
Chen, Kaige, 164
chiaroscuro, 149
Children of Men, 19, 75, 124, 125, 127, 128–139, 173
Chion, Michel, 151, 152, 162, 164, 165, 167
chrononormativity, 38, 40
cinema of attractions, 77
cinematography, 44, 55, 63, 85, 130
Clayton, Amie, 67
Clennon, David, 49
cloud, 8
clone, 8, 16, 18, 80, 82, 86, 96, 117, 124, 127, 160
Cold War, 103, 104
Colebrook, Claire, 38, 85
Coleman, Jenna, 35
Coley, Rob, 141
Commando Cody: Sky Marshal of the Universe, 104
commodification, 5, 13, 33, 42, 43, 46, 47, 50, 55, 56, 57
computer-generated imagery (CGI), 2, 3, 4, 33, 49, 58, 78, 174
Conran, Kerry, 124
conspiracy
consumption, 17, 18, 40, 42, 50, 57, 58, 69, 76, 107, 131, 144
Containment, 124
continuity, 14, 15
 post-continuity, 15
 traditional, 16
Continuum, 11
convergence, 31, 32, 33, 181
 culture, 22
Copley, Sharlto, 116
Cornell, Alex, 141
Cotton, Maxwell Perry, 114
coverage, 10
Cranny-Francis, Anne, 87
crime, 36, 37, 63
Cruise, Tom, 61, 125, 170
Cuarón, Alfonso, 19, 65, 75, 124, 131

INDEX 193

Cubitt, Sean, 8, 47
cultural praxis, 8
Cumberbatch, Benedict, 121
cybernetic, 3, 11
cyborg (AI), 3, 18, 80, 82, 89, 90, 91, 92, 94, 95, 96, 111, 124, 144, 150, 159, 172, 181
  cyborgian life, 4
  humanist, 92, 93
  pathological, 93

D-BOX, 76, 77, 78
da Vinci, Leonardo, 27
D'Adamo, Amedeo, 80
Dallas, 24
Damon, Matt, 15, 115, 116
Dances With Wolves, 118
data (information), 1, 8–9, 11, 18, 19, 61, 81, 141
Day After Tomorrow, The, 124
Day the Earth Stood Still, The (1951), 104, 105
Day the Earth Stood Still, The (2008), 14, 91
De Benedictis, Sara, 168
Debord, Guy, 35, 47, 56, 57
del Toro, Guillermo, 48
Deleuze, Gilles, 13, 45, 54, 58, 74, 78, 83, 86, 88, 147, 149, 155, 177
  movement image, 13
  time image, 13, 54
dematerialisation, 9, 78, 89, 181
  digital, 8
Dern, Bruce, 111
Derrickson, Scott, 14
Desai, Tina, 67
Destination Moon, 106
deterritorialisation, 5, 6, 18, 60, 61, 62, 66, 68, 72, 73, 75, 78, 133, 143, 146, 151, 162, 167, 177
digital *see* liquid
District 9, 116, 173
distribution, 12
Doane, Mary Anne, 160
Doctor Who (*Dr Who*), 14, 21, 22, 26, 30, 33, 119, 169, 180
  'Big Bang, The', 34
  'Blink', 34
  'City of Death, The', 27
  'Doctor Dances, The', 91

'Empty Child, The', 91
'Forest of the Dead', 34
'God Complex, The', 34
'Night Terrors', 34
'Robots of Death, The', 27
'Smith and Jones', 34
'Waters of Mars', 14
Donaldson, Roger, 88, 159, 172
Doona, Bae, 67
doubling, 92, 152, 155, 161, 162
Downey, Christine, 37
dreamscapes, 4, 17
Drone Shadows, 141
drones, 140–142
du Gay, Paul, 73
Dyer, Richard, 100, 101, 109, 113, 114, 117, 132
dystopia, 3, 13, 48, 60, 80, 82, 85, 92, 93, 124

Eagleton, Terry, 19
Edge of Tomorrow, 170, 180
editing, 10, 11, 13, 14, 15, 36, 74
effect, 4, 5, 15, 25, 26, 32, 64, 77, 106, 165
  analogue (mechanical) (plastic), 25, 32, 36
  audio (sound), 1
  digital, 5, 32, 33, 34, 40, 49, 64, 77, 174
  liquid, 18, 41, 59
  science fiction, 49
  sound, 148, 164
  special, 1, 4, 5, 6, 7, 11, 14, 16, 18, 21, 22, 23, 24, 25, 26, 27, 28, 29, 31, 32, 33, 34, 35, 36, 40, 41, 44, 47, 49, 57, 59, 64, 66, 78, 80, 102, 103, 105, 144, 145, 146, 172, 174, 175, 177
  visual, 11, 49, 106
Ejiofor, Chiwetel, 129
Ellsworth, Elizabeth, 109
Elsaesser, Thomas, 134, 150
Elysium, 102, 114–116
embodiment, 19, 20, 29, 30, 35, 38, 39, 42, 43, 60, 68, 71, 75, 76, 84, 85, 89, 90, 99, 128, 129, 133, 146, 150, 151, 154, 155, 156, 160, 162, 165, 172
  erotic, 89
  radical, 4
Emery, John, 104
Emmerich, Roland, 43, 50, 124
enchantment, 57–58, 156

INDEX

Enemy Mine, 87
Enticknap, Leo, 77
Equilibrium, 60, 124
Eternal Sunshine of the Spotless Mind, 126
eugenics, 97, 99, 133
Ever Since the World Ended, 124, 125
Evil Aliens, 87
Ex Machina, 96
Extraterrestrial, 151
extraterrestrial see alien
eye-tracking, 18, 40, 42–45, 47, 50, 51, 52, 55, 60, 61, 99
Ezban, Isaac, 170

Facebook, 5
Faculty, The, 87
Falling Skies, 124
fantasy, 77
Farrell, Colin, 83
fastness, 16, 17
feminine, 94, 156, 160
 monstrous-feminism, 158
feminism, 39, 167
 material, 39
 post-feminism, 168
Ferris, Pam, 129, 135
Feuer, Jane, 23
film (cinema), science fiction, 2, 3, 4, 5, 6, 7, 9, 10, 11, 12, 13, 15, 16, 17, 18, 19, 29, 41, 42, 43, 44, 46, 48, 49, 54, 59, 60, 62, 64, 65, 66, 73, 79, 82, 85, 87, 89, 92, 93, 96, 100, 101, 102, 103, 104, 105, 106, 108, 111, 114, 120, 121, 123, 124, 125, 127, 131, 140, 143, 144, 145, 148, 151, 152, 153, 159, 168, 169, 171, 172, 173, 174, 181
film and television industry, 7
filmmaking, 2, 6, 10, 15, 17, 63
Finnegan, Ruth, 20
Fiske, John, 23
Flash Gordon, 178
flow, 6, 7, 9, 10, 13, 14, 23, 32, 52, 62, 74
 overflow, 31, 32, 33
Fly, The, 173
Forbidden Planet, 110, 111, 112
Ford, Harrison, 113
Forkert, Kirsten, 69
Foster, Jodi, 116
Foucault, Michel, 23, 60, 98
Freeman, Elizabeth, 39

Friedberg, Anne, 77

gaming, 42
 4D, 76
Gardner, Jared, 118
Garland, Alex, 96
Gattaca, 97–99
Gelder, Ken, 107
gender, 18, 93, 96, 97, 98, 156, 157, 160, 161, 168, 172
genre, 77, 103, 148, 164, 173, 174
gestalt, 23
Giddens, Anthony, 66
Gillan, Karen, 35
Giron, Valentina, 114
Glazer, Jonathan, 68
Gleeson, Domnhall, 96
Glenister, Philip, 36
globalisation, 66, 124, 128, 131
Godfather, The, 47
Godzilla, 43, 45, 50, 55, 57, 58, 59
GoggleBox, 179
Golad, Ori, 1
Golding, Sally, 175
Gordon, Andrew, 29
Grant, Barry Keith, 44
Grant, Calum, 124
gravity, 62, 63, 64, 65, 66, 75
Gravity, 65, 78
Greene, Brian, 38
Greengrass, Paul, 15
Guattari, Félix, 74, 86, 147, 155
Gunning, Tom, 77
Gutierrez, Chris, 133

Hagener, Malte, 150
Hales, Kathryn
Hall, Stuart, 70
Hamilton, Linda, 148
haptics, 4, 5, 42, 44, 52, 59, 78, 134, 177
Harris, Richard, 23
Hawke, Ethan, 97, 99
Hayles, N. Katherine, 4, 172
hegemony, 101, 134
Helix, 124
Henstridge, Natasha, 88
Her, 89, 90, 94
heterotopia, 25, 35, 38
Hillcoat, John, 16, 80
Hirschbiegel, Oliver, 87
Hitchcock, Alfred, 63

INDEX

Hobson, Janell, 108
Hollywood, 6, 12, 14, 40, 107, 114, 118, 119, 157, 167, 174
  New Hollywood, 14, 47
Holocaust, 134
hooks, bell, 109
horror, 77, 85
Hostel, 134
Humans, 95, 124
Hunger Games, The, 74, 123

I, Robot, 91, 124
identity, 18, 19, 82, 93, 101, 111, 113, 115, 122, 132, 134, 150, 155, 156, 157, 160, 161, 172
In Time, 13
Inception, 126
Incident, The (El Incidente), 170, 180
Independence Day, 50
Industrial Revolution, 95
information *see* data
interface, 3, 4, 8, 11, 32, 35, 66, 89
  para-interface, 8
Interstellar, 80, 124, 147, 169, 171
intertext, 46, 47, 57
Invasion, (2005), 87, 130
Invasion, The (2007), 87
Invasion of the Body Snatchers, 152
Iron Man, 173–174
Isaac, Oscar, 96
Island, The, 16, 60, 124
isolation *see* loneliness
It! The Terror from Beyond Outer Space, 107

Jameson, Fredric, 59
Jameson, Louise, 27
Jankovich, Mark, 103, 104–105
Jansson, André, 8
Jaws, 47
Jenkins, Henry, 32
Jha, Manish, 124
Johansson, Scarlet, 70, 71, 73, 89, 168
Jones, Duncan, 117
Jonze, Spike, 89

Kakoudaki, Despina
Kant, Immanuel, 48
Kaplan, E. Ann, 104, 106
Kavanagh, H. James, 112
Keane, Stephen, 11, 12
Kehr, Dave, 10

Kellner, Douglas, 48, 164
Kemmer, Ed, 107
Kirby, David, 97, 98
Klinger, Barbara, 77
knowledge, 5, 19, 49, 71, 127
  commercialised, 5
  exterior
Knight, Deborah, 126
Knight, Peter, 61
Kolker, Robert, 169
Kompare, Derek, 130
Kosinski, Joseph, 48
Kristeva, Julia, 40
Kubrick, Stanley, 64, 108, 145, 169
Kuhn, Annette, 76
kung fu, 73

Lanthimos, Yorgos, 82
Larkham, Peter, 23
Lazard, Justin, 88
Lazo, Daniel, 1
Levi, Mica, 165, 168
Levy, Emmanuel, 85
Libertines, The, 135
Life on Mars, 22, 36, 37, 38
Liman, Doug, 170
liquefaction, 9, 129
liquid, 2, 9, 10, 11, 13, 14, 15, 17, 18, 19, 21, 22, 25, 28, 29, 32, 42, 46, 54, 60, 62, 70, 78, 80, 86, 88, 98, 99, 101, 128, 143, 144, 145, 146, 150, 154, 162, 163, 165, 171, 172, 176
  bodies, 18, 79, 80, 82, 123
  modernity, 9, 14, 15, 19, 21, 22, 31, 32, 33, 34, 35, 36, 37, 38, 39, 40, 41, 42, 43, 50, 54, 55, 57, 58, 59, 60, 61, 62, 68, 70, 71, 84, 86, 90, 94, 99, 100, 101, 102, 103, 115, 116, 118, 119, 120, 121, 122, 127, 129, 131, 135, 139, 147, 156, 162, 169, 170, 171, 174, 177, 181
  terror, 19, 123, 142
liquid age, 13, 72, 73, 81, 82, 90, 92, 96, 116, 123, 143, 150, 172, 173, 174, 175
liquidity, 9, 10, 11, 13, 16, 18, 80, 82, 96, 116, 148
literature, 42, 67
Litle, Joshua Atesh
Lloyd Wright, Frank, 98
Lobster, The, 82–84, 90
location, 6, 28
Lockout, 34

Lockwood, Dean, 141
loneliness, 18, 19, 20, 62, 65, 67, 68, 69, 70, 71, 72, 74, 83, 85, 90, 96, 143, 162–169, 171, 176, 179
Looking for Mr. Goodbar, 168
Looper, 126
Lost, 134, 140
Lottery, The, 124
Lucas, George, 111, 125
Lumière Brothers, 63
Lumley, Joanna, 24
Luna I, 103
Lyon, David, 8
Lyotard, Jean-François, 5

MacCormack, Patricia, 84
Mann, Terrence, 67
Manovich, Lev, 2, 81
Marks, Laura U., 5, 134
Martian, The, 169
Marx, Karl, 75, 138
masculinity, 19, 94, 98, 109, 113, 115, 116, 126, 132, 133, 156, 157, 160, 167, 173
Matrix, The, 12, 34, 92, 120
Matrubhoomi: A Nation Without Women, 124
May-raz, Eran, 1
McAfee, Andrew, 95
McGoohan, Patrick, 34
McKnight, George, 126
McMahan, Alison, 47, 65
McTeigue, James, 124
McTiernan, John, 155
Mecha, 94
Medak, Peter, 88
Méliès, George, 169
memory, 38
  cultural, 8
Metz, Christopher, 76
Milburn, Colin, 81, 91
Minihan, Colin, 151
Minority Report, 11, 60, 61, 124, 126, 142
Mirrlees, Tanner, 174
mise en scène, 50, 51, 55, 62, 65, 70, 90, 113, 125, 144, 151, 165, 169
Mitchell, William J., 3, 81
Mittag, Martina, 6
Monbiot, George, 69
monomyth, 30, 74, 132
Moon, 117

Moore, Juliane, 129
Morel, Pierre, 124
Mortensen, Viggo, 85
Mostow, Jonathan, 91
motion-capture, 49
Moulton, Carter, 77
Moulton, Forest Ray
Moura, Wagner, 115
Mr Ben, 178
Mulvey, Laura, 76
Munch, Edvard, 162
Murphy, Cillian, 50, 121

nanoscience (nanotechnology), 81–82, 91
Napier, Susan J., 94
narrative, 3, 5, 11, 13, 15, 16, 19, 21, 24, 28, 29, 30, 33, 34, 36, 42, 47, 49, 51, 54, 55, 62, 64, 66, 71, 72, 76, 77, 92, 94, 102, 105, 106, 110, 115, 117, 121, 123, 125, 130, 135, 136, 140, 149, 164, 167, 174, 179
Natural City, 124
Ndalianis, Angela, 77, 78
Neale, Steve, 49
Neimanis, Astrida, 39
Never Let Me Go, 96
Netflix, 12, 66
Neveldine, Mark, 15
Niccol, Andrew, 13, 97
Nichols, Bill, 33
Nichols, Rachel, 11
Nietzsche, Friedrich, 40
Night of the Living Dead, 109
Nolan, Christopher, 80, 124, 147, 169, 171
Nolfi, George, 15
nostalgia, 29, 36, 38, 58, 59, 69, 154, 178
novum (cognitive innovation), 105
Nuemann, Kurt, 104
Nye, David, 48

Oblivion, 48
obsolescence, 19
ocular-generated data, 1
Olsen, Brad, 125
One, The, 124
Only Fools and Horses, 179
ontology, 46
Osborn, Lyn, 107
Other, 25, 70, 71, 87, 94, 102, 107, 109, 112, 113, 118, 119, 130, 132, 133, 134, 143, 148, 151, 156, 160, 162, 171
  Minoritarian, 101

INDEX

Our Drone Future, 141
Owen, Clive, 19, 75, 128

Pacific Rim, 48
para-social, 3, 37
pataphysical, 47
Pate, Jonas, 130
patriarchy, 96, 143, 157, 161, 167
Patrick, Robert, 11
Petersen, Christina, 76, 77
Petersen, Wolfgang, 87
Pheasant-Kelly, Fran, 123, 173
phenomenology, 71, 180
Phoenix, Joaquin, 89
Pichel, Irving, 106
Pidgeon, Walter, 110
Pierson, Michele, 35, 49
Pieterse, Jan Neverdeen, 73
Pine, Chris, 121
Pink, Sarah, 19
Piper, Billie, 35
piracy, 12
plastic, 4, 5
Post-Cinematic Affect, 15
posthuman, 3, 4, 19, 41, 42, 43, 78, 80, 81, 82, 91, 94, 96, 124, 172
pre-modernity, 5
precipice, 63, 65
Predator, 155
Prince, Stephen, 2, 3, 33
Prisoner, The, 34
production, 6, 10, 17, 32, 33, 41, 42, 57, 141
  post-production, 2, 11, 174
Prometheus, 123
Proyas, Alex, 91, 124

Quantum Leap, 21, 29, 30

race *see* whiteness
Ravich, Rand, 87
realism, 1, 2, 21, 26, 33, 129, 165
  hyper-realism, 71, 135
  indexical, 2, 33
  perceptual, 2, 3
  referential, 3
reception, 12, 13, 32, 76, 77
Reed, Peyton, 41
Reeves, Keanu, 120
Redmond, Sean, 52, 71, 75, 125, 138
rematerialisation, 8, 80, 89, 90

remixability, 2, 10
Resident Evil, 124
reterritorialisation, 6, 74, 87
Revolution, 80
Rhoden, Maureen, 26
Road, The, 16, 80, 85, 173
Robbins, Tim, 126
Robins, 73
Rocketship X-M, 104, 106, 110
Rockwell, Sam, 117
Rodriguez, Michelle, 48
Rodriguez, Robert, 87
Romanek, Mark, 96
Romero, George A., 109
Ross, Miriam, 74, 77
Roth, Eli, 134
Rowe, P. G., 23
Royal Variety Show, 24
Royle Family, 179
Ryan, Michael, 48

Sapir, Esteban, 153
Sapphire and Steel, 21, 24, 30
  'Assignment 1: Escape Through a Crack in Time', 24, 30
Sarah Jane Adventures, The, 33
Sardar, Ziauddin, 117
Saw, 134
science fiction, 5, 10, 11, 13, 16, 17, 19, 20, 24, 28, 30, 36, 38, 39, 40, 41, 42, 49, 58, 61, 76, 77, 78, 87, 91, 92, 105, 107, 108, 117, 130, 144, 146, 148, 151, 152, 156, 162, 174, 175, 177, 181
  digital age, 2, 3, 4, 5, 6, 7, 9, 10, 11, 15, 16, 17, 18, 19, 22, 34, 42, 43, 46, 60, 62, 64, 65, 73, 74, 75, 79, 80, 82, 89, 99, 114, 124, 125, 127, 128, 140, 143, 175, 176, 181
  liquid, 7, 12, 13, 19, 60, 61, 62, 73, 79, 81, 82, 90, 92, 96, 143, 144, 153, 171, 172, 173, 174, 175, 176
  spectacular, 18, 41, 42, 43, 44
Schatz, Thomas, 47
Schut, Bragi F.
Schwarzenegger, Arnold, 160
Scott, Ridley, 43, 101, 108, 112, 113, 144, 169
Scott, Tony, 15
Scream, The, 162
screenmaking *see* filmmaking
Second Machine Age, 95

Sense8, 12, 66–68, 73, 74, 181
Sensurround, 76
Shaviro, Stephen, 15, 86–87
Shyamalan, M. Knight, 124
Siegel, Don, 152
Sight, 1–2, 3, 4, 5, 6, 7, 8, 9
Signs, 124
Silent Running, 111
Silverman, Kaja, 157, 158, 159, 162, 167
Simm, John, 36
Sita, Jodi, 52
Sky Captain and the World of Tomorrow, 124
Sliders, 22, 32
slow-motion, 51
Smit-McPhee, Kodi, 85
Smith, Brian J., 67
Sobchack, Vivian, 11, 20, 31, 131, 140, 144, 145, 147, 149, 153, 177
social media (networks), 35, 66, 67, 69
society, 5, 23, 25, 26, 35, 103, 123, 124, 132, 133
  networked, 6, 8
Society, 87
Soderbergh, Steven, 10
software, 2
  gaming, 1
Sontag, Susan, 103
soundscape, 19, 71, 136, 138, 143, 145, 155, 164, 166
Source Code
Soviet Union, 103
space, 2, 6, 11, 18, 19, 21, 22, 23, 25, 26, 27, 28, 29, 31, 33, 34, 36, 37, 38, 39, 44, 50, 51, 61, 62, 63, 64, 65, 66, 73, 78, 81, 86, 88, 89, 90, 108, 128, 129, 131, 135, 137, 138, 145, 146, 147, 153, 154, 173, 175, 178, 179, 180, 181
  3D, 2
  (cinematic) outer, 18, 64, 65, 100, 101, 102, 104, 105, 106, 107, 111, 112, 113, 114, 120, 121, 122
  liquid, 19, 29, 60, 73, 75
  space-shift, 35
Space Patrol, 107
Space Race, 19
spastic, 4
spatialisation, 6
Specials, The, 164
Species, 88, 159
Species 2: Offspring 88

spectacle, 16, 24, 29, 32, 42, 43, 46, 47, 48, 49, 50, 52, 53, 54, 55, 56, 57, 58, 59, 65, 76, 77, 78, 144, 145, 172, 173
  active (dynamic), 50, 55
  contemplative (immersive), 50, 55
  natural, 50, 53
  science fiction, 41, 42, 44, 45, 47, 59, 76
  self-reflexive, 49
  society of, 35, 47, 57
  spectacle-driven, 24
  sublime, 42, 45, 52, 53, 58, 59, 64
  technological, 47, 48, 50
  technophilia, 47, 48
  technophobia (-ic), 48, 50
  television, 11
speed *see* velocity
Spielberg, Stephen, 11, 48, 60, 124, 125
Spielman, Y., 11, 64
Spiner, Brent, 93, 111
Spivak, Gayatri Chakavorty, 134
Splice, 172
Spottiswoode, Roger, 124
Sputnik, 103
Stacey, Jackie, 76, 98, 117, 118
Star Trek, 48, 101
Star Trek: The Next Generation, 64, 87, 91, 92, 93, 111
Star Trek Into Darkness, 121
Star Wars: Episode III - Revenge of the Sith, 125
Star Wars: Episode IV - A New Hope, 47, 111
stardom *see* celebrity
Steers, Mai-Ly N., 69
Stewart, Garret, 49
Strange Days, 63
Strauss, Johann, 108
Strauss, Richard, 108
sublime, 4, 18, 22, 28, 29, 31, 35, 40, 41, 43, 44, 45, 46, 47, 48, 49, 50, 51, 52, 53, 57, 58, 71, 78, 102, 145, 146
  spectacle, 42, 45, 52, 53, 58, 59
Sunshine, 43, 45, 50–55, 58, 124, 145
Surface, 130
Surnow, Joel, 134
surveillance, 4, 5, 9, 18, 26, 35, 37, 40, 43, 60, 98, 99, 131, 141, 160
  hyper-surveillance, 98
Suvin, Darko, 105, 174
synaesthesia, 20, 29, 78, 88, 90, 164, 177
synergetic, 8, 32

INDEX

Tate, Catherine, 35
Taubin, Amy, 108
Tavener, John, 136
Taylor, Alan, 91
Taylor, Brian, 15
technocrat, 5
television, 10, 11, 12, 13, 21, 22, 24, 31, 32, 34, 35, 42, 60, 63, 76, 150, 152, 157, 175, 177–181
    digital age, 15, 16, 17, 18, 19, 62, 64, 124, 140, 143
    liquid, 12, 13, 79, 92, 143, 144, 171, 172, 173, 174
    science fiction, 2, 3, 4, 5, 6, 7, 9, 10, 11, 12, 13, 15, 16, 17, 18, 19, 30, 35, 59, 60, 61, 62, 64, 66, 79, 82, 85, 87, 89, 93, 101, 102, 103, 104, 105, 106, 111, 123, 124, 140, 143, 144, 145, 148, 151, 159, 171, 172, 173, 174, 181
    of special attractions, 28, 29
    time travel, 18, 21, 22, 28, 29
Telotte, J. P., 92
Terminator, The, 91, 92, 93
Terminator 2: Judgement Day, 11, 80, 148, 159
Terminator 3: Rise of the Machines, 91
Terminator Genisys, 91
Tester, Keith, 9
Tetsuo, 149–150
Thatcher, Margaret, 25, 164
    UK government (1979–1987), 25
theory
    accumulation, 39
    queer, 39
    screen, 76
Thing, The, 49
Thompson, Kirsten Moana, 130, 137
Threshold, 130
Timberlake, Justin, 13
time, 6–7, 11, 12, 13, 15, 21, 22, 23, 24, 25, 26, 27, 28, 29, 30, 31, 32, 33, 34, 35, 36, 38, 39, 40, 50, 51, 61, 62, 78, 81, 147, 153, 154, 170, 179
    linear (chronological), 7, 38, 40, 57
    monumental, 40, 41
    thick, 39, 41
    time-shift, 13, 22, 33, 35
Torchwood, 33
torture, 128, 130, 133, 134, 148
Total Recall, 160
Train Arrived at the Station, The, 63

transcendence, 28, 62, 96, 101, 108, 135
    embodied, 42
Transformers, 16, 124
transmedia, 76
travel, 29, 35, 78, 102, 119, 153, 154, 162, 169
    space, 19, 101, 102, 103, 105, 106, 108, 143
    time, 17, 18, 21, 22, 24, 28, 29, 30, 31, 32, 33, 35, 36, 38, 39, 40, 41, 54, 59, 102, 146, 177
Trip to The Moon, A, 169
Trumball, Douglas, 111
Tsukamoto, Shin'ya, 149
Tuck, Greg, 46
Tyler, Imogen, 168
typography, 2

Ultraviolet, 124
uncanny valley, 25
Under the Dome, 34
Under the Skin, 68, 70–73, 80, 96, 143, 162, 164, 165–168, 169
utopia, 4, 22, 48, 59, 75, 138

V for Vendetta, 124
Van Damme, Jean-Claude, 67
Vanderbeek, Stan, 175
velocity, 9, 10, 11, 12, 13, 14, 43, 63, 144
Verhoeven, Paul, 160
verisimilitude, 25
verticality, digital, 6, 63
Vertigo, 63
Vint, Sheryl, 126
Virilio, Paul, 4, 123
virtual, 1, 4, 7, 8, 17
vision, 44, 45, 57, 59, 60, 106, 134, 177
    embodied, 43, 55

Wachowskis, 12, 92, 120
Waldby, Catherine, 89
Walker, Ben, 5, 106
Walking Dead, The, 16, 80, 86, 127
Wan, James, 134
War on Terror, 19, 123, 125, 128, 129, 130, 132, 133, 134, 136, 138, 140
War of the Worlds, 48, 124, 125–126, 127, 133, 173
Ward, Lalla, 27
Watts Riots, 108

Weaver, Sigourney, 81
Web 2.0, 7
Weisz, Rachel, 83
Wellywood, 7
Weltanschauung, 59
West, Jake, 87
Whissel, Kirsten, 6, 63
whiteness, 18, 19, 99, 100–122, 128, 132, 133
   hyper-whiteness, 112, 115
   millennial, 18, 114
   naturalised (normalised,), 109, 110
   pathological, 109
Whittington, William, 129, 135, 136, 137, 145
Wickham, Robert E., 69
Wilcox, Fred M., 110
Wilcox, Rhonda, 93, 111
Wilde, Olivia, 13

Williams, Raymond, 23
Wimmer, Kurt, 60, 124
Wise, Robert, 104
Without A Trace, 134
Wong, James, 124
Wood, Alison, 32
world-building, 3, 4, 145, 153
World War II, 135
   post-World War II, 23
Worthington, Sam, 118

Yellow Earth, 164
Yip, Man-Fung 77
Yuzna, Brian, 87

Zavitz, Lee, 105
Zizek, Slavoj, 131
zombie, 14, 80, 86–87, 91, 109, 121, 126–127